GOD
I AM

700 Names of God Titles and Attributes

Compiled, Written and Illustrated
by

T. L. Steele

Library of Congress Control Number: 2018941618
ISBN-13: Paperback: 978-1-64151-698-3
             PDF: 978-1-64398-990-7
             E-pub: 978-1-64398-992-1
             Kindle: 978-1-64398-991-4

Printed in the United States of America

PUBLISHING

LitFire LLC
1-800-511-9787
www.litfirepublishing.com
order@litfirepublishing.com

I wish to acknowledge my loving parents, Ernest and Christina D'Ambrosie, and my late brothers Joe and David, to honour their memory.

I also acknowledge my sister, Margherita Marcus for coming up with the inspiring book title itself. Also thanks to my nephew Andrew Marcus for his continuing support as well as the other members of my family, especially Anita, my sister, Michael, my brother, and friends for their encouragement.

Illustrations by Teresa L. Steele

Trust in the Lord Prov. 3:5-6
In the Beginning Gen.1:1
The Lord's Prayer Matt.6:9-13
Highly Exalted Phil. 2:9-10a
Lion of Judah Rev. 5:5
Be Still and Know Ps. 46:10
Sun of Righteousness Mal. 4:2
The Vine and branches Jn. 15:1

www.artisancreations-god.com

That I may know Him and the power of His resurrection
Phil. 3:10a

INTRODUCTION

For every single need we have, there is a name or title of God that covers that need. This book is aimed at helping the reader to know more about God and grow in the understanding of who He is. The names of God can be learned and used in prayer for specific situations you are facing. They are easily cross-referenced using the index at the back of the book which is in biblical order. This is a compilation, with the names, titles and attributes of God in alphabetical order with Scriptural illustrations both inspired by the Holy Spirit and created by the author for the glory of God.

The most important and most often written name of God in the Hebrew Bible is YHWH or YHVH, the four-letter name of God, it is also known as the Tetragrammaton, which derives from the prefix Tetra "four" and "Gramma" letter. The Hebrew letters are named Yod-Heh-Vav-Heh. It appears 6,828 times in the Masoretic text of the Hebrew Bible and is first mentioned in Genesis 2:4. In English language Bibles it is traditionally translated as "The LORD". The chief meaning of Jehovah is derived from the Hebrew word Havah meaning "to be". The following names of God are described in Rabbinic Judaism to be so holy that once written should not be erased: YHWH, El, El Elohim, Elohay, El Shaddai, Jehovah Tzeva'ot, and YAH.

I found this book to be similar to painting a portrait. The names, titles and attributes of God are listed in alphabetical order and there are descriptions of the various qualities of God, something like the background and foreground detail of a canvas. As an artist, when painting a canvas, I begin by painting the background, then add the subject matter by sketching it in before finishing it and adding the detail. I work overall in general terms, so that no one area becomes finished-looking over another area and build in layers increasing the detail and finer features of the painting whilst working overall towards the top layers, thus forming unity. Writing about God has not been much different. I have been building a picture of our Creator using words to describe who He is. Mostly, His own words have been used through listing those qualities and character traits in an orderly fashion, and through writing in descriptive detail about these qualities in the second part, thereby building a visual idea in order to allow the viewer a window into the throne room of God.

I have never tried to draw or paint a picture of God, for who He is, is indescribable. Nor have I tried to physically define His Son, Jesus, who is so often portrayed in ways that do Him a disservice with features limited to the artist's finite and sketchy understanding. I believe it to be relevant to make a disclaimer here. I do not profess to be particularly divinely inspired, or claim to be a prophet, by any stretch of the imagination; Most of this book is based upon either Scriptural quotations, or information that I have either learned from my studies of the Bible or gleaned from men and women of God. And may I say with St. Thomas Aquinas: "The end of my labour has come. All that I have written appears to be so much straw after the things that have been revealed to me."

Upon finishing the writing of this book, I received a word of confirmation from the Word of God, in Exodus 9:16: "And in very deed have I raised thee up, for to show in thee my power; and that my name may be declared throughout all the earth." This seems as profound and relevant for me as it must have been for Moses when the Lord spoke these words to him.

In the Old Testament times, a name was not only an identification, it was an identity also. Often with a special meaning attached to the name. Throughout Scripture God reveals Himself to us through His names. As we study these names as revealed in the Bible, we will better understand who He really is. The meaning behind God's names and titles reveal the central personality and nature of the One who bears them. To hallow the name of God is to regard Him with complete devotion and loving admiration. God's name is of the utmost importance. The Levites in Nehemiah said: "Stand up and bless the Lord your God for ever and ever: and blessed be thy glorious name, which is exalted above all blessing and praise" (Neh. 9:5b). We ought never to take the name of God lightly, but to rejoice in it and think upon it deeply, with reverence and awe, giving it a place of grave significance in our minds and hearts. Each of the names of God describes a different aspect of His many-faceted character. There is no better way to discover what God is like, than to look deeply at His names, and seek to understand how He cares for us, His creation. The Bible shows us of the nature and character of God. His moral character, which is reflected in His words and deeds- his holiness, His love and mercy, His truthfulness, His faithfulness, His goodness, His patience and His justice. In the Westminster Catechism "What is God?" it reads: "God is (a) Spirit, infinite, eternal and unchangeable in His being, wisdom, power, holiness, justice, goodness and truth." It has also been said: "God is King over His world; He rules all things for His own glory, displaying His perfections in all that He does, in order that men may worship and adore Him." God is so wonderfully multifaceted that He has many names that communicate His capabilities and character. When we reflect on God's names and pray accordingly, we can be sure that He will answer and be faithful to His name.

Our aim in studying the Godhead must be to know Himself better, to know the living God, whose attributes they are. There is a vast difference between knowing about God and knowing Him in a deeply personal way. Man's prayers are always the best evidence for a person's view of God. A little knowledge *of* God is worth more than a great deal of knowledge *about* Him. To know God is distinctly separate, therefore, from knowing about Him. The Westminster Catechism says: "The chief end of man is to glorify God and enjoy Him forever." Knowing God is our chief aim as believers, and to experience intimacy with Him in this life. Intimacy with God is not about "holy handouts." God is not a "cosmic sugar-daddy," but we can and ought to seek Him for all our needs.

Intimacy is about a relationship, not a gift exchange. Our primary purpose in life is to embrace the transcendent God by faith and to worship Him in purity and service. Our relationship with Jesus Christ ought to be marked with awe and respect. Full surrender means that we live with an attitude of unlimited obedience.

There is not much mention in the Bible of either giants or aliens, and no one knows for sure the age of the planet or when the human race first began, so in my presentation I have sought to convey what the Bible has to say about God and life itself, not what it does not say. The Bible does not enter into scientific details or accounts.

I believe that God is the Master scientist. We can see His mastery in the formations of the snowflake; apparently there is not one alike, yet under a microscope the beauty and intricately unique design is unparalleled. The Holy Scriptures simply declare: "In the beginning God…" As stated in the introduction, I have selected a verse of Scripture, or a part of the relevant verse, to describe best a particular attribute, name or title of God. For a deeper understanding it is best to read not only the selected Scripture, but the preceding and following verses in your Bible in order to grasp the fuller meaning. For example: "The Lord is great" is mentioned in 1 Chronicles 16:25, or more precisely, "Great is the Lord." However, in context, the passage referring to God's greatness actually begins in verse 23 and goes on to declare how great God is through to verse 36. This passage is referred to as a Psalm of gratitude, and it speaks of God's glory and greatness, His holiness and mercy, and that He is to be feared above all gods, meaning with reverential awe and respect.

Adoration and thanksgiving for God's attributes and actions are very important, as are clean hands and a pure heart. In the 23rd Psalm alone, we see many of God's names. There are two classes or categories of attributes; the negative class which is absolute, referring to God's simplicity, infinity, eternality and immutability, and the positive class, which are relative attributes relating to God's power, knowledge, holiness, justice, goodness and truth. Every attribute has its special significance for man. God is indivisibly one and perfect and cannot contradict himself. Even the Holy Scriptures, which reveal God to us, do not fully supply the elementary conceptions necessary to a perfect knowledge of God. His attributes are, in effect, incomprehensible to us. Some of the key known attributes of God are that he is eternal, holy, unchanging, impassable, infinite, all-powerful, omnipresent, all-wise, all-knowing, simple, self-existent, self-sufficient, immaterial, good, loving, gracious and merciful. He is justice, freedom, jealous and sovereign. The names of God are revealed in life-making encounters with God throughout the Scriptures.

The Authorized version of the Bible is used throughout this book. In some cases only the relevant part of the scripture verse has been written for easier understanding of the subject. Words in italics are Greek. It is my prayer that you find great pleasure in growing in your knowledge of God as you read this book prayerfully as a Bible companion and may your joy increase and be full as you take delight in renewed worship of the Lord our God and Saviour Jesus Christ.

T. L. Steele 2018

CONTENTS

PART ONE

INDEX TO NAMES OF GOD

51	El Mauzi	Psalm 43:2a
51	El Mohshahgoth	Psalm 68:20
51	El Mishpat	Isaiah 30:18b
51	El Nahsah	Psalm 99:8
52	El Nathan N'Qamah	Psalm 18:47
52	El Olam	Jer. 31:3b
52	El Palet, Jehovah Mephalti	Psalm 18:2
52	El Rachum	Deut. 4:31
52	El Roi, the God who sees	Gen. 16:13
52	El Sal'i	2 Sam. 22:47
53	El Sehlag	Psalm 42:9
53	El Selichot	Neh. 9:17b
53	El Shaddai	Psalm 91:1
53	El Shama	Psalm 17:6
53	El Shamar	Neh. 1:5
53	El Shaphat	Gen. 18:25b
54	El Simchah Giyl	Psalm 43:3-4
54	El Tehilati	Psalm 109:1
54	El Tsaddik	Psalm 7:9b
54	El Tzur	Isaiah 30:29
54	El Yehuatenu	Psalm 68:19
55	El Yehuati	Isaiah 12:2
55	El Yerushlem	Ezra 7 :19
55	El Yeshurun	Deut. 33:26
55	Eli Maelekhi	Psalm 68:24
55	Eloah	Job 22:12
55	Elohenu Olam	Psalm 48:14
55	Elohim	Gen. 1:1
56	Elohim Bashamayin	Deut.4:39
56	Elohim Ben Yachad	John 1:18
56	Elohim Kedoshim	Josh. 24:19a
56	Elohim Machase Lanu	Psalm. 62:8
56	Elohim Misgab, Elohei Chasdi	Psalm 59:17
57	Elohim of all Flesh	Jer. 32:27
57	Elohim Ozer Li	Psalm 54:4
57	Elohim Shofet Tsadik	Psalm 7:11
57	Elohim Shoptim Ba-arets	Psalm 58:11b

70	Glorified	John 13:31
70	Glorious	Titus 2:13
71	Glory of Israel	Isaiah 60:1
71	God	John 1: 1-2
71	God's Anointed	Acts 10:38a
71	God's Countenance	Num. 6:24-26
71	God's Glory Thunders	Psalm 29:2-3
71	God's Holy Child Jesus	Acts 4:26-27a
71	God of gods	Josh 22:22a
71	God of Holiness	Ex.28:36b
72	God of Hosts	Amos 4:13
72	God of Israel	Luke 1:68
72	God of thy Father	Isaiah 63:16b
72	Go'el	Ex. 15:13
72	Good	Psalm 145:8-9
72	Good Shepherd	John 10:11
73	Governor	Matt. 2:6
73	God Most High	Psalm 47:2
73	God of the Whole Earth	Isaiah 54:5
73	God of Wonders	Acts 2:19
73	Gracious	Ex.34:6
73	Grants Favour	Jer. 3:12b
73	Great; To be Feared; Revered	1 Chron. 16:25
74	Great High Priest	Heb. 10:19-22
74	Great Shepherd	Heb. 13:20-21a
74	Guide	Psalm 32:8
74	Ha Adonai	Ex. 23:17
74	Ha'Av l'Yeshua HaMashiach	2 Cor. 11:31a
74	Ha Kadosh Barukh Hu	Rev. 19:16
75	Hallowed	Luke 11:2
75	Hashem	Deut. 28:58
75	Hates Iniquity	Prov. 6:16-19
75	He that fills all in all	Eph. 1:23
75	Head of All Things	Eph. 4:15
75	Head of the Church	Col. 1:18
76	Healer	Matt. 8:16
76	Healer of the brokenhearted	Isaiah 61:1

88	Justice	Rev. 19:2a
88	Kadosh	Isaiah 40:25
89	Keeps silent	Psalm 28:1
89	Kind	Luke 6:35
89	King	Luke 19:38
89	King Eternal, Immortal, Invisible	1 Tim. 1:17
89	King of Glory	Psalm 24:9
89	King of Israel	John 12:13b
89	King of the Jews	John 19:19
90	King of Kings	Rev. 17:14a
90	King of Nations	Jer. 10:7
90	King of Peace	Heb. 7:2
90	King of Saints	Rev. 15:3
90	Kurios	Rom. 10:9
90	Lamb	Rev. 22:1
91	Lamb of God	John 1:29b
91	Lamb Who was Slain	Rev. 5:12
91	Lamb Upon the Throne	Rev. 5:13
91	Lamp	2 Sam. 22:29
91	Last Adam	1 Cor. 15:45
91	Laughs	Psalm 2:4
91	Life	John 1:4
92	Life's Guarantor	Jer. 33:6
92	Lifter of my Head	Psalm 3:3
92	Light	John 8:12
92	Light of the Gentiles	Luke 2:32
92	Light of Israel	Isaiah 10:17a
92	Light of the World	John 1:9
92	Lily of the Valleys, Rose of Sharon	Song of Sol 2:1
93	Illustration	Rev. 5:5
93	Lion of the Tribe of Judah	Rev. 5:5
94	Listens and Hears	2 Chron. 7:14
94	Lives for Ever	Rev. 4;10-11
94	Living God	Heb. 10:31
94	Living Bread	John 6:51
94	Israel's Living Star	Num. 24:17
94	Living Stone	1 Pet. 2:4

94	Living Water of Life	John 4:14
95	Lo Ammi	Hos. 2:23
95	Longsuffering	Num. 4:18a
95	The LORD	Psalm 106:1
95	Lord of all	Acts 10:36
95	Lord of the Dead	Rom. 14:9
95	Lord of the Earth	Zech. 14:9
95	Lord of Glory	1 Cor. 1:6-8
95	Lord of the Sabbath	Luke 6:5
95	Lord from Heaven	1 Kings 18:38-39
96	Lord Jehovah	Jer. 16:21
96	Our Lord	Rom. 6:23
96	Lord Adon	Psalm 12:5
96	The LORD God	Ex. 15:2
96	The Lord of Hosts	1 Chron. 17:24
96	Lord God of Hosts	Psalm 84:12
97	The Lord Jesus	Col. 1:2b
97	The Lord's Christ	Luke 2:26
97	The Lord of the Living	Matt. 23:32
97	LORD of Lords	Psalm 136:3
97	My Lord and my God	John 20:28
97	Love	1 John 4:8
98	Lovingkindness	Psalm 63:3
98	Machaceh	Psalm 61:3
98	Machseh, Fortress	Psalm 91:2
98	Majestic	Psalm 145:5
98	The Majesty	Heb. 8:1b
98	Makes Everything Beautiful	Eccl. 3:11
98	Makes Known His Salvation	Psalm 98:2
99	Makes Wise the Simple	Psalm 19:7
99	Malakh Adonai	Ex. 23:20
99	Manifest in the flesh	1 Tim. 3:16
99	Man of Sorrows	Isaiah 53:3
99	Manna	Rev. 2:17
99	Ma'on	Psalm 90:1
100	Maowz-Dal	Isaoah 25:4
100	Marvelous	1 Chron. 16:12

100	Mashiach	Zech. 9:9
100	Mashiach Ha Elohim	Luke 9:20
100	Master	Matt. 23:8
100	Mediator	1 Tim. 2:5
101	Meek and Lowly in Heart	Matt.11:29
101	Meets Every Need	Phil. 4:19
101	Melech Ha Melachim	Rev. 19:16
101	Melekh	Psalm 10:16a
101	Mercies are Great	Lam. 3:22-23
101	Merciful	Luke 6:36
101	Merciful and Gracious	Psalm 103:8
102	Messenger	Mal. 3:1
102	Messiah	John 1:41
102	Mighty God	Jer. 32:18
102	Mighty in Battle, Gibbor Milchamah	Psalm 24:8
102	Mighty in Power	Eph. 3:20-21
102	Mighty One of Israel	Isaiah 60;16b
103	Mighty Warrior	Isaiah 42:13
103	Miqweh Y'Israel	Jer. 17:13
103	My God and my Lord	Psalm 35:23
103	Mystery of God	Col. 2:2
103	The Name	Psalm 135:13
103	The Name above every name	Eph 1:21
104	Name Endures Forever	Psalm 72:17
104	Name is Excellent	Psalm 148:13
104	Name is Pleasant	Psalm 135:3
104	Nazarene	Matt. 2:23
104	Never Leaves us	Heb.13:5b
104	Never Sleeps	Psalm 121:4
104	New Name	Rev.3:12
105	Not Mocked	Gal. 6:7
105	Not Religious	James 1:27
105	Olam Zerowa	Deut. 33:26-9
105	Omnipotent	Rev. 19:6b
105	Omniscient	Psalm 44:21
105	Omnipresent	Psalm 139:7
106	One	Eph. 4:5-6

THE NAMES, TITLES AND ATTRIBUTES OF GOD

God is

But without faith it is impossible to please him: for he
that cometh to God must believe that he is, and that
he is a rewarder of them that diligently seek him
Heb. 11:6

God is Abba

And Jesus said, "Abba all things are possible unto thee"
Mark 14:36a

God is Abba Avinu
The LORD our Father

For ye have not received the spirit of bondage again to fear; but ye
have received the Spirit of adoption, whereby we cry, Abba, Father
Romans 8:15

God is Abir Jacob, Jehovah Goelekh
The LORD thy Redeemer

Thou shalt also suck the milk of the Gentiles, and shalt suck
the breast of kings: and shalt know that I the LORD am thy
Saviour and thy Redeemer, the mighty One of Jacob
Isaiah 60:16

God is Able

Now unto him that is able to keep you from falling, and to
present you faultless before the presence of his glory with
exceeding joy, to the only wise God our Saviour, be glory and
majesty, dominion and power, both now and for ever, Amen.
Jude 24-25

God is the God of Abraham, Isaac and Jacob
Moreover he said, I am the God of thy father, the God of
Abraham, the God of Isaac and the God of Jacob
Ex. 3:6a

God is Addiyr Jehovah
Glorious LORD
But there the glorious LORD will be unto us
a place of broad rivers and streams
Isaiah 33:21a

God is Addiyr Mahrom Jehovah
Mighty is the LORD on High
The LORD on high is mightier than the noise of many
waters, yea, than the mighty waves of the sea.
Psalm 93:4

God is Adon
LORD, Master
The hills melted like wax at the presence of the LORD,
at the presence of the Lord of the whole earth
Psalm 97:5

God is Adoni
My Lord
The LORD said unto my Lord, Sit thou at my right
hand, until I make thine enemies thy footstool
Psalm 110:1

God is Adoneinu
Our LORD
O LORD our Lord, how excellent is thy name in all the
earth! Who hast set thy glory above the heavens
Psalm 8:1

God is Adon Jehovah Tsaba
The LORD, the LORD Almighty
FOR, BEHOLD, the LORD, the LORD of hosts, doth take
away from Jerusalem and from Judah the stay and the staff,
the whole stay of bread, and the whole stay of water.
Isaiah 3:1

God is Adon Kol-ha'arets
Lord of all the earth
And the angel answered and said unto me, These are
the four spirits of the heavens, which go forth from
standing before the Lord of all the earth
Zech. 6:5

God is Adonai
The LORD
I am he that liveth, and was dead; and behold, I am alive
forevermore, Amen; and I have the keys of hell and of death.
Rev. 1:18

God is Adonai-Adonai
The Lord YHWH or Lord God
O Lord God, thou hast begun to show thy servant thy greatness
and thy mighty hand: for what God is there in heaven or in earth,
that can do according to thy works, and according to thy might?
Deut 3:24

God is Adonai Elohay

The LORD my God
Consider and hear me, O LORD my God: lighten
my eyes, lest I sleep the sleep of death
Psalm 13:3

God is Adonai Elohe David
Thus saith the LORD, the God of David thy Father,
I have heard thy prayer, I have seen thy tears
Isaiah 38:5

God is Adonai Elohim
He will swallow up death in victory; and the LORD
God will wipe away tears from off all faces
Isaiah 25:8a

God is Adonai El Elyon
The LORD Most High God
I will praise the LORD according to his righteousness: and
will sing praise to the name of the LORD most high
Psalm 7:17

God is Adonai Elohei Y'Israel
The LORD God of Israel
At that day shall a man look to his Maker, and his eyes
shall have respect to the Holy One of Israel
Isaiah 17:7

God is Adonai Eloheikhem
The LORD your God
Ye shall fear every man his mother, and his father, and
keep my sabbaths: I am the LORD your God
Lev. 19:3

God is Adonai Eloheinu
One LORD
Hear, O Israel: The LORD our God is one LORD
Deut. 6:4

God is Adonai Jehovah Tsaba Israel
Therefore saith the LORD, the LORD of hosts, the
mighty One of Israel, Ah, I will ease me of mine
adversaries, and avenge me of mine enemies.
Isaiah 1:24

God is Adonai Mekaddishkem
The Lord your sanctifier
Speak thou also unto the children of Israel, saying,
Verily my sabbaths ye shall keep: for it is a sign between
me and you throughout your generations; that ye may
know that I am the LORD that doth sanctify you
Ex. 31:13

God is Adonai Nissi
The Lord my Miracle or Banner
Thou hast given a banner to them that fear thee, that
it may be displayed because of thy truth. Selah
Psalm 60:4

God is Adonai Osenu
The LORD our Maker
O come, let us worship and bow down: let us
kneel before the LORD our maker
Psalm 95:6

God is Adonai Sal'i
The Lord our Rock
There is none holy as the LORD: for there is none
beside thee: neither is there any rock like our God
1 Sam. 2:2

God is Adonai-Tzva'ot
The LORD of Armies or Hosts
Who is this King of glory? The LORD of
hosts, he is the King of glory. Selah
Psalm 24:10

God is Adonai Tsuri v'goali
The LORD my Rock and Redeemer
Let the words of my mouth, and the meditation of my heart, be
acceptable in thy sight, O LORD, my strength, and my redeemer
Psalm 19:14

God is Adonai Tsuvah
The LORD my Salvation
Make haste to help me, O Lord my salvation
Psalm 38:22

God is Adonai Yishmarkha Mikol Ra
The LORD thy Protector
The LORD shall preserve thee from all evil: he shall preserve thy soul
Psalm 121:7

God is Advocate
And if any man sin we have an advocate with
the Father, Jesus Christ the righteous
1 John 2:1b

God is Alive Forevermore
I am he that liveth and was dead; and, behold,
I am alive for evermore, Amen
Rev. 1:18a

God is our All in All
And he is before all things, and by him all things consist
Col. 1:17

God is All-Glorious
Incarnate One
And the Word was made flesh, and dwelt among
us, (and we beheld his glory, the glory of the only
begotten of the Father,) full of grace and truth
John 1:14

God is All Sufficient

And God is able to make all grace abound toward you; that ye, always having all sufficiency in all things, may abound to every good work
2 Cor. 9:8

God is Almighty

Holy, holy, holy, Lord God Almighty, which was, and is,
and is to come
Rev. 4:8b

God is the Alpha and the Omega

And he said unto me, It is done. I am Alpha and Omega,
the beginning and the end. I will give unto him that is
athirst of the fountain of the water of life freely
Rev 21:6

God is The Amen

These things saith the Amen, the faithful and true witness,
the beginning of the creation of God
Rev. 3:14b

God is Ancient of Days

I saw in the night visions, and, behold, one like the Son
of man came with the clouds of heaven, and came to the
Ancient of days, and they brought him near before him
Daniel 7:13

God is the Angel of the Lord

And the angel of the LORD appeared unto him, and said unto
him, The LORD is with thee, thou mighty man of valour
Judges 6:12

The Angel of His Presence
Malach Panav
In all their affliction he was afflicted, and the angel of his
presence saved them: in his love and in his pity he redeemed
them; and he bare them, and carried them all the days of old
Isaiah 63:9

God is the God of the Angel-Armies
Then said David to the Philistine, Thou comest to me with a sword, and
with a spear, and with a shield: but I come to thee in the name of the
LORD of hosts, the God of the armies of Israel, whom thou hast defied
1 Sam. 17:45

Angels are Subject to God
Jesus Christ who is gone into heaven, and is on the right hand of God;
angels and authorities and powers being made subject unto him
1 Pet. 3:22

Anger of God
And he (Jehoahaz) did that which was evil in the sight of
the LORD, and followed the sins of Jeroboam the son of
Nebat, which made Israel to sin; he departed not therefrom.
And the anger of the LORD was kindled against Israel
2 Kings 13:2-3a

God Annihilates Satan's Plans
For he must reign, till he hath put all enemies under
his feet. The last enemy to be destroyed is death
1 Cor. 15:25-26

God is the Anointed One
The kings of the earth set themselves, and he rulers take counsel
together, against the LORD and against his anointed
Psalm 2:2

God is the Anointing Oil

The crown of the anointing oil of his God is upon him: I am the LORD
Lev. 21:12b

God is the Apostle

Wherefore, Holy brethren, partakers of the heavenly calling, consider
the Apostle and High Priest of our profession, Christ Jesus
Heb. 3:1

God is Architect

God hath is these last days spoken unto us by his Son, whom he hath
appointed heir of all things, by whom also he made the worlds
Heb. 1:2

God is the Ark of the Covenant

Arise, O LORD, into thy rest; thou, and the ark of thy strength
Psalm 132:8

God is Ascended

Wherefore he saith, When he ascended up on high, he
led captivity captive, and gave gifts unto men
Eph. 4:8

God is the Author of Eternal Salvation

And being made perfect, he became the author of
eternal salvation unto all them that obey him
Heb. 5:9

God is Aveer Jacob

Mighty One of Jacob
LORD, remember David, and all his afflictions: How he sware
unto the LORD, and vowed unto the mighty God of Jacob.
Psalm 132:1-2

God is Avi, 'Ab
Father
A Father of the fatherless, and a judge of the
widows, is God in his holy habitation
Psalm 68:5

God is Avi'ad
Everlasting Father, Father of Eternity
But to us there is but one God, the Father, of whom
are all things, and we in him, and one Lord Jesus
Christ, by whom are all things, and we by him
1 Cor. 8:6

God is Avi HaRachamim
Blessed be God, even the Father of our Lord Jesus Christ,
the Father of mercies, and the God of all comfort
2 Cor. 1:3

God is Avi Ha Ruchot
Furthermore we have had fathers of our flesh which corrected
us, and we gave them reverence: shall we not much rather
be in subjection to the Father of spirits, and live?
Hebrews 12:9

God is Avi Yeshua Hamaschiach Adoneinu
Father of our LORD Yeshua (Jesus) the Messiah
Blessed be the God and Father of our Lord Jesus Christ, which
according to his abundant mercy, hath begotten us again unto a
lively hope by the resurrection of Jesus Christ from the dead
1 Peter 1:3

The Babe
And this shall be a sign unto you; Ye shall find the babe
wrapped in swaddling clothes lying in a manger
Luke 2:12

God is Ba Elim Adonai
Awesome Faithful God
Who is like unto thee, O LORD, among the gods? Who is like
thee, glorious in holiness, fearful in praises, doing wonders?
Ex. 15:11

God is the Balm of Gilead
Is there no balm in Gilead? Is there no physician there?
Jer. 8:22a

God is Bamah
High Place
Then I said unto them, What is the high place whereunto ye
go? And the name thereof is called Bamah unto this day
Ezek. 20:29

God is our Banner
He brought me to the banqueting house,
and his banner over me was love
Song of Sol. 2:4

God is Bara Y'Israel
Creator of Israel
I am the LORD, your holy one, the creator of Israel, your King
Isaiah 43:15

God is our Battle Cry
The righteous cry, and the LORD heareth, and
delivereth them out of all their troubles
Psalm 34:17

God is Beautiful
One thing have I desired of the LORD, that will I seek after; that
I may dwell in the house of the LORD all the days of my life, to
behold the beauty of the LORD, and to inquire in his temple
Psalm 27:4

God is the Beginning and Ending

I am Alpha and Omega, the beginning and the ending, saith the
Lord, which is, and which was, and which is to come, the Almighty

Rev. 1:8

God is the Beloved

To the praise of the glory of his grace, wherein he
hath made us the accepted in the beloved

Eph. 1:6

The Beloved Son

And lo a voice from heaven, saying, This is my
beloved Son, in whom I am well pleased

Matt. 3:17

The Beloved Son of God

And a voice came out of the cloud, saying,
This is my beloved Son: hear him

Luke 9:35

God is Beni Yedidi

While he yet spake, behold, a bright cloud overshadowed
them: and behold a voice out of the cloud, which said, This is
my beloved Son, in whom I am well pleased; hear ye him

Matt. 17:5

God of Beth-el

The house of God
And he called the name of that place Beth-el

Gen. 28:19a

God is One Who Blesses us

The Lord bless thee and keep thee

Num. 6:24

God is Blessed
And they that went before, and they that followed, cried,
saying, Hosanna; Blessed is he that cometh in the name of
the Lord: Blessed be the kingdom of our father David, that
cometh in the name of the Lord: Hosanna in the highest
Mark 11:9-10

The Blessedness of God
Blessed be God, even the Father of our Lord Jesus Christ,
the Father of mercies, and the God of all comfort
2 Cor. 1:3

God is the Bishop of Souls
For ye were as sheep going astray; but are now returned
unto the Shepherd and Bishop of your souls
1 Pet. 2:25

God is the Blood Atonement
And not only so, but we also joy in God through our Lord Jesus
Christ, by whom we have now received the atonement
Rom. 5:11

God is He Who Blots out Transgressions
I, even I, am he that blotteth out thy transgressions for mine own sake,
and will not remember thy sins
Isaiah 43:25

The Body
Take, eat: This is my body, which is broken for you:
This do in remembrance of me
1 Cor. 11:24

God is the Bow of Battle
Out of him came forth the corner, out of him the nail, out of
him the battle bow, out of him every oppressor together
Zech. 10:4

God is the **BRANCH**

Tsemach

Thus speaketh the LORD of hosts, saying, Behold the man
whose name is the BRANCH; and he shall grow up out of
his place, and he shall build the temple of the LORD
Zech. 6:12

The Bread of God

For the bread of God is he which cometh down from heaven,
and giveth life unto the world
John 6:33

God is the Bread of Heaven

Then Jesus said unto them, Verily, verily, I say unto you,
Moses gave you not that bread from heaven; but my
Father giveth you the true bread from heaven
John 6:32

The Bread of Life

Artos Zoes

And Jesus said unto them, I am the bread of life: he that cometh to
me shall never hunger; and he that believeth on me shall never thirst
John 6:35

God is the Breath that Gives Life

The spirit of God hath made me, and the breath
of the Almighty hath given me life
Job 33:4

The Bridegroom

As the bridegroom rejoiceth over the bride,
so shall thy God rejoice over thee
Isaiah 62:5b

God is the Bright and Morning Star

Aster Lampros Proinos

I am the root and offspring of David, and the bright and morning star

Rev. 22:16b

God is a Buckler

He layeth up sound wisdom for the righteous: he
is a buckler to them that walk uprightly

Prov. 2:7b

God is the Builder

For he looked for a city which hath foundations,
whose builder and maker is God

Heb. 11:10

God is Builder of All Things

For every house is builded by some man;
but he that built all things is God

Heb. 3:4

God is One Who Can Be Known

That I may know him, and the power of his resurrection, and the
fellowship of his sufferings, being made conformable unto his death

Phil. 3:10

God Can Be Trusted

They that trust in the LORD shall be as mount Zion,
which cannot be removed, but abideth for ever

Psalm 125:1

God Cannot Lie

wherein God, willing more abundantly to show unto the heirs
of promise the immutability of his counsel, confirmed it by an
oath; that by two immutable things, in which it was impossible
for God to lie, we might have a strong consolation, who have
fled for refuge to lay hold upon the hope set before us

Heb. 6:17-18

God Cannot Sin
And ye know that he was manifested to take
away our sins; and in him is no sin
1 John 3:5

God Cannot Be Thwarted
There is no wisdom nor understanding nor counsel against the LORD
Prov. 21:30

God is the Captain of Man's Salvation
For it became him, for whom are all things, and by whom
are all things, in bringing many sons to glory, to make the
captain of their salvation perfect through sufferings
Heb. 2:10

God is One Who Cares
Casting all your care upon him; for he careth for you
1 Peter 5:7

The Carpenter
Is not this the carpenter, the son of Mary?
Mark 6:3

The Carpenter's Son
Is not this the carpenter's son? Is not his mother called Mary?
Matt. 13:55

God is One Who Celebrates
Concerning the feasts of the LORD,
which ye shall proclaim to b holy convocations, even these are my feasts
Lev. 23:2b

God is Cether
My Hiding Place
Thou art my hiding place; thou shalt preserve me from trouble;
thou shalt compass me about with songs of deliverance. Selah
Psalm 32:7

God is One Who Chastens
For whom the Lord loveth he chasteneth, and
scourgeth every son whom he receiveth
Heb. 12:6

The Chief Cornerstone
Jesus Christ himself being the chief corner stone
Eph. 2:20b

The Chief Shepherd
And when the chief Shepherd shall appear, ye shall
receive a crown of glory that fadeth not away
1 Pet.5:4

The Chosen of God
But ye are a chosen generation, a royal priesthood, an holy nation,
a peculiar people; that ye should show forth the praises of him
who hath called you out of darkness into his marvelous light
1 Peter 2:9

The Christ
Christos
And Jacob begat Joseph the husband of Mary, of
whom was born Jesus, who is called Christ
Matt. 1:16

The Christ Child
Child -Yeled, *Pais*
And when they were come into the house, they saw the young
child with Mary his mother, and fell down, and worshipped him
Matt. 2 :11a

Trust in the Lord...

The Christ of God

He said unto them, But whom say ye that I am?
Peter answering said, The Christ of God
Luke 9:2

Christ the Lamb

These were redeemed from among men, being the
firstfruits unto God and to the Lamb
Rev 14:4b

Christ's Anointed

And I heard a loud voice saying in heaven, Now is come
salvation, and strength, and the kingdom of our God, and
the power of his Christ: for the accuser of our brethren is cast
down, which accused them before our God day and night
Rev. 12:10

Christ's Coming is Near

Be ye also patient; stablish your hearts: for the
coming of the Lord draweth nigh
James 5:8

God is the Comforter

And I will pray the Father, and he shall give you another
Comforter, that he may abide with you for ever
John 14:16

God is Commander

Behold, I have given him for a witness to the people,
a leader and commander to the people
Isaiah 55:4

God is Compassionate

But thou, O Lord, art a God full of compassion, and gracious
longsuffering, and plenteous in mercy and truth
Psalm 86:15

God is our Confidence
For the LORD shall be thy confidence, and
shall keep thy foot from being taken
Prov. 3:26

God is the Consolation of Israel
And, behold, there was a man in Jerusalem, whose name was
Simeon; and the same man was just and devout, waiting for the
consolation of Israel: and the Holy Ghost was upon him
Luke 2:25

God is a Consuming Fire
Esh Oklah
For the LORD thy God is a consuming fire, even a jealous God
Deut. 4:24

God is Conqueror of Death, Hell and the Grave
O death, where is thy sting? O grave, where is thy victory?...But thanks
be to God, which giveth us the victory through our Lord Jesus Christ
1 Cor. 15:55,57

The Cornerstone
Akrogoniaios Lithos
The same is made the head of the corner
1 Peter 2:7

God Corrects and Disciplines His Children
Thou shalt also consider in thine heart, that as a man
chasteneth his son, so the LORD thy God chasteneth thee
Deut. 8:5

God Counsels us
O Lord, thou art my God; I will exalt thee, I will
praise thy name; for thou hast done wonderful things;
thy counsels of old are faithfulness and truth
Isaiah 25:1

God's Countenance

The LORD bless thee, and keep thee: The LORD make his
face shine upon thee, and be gracious unto thee: The LORD
lift up his countenance upon thee, and give thee peace
Num. 6:24-26

God's Covenant of the People

Thus saith the LORD, In an acceptable time have I heard
thee, and in a day of salvation have I helped thee: and I will
preserve thee, and give thee for a covenant of the people, to
establish the earth, to cause to inherit the desolate heritages
Isaiah 49:8

God is Creator

For by him were all things created, that are in heaven, and that are in
earth, visible and invisible, whether they be thrones, or dominions, or
principalities or powers: all things were created by him, and for him
Col. 1:16

God is Creator of All Things

Of old thou hast laid the foundation of the earth:
and the heavens are the work of thy hands
Psalm 102:25

God is Crowned with Many Crowns

His eyes were as a flame of fire, and on his head were many crowns;
and he had a name written, that no man knew, but he himself
Rev. 19:12

God is the Cup

Thou prepares a table before me in the presence of mine enemies:
thou anointest my head with oil; my cup runneth over
Psalm 23:5

The Cup of the Blood
Likewise also the cup after supper, saying, This cup is the
new testament in my blood, which is shed for you
Luke 22:20

The Day of the Lord
For the day of the LORD is near upon all the heathen:
as thou hast done, it shall be done unto thee: thy
reward shall return upon thine own head
Obad. 15

The Dayspring
Through the tender mercies of our God; whereby
the dayspring from on high hath visited us
Luke 1:78

The Daystar
Until the day dawn and the day star arise in your hearts
2 Peter 1:19b

God is Defender of Widows and fatherless
Defend the poor and fatherless: do justice to the afflicted and needy
Psalm 82:3

God Delights in our Praises
Praise ye the LORD: for it is good to sing praises unto
our God; for it is pleasant; and praise is comely
Psalm 147:1

God is Deliverer
There shall come out of Zion the Deliverer and
shall turn away ungodliness from Jacob
Romans 11:26

God is the Desire of Nations

And I will shake all nations, and the desire of all nations shall come:
and I will fill this house with glory, saith the LORD of hosts
Haggai 2:7

God is Despotes

Lord

And they cried with a loud voice, saying, How long, O
Lord, holy and true, dost thou not judge and avenge
our blood on them that dwell on the earth?
Rev. 6:10

God is Divine

According as his divine power hath given unto us all
things that pertain unto life and godliness
2 Pet. 1:3a

God is the Divine Judge of all Things

Let the sea roar, and the fulness thereof; the world, and they that
dwell therein. Let the floods clap their hands: let the hills be joyful
together before the LORD; for he cometh to judge the earth: with
righteousness shall he judge the world, and the people with equity
Psalm 98:7-9

The Divine Son

Whereby are given unto us exceeding great and precious promises:
that by these ye might be partakers of the divine nature
2 Pet. 1 :4a

The Door of the Sheep

Then said Jesus unto them again, Verily, verily, I
say unto you, I am the door of the sheep
John 10:7

God does not show Partiality

But the wisdom that is from above is first pure, then
peaceable, gentle and easy to be entreated, full of mercy and
good fruits, without partiality and without hypocrisy
James 3:17

God is our Dwelling Place

The LORD is high above all nations, and his glory above
the heavens. Who is like unto the LORD our God,
who dwelleth on high, who humbleth himself to behold
the things that are in heaven, and in the earth!
Psalm 113:4-6

God is Eben

The Stone

But his bow abode in strength, and the arms of his hands
were made strong by the hands of the mighty God of Jacob;
(from thence is the shepherd, the stone of Israel)
Gen. 49:24

God is the Earnest of our Inheritance

Ye were sealed with that holy Spirit of promise, Which is
the earnest of our inheritance until the redemption of the
purchased possession, unto the praise of his glory
Eph. 1:13b, 14

God is Ehyer-asher-Ehyer

I AM that I AM, the Great I AM

And God said unto Moses, I AM THAT I AM: and he said, Thus shalt
thou say unto the children of Israel, I AM hath sent me unto you
Ex. 3:14

God is El

Mighty, Strong, Prominent

And God Almighty bless thee, and make thee fruitful, and
multiply thee, that thou makest be a multitude of people
Gen. 28:3

God is Elah-avahati
God of my fathers
I thank thee, and praise thee, O thou God of my fathers,
who hast given me wisdom and might, and hast made
known unto me now what we desired of thee: for thou
hast now made known unto us the king's matter
Dan. 2:23

God is Elah Elahin
God of gods
Of a truth it is, that your God is a God of gods, and a Lord of kings
Dan. 2:47b

God is Elah Shemaya
God of Heaven
Whatsoever is commanded by the God of heaven, let it be
diligently done for the house of the God of heaven
Ezra 7:23a

God is Elah Yerush'lem
The vessels also that are given thee for the service of the house
of thy God, those deliver thou before the God of Jerusalem
Ezra 7:19

God is Elah Y'Israel
God of Israel
Then the prophets, Haggai the prophe, and Zechariah the
son of Iddo prophesied unto the Jews that were in Judah and
Jerusalem in the name of the God of Israel, even unto them
Ezra 5:1

God is El Aoreok
Longsuffering, Slow to Anger
He is the Rock, his work is perfect: for all his ways are judgment:
a God of truth and without iniquity, just and right is he
Deut. 32:4

God is El Chaiyai
The God of my Life
Yet the LORD will command his lovingkindness in
the daytime, and in the night his song shall be with
me, and my prayer unto the God of my life
Psalm 42:8

God is El Chayil, Elohei Ma'uzzi
God my Power, God of my Strength God is my strength
and my power: and he maketh my way perfect
2 Sam. 22:33

God is El Chaiyim
The Living God or God of my life But the LORD is the
true God, he is the living God, and an everlasting king
Jer.10:10a

God is El Channun
The Gracious God
For I knew that thou art a gracious God, and meciful, slow to
anger, and of great kindness, and repentest thee of the evil
Jonah 4:2b

God is El Chay, El Ghah'y
The Living God
And Joshua said, Hereby ye shall know that
the living God is among you.
Joshua 3:10a

God is El Chuwl
The LORD who gave you birth
Of the Rock that begat thee thou art unmindful,
and hast forgotten God that formed thee
Deut. 32:18

God is El De'ot, El Deah
The God of Knowledge, Omniscient God
For the LORD is a God of knowledge, and by him actions are weighed
1 Sam. 2:3b

God is El Derek Tamiym
God Whose Way is Perfect
As for God, his way is perfect; the word of the LORD is
tried: he is a buckler to all them that trust in him
2 Sam. 22:31

God is El Echad
The One God
Have we not all one father? Hath not one God created us?
Mal. 2:10a

God is El Emet
The God of Truth
Into thine hand I commit my spirit: thou hast
redeeemed me, O LORD God of truth
Psalm 31:5

El Erekh Apayim avi ha tanchumim
God of Patience and Consolation
I have seen his ways, and will heal him: I will lead him also,
and restore comforts unto him and to his mourners
Isaiah 57:18

God is El Gadol Gibohr Yare, El Ha Elohim
The Great, Mighty and Awesome God, the God of gods
For the LORD your God is God of gods, and Lord
of lords, a great God, a mighty and a terrible, which
regardeth not persons, not taketh reward.
Deut. 10:17

God is El Gaol
God is Redeemer
For I know that my redeemer liveth, and that he
shall stand at the latter day upon the earth
Job 19:25

God is El Gibor
The Mighty God
The remnant shall return, even the remnant
of Jacob, unto the mighty God
Isaiah 10:21

God is El G'moolah Jehovah
The LORD, God of Vengeance
Because the spoiler is come upon her, even upon Babylon, and
her mighty men are taken, every one of their bows is broken:
for the LORD God of recompenses shall surely requite.
Jer. 51:56

God is El Haggadol
The Great God
And Ezra blessed the LORD, the great God. And all the people
answered, Amen, Amen, with lifting up their hands: and they bowed
their heads and worshipped the Lord with their faces to the ground
Neh. 8:6a

God is El Hakkadosh
The Holy God
But the LORD of hosts shall be exalted in judgment, and
God that is holy shall be sanctified in righteousness
Isaiah 5:16

God is El Hakkarod, El Hakabodh, El Kahvohd
The God of Glory
The voice of the LORD is upon the waters: the God of
glory thundereth: the LORD is upon many waters
Psalm 29:3

God is El Hanne'eman
The Faithful God

Know therefore that the LORD thy God, he is God, the faithful God, which keepeth covenant and mercy with them that love him and keep his commandments to a thousand generations
Deut. 7:9

God is El Hannora
The Awesome God

Now therefore, our God, the great, the mighty, and the terrible God, who keepest covenant and mercy, let not all the trouble seem little before thee
Neh. 9:32a

God is El Hashamayim
The God of the Heavens

And it came to pass when I heard these words, that I sat down and wept, and mourned certain days, and fasted, and prayed before the God of heaven, and said, I beseech thee, O LORD God of heaven, the great and terrible God, that keepeth covenant and mercy for them that love him and observe his commandments
Neh. 1:4-5

God is El Kadosh
Holy

Who is able to stand before this holy LORD God?
1 Sam. 6:20b

God is El Kanno, El Qanna
the Jealous God

For thou shalt worship no other god: for the LORD, whose name is Jealous, is a jealous God
Ex. 34:14

God is El Kedem
God of the Beginning or Eternal God
The eternal God is thy refuge, and underneath are the everlasting arms
Deut. 33:27a

God is El Magen
Shield
Our soul waiteth for the LORD: he is our help and our shield
Psalm 33:20

God is El Mauzi
God of my Strength
For thou art the God of my strength
Psalm 43:2a

God is El Mishpat
God of Justice
For the LORD is a God of judgment: blessed
are all they that wait for him
Isaiah 30:18b

God is El Mohshahgoth
God of Salvation
He that is our God is the God of salvation; and unto
God the Lord belong the issues from death
Psalm 68:20

God is El Nahsah
The God who Forgives
Thou answeredst them, O LORD our God: thou wast a God that
forgavest them, though thou tookest vengeance of their inventions
Psalm 99:8

God is El Nathan N'Qamah
The God who avenges me
It is God that avengeth me, and subdueth the people under me
Psalm 18:47

God is El Olam
The Everlasting God
Yea, I have loved thee with an everlasting love: therefore
with lovingkindness have I drawn thee
Jeremiah 31:3b

God is El Palet, Jehovah Mephalti
The LORD my Deliverer
The LORD is my rock, and my fortress, and my deliverer;
my God, my strength, in whom I will trust; my buckler,
and the horn of my salvation, and my high tower
Psalm 18:2

God is El Rachum
The Merciful God
For the LORD thy God is a merciful God; he will
not forsake thee neither destroy thee, not forget the
covenant of thy fathers which he sware unto them
Deut. 4:31

God is El Ro'i
The Strong One Who Sees
And she called the name of the LORD that
spake unto her, Thou God seest me
Gen. 16:13

God is El Sal'i, El Sela
God of my Strength, my Rock, Bountiful
The LORD liveth; and blessed be my rock; and
exalted be the God of the rock of my salvation
2 Sam. 22:47

God is El Sehlag
God my Rock
I will say unto God my rock, Why hast thou forgotten me? why
go I mourning because of the oppression of the enemy?
Psalm 42:9

God is El Selichot
God of Forgiveness
But thou art a God ready to pardon, gracious and merciful, slow
to anger, and of great kindness, and forsookest them not
Neh. 9:17b

God is El Shaddai
The all-sufficient God, Almighty
He that dwelleth in the secret place of the most High
shall abide under the shadow of the Almighty
Psalm 91:1

God is El Shama
God who Hears me
I have called upon thee, for thou wilt hear me, O God:
incline thine ear unto me, and hear my speech
Psalm 17:6

God is El Shamar
God Who Keeps Covenant
I beseech thee, O LORD God of heaven, the great and
terrible God, that keepeth covenant and mercy for them
that love him and observe his commandments
Neh. 1:5

God is El Shaphat
God is Divine Judge
Shall not the judge of all the earth do right?
Gen. 18:25b

God is El Simchah Giyl
God my Exceeding Joy
O send out thy light and thy truth: let them lead me; let them
bring me unto thy holy hill, and to thy tabernacles. Then
will I go unto the altar of God, unto God my exceeding joy:
yea, upon the harp will I praise thee, O God my God
Psalm 43:3-4

God is El Tehilati
The God of my Praise
Hold not thy peace, O God of my praise
Psalm 109:1

God is El Tsaddik
The Righteous One
For the righteous God trieth the hearts and reins
Psalm 7:9b

God is El Tzur
God our Rock
Ye shall have a song, as in the night when a holy solemnity is kept;
and gladness of heart, as when one goeth with a pipe to come
into the mountain of the LORD, to the mighty One of Israel
Isaiah 30:29

God is El Yehuatenu
The God of our Salvation
Blessed be the Lord, who daily loadeth us with
benefits, even the God of our salvation. Selah
Psalm 68:19

God is El Yehuati
The God of my Salvation
Behold, God is my salvation; I will trust, and not
be afraid: for the LORD JEHOVAH is my strength
and my song; he also is become my salvation
Isaiah 12:2

God is El Yerush'lem, Elah Yerushelem
God of Jerusalem
The vessels also that are given thee for the service of the house
of thy God, those deliver thou before the God of Jerusalem
Ezra 7:19

God is El Yeshurun
The Righteous God
There is none like unto the God of Jeshurun, who rideth upon
the heaven in thy help, and in his excellency on the sky
Deut. 33:26

God is Eli Maelekhi
God my King
They have seen thy goings, O God; even the goings
of my God, my King, in the sanctuary
Psalm 68:24

God is Eloah
God
Is not God in the height of heaven? and behold
the height of the stars, how high they are!
Job 22:12

Elohenu Olam
Our Everlasting God
For this God is our God for ever and ever: he
will be our guide even unto death
Psalm 48:14

God is Elohim
God's Power and Might
In the beginning God created the heaven and the earth
Gen 1:1

God is Elohim Bashamayin
God in Heaven
Know therefore this day, and consider it in thine
heart, that the LORD he is God in heaven above,
and upon the earth beneath: there is none else
Deut. 4:39

God is Elohim Ben Yachad
No man hath seen God at any time; the only begotten Son,
which is in the bosom of the Father, he hath declared him
John 1:18

God is Elohim Kedoshim
Holy God
And Joshua said unto the people, Ye cannot serve the
LORD: for he is an holy God; he is a jealous God
Joshua 24:19a

God is Elohim Machase Lanu
God our Refuge
Trust in him at all times; ye people, pour out your
heart before him: God is a refuge for us Selah
Psalm 62:8

God is Elohim Misgab, Elohei Chasdi
God of my Kindness, Goodness and Faithfulness
Unto thee, O my strength, will I sing: for God is
my defense, and the God of my mercy
Psalm 59:17

God is Elohim of all flesh

Elohay Kol Basar
Behold, I am the LORD, the God of all flesh:
is there anything too hard for me?
Jer. 32:27

God is Elohim Ozer Li
God my Helper
Behold, God is mine helper: the Lord is with them that uphold my soul
Psalm 54:4

God is Elohim Shofet Tsadik
God is Righteous Judge
God judgeth the righteous, and God is angry with the wicked every day
Psalm 7:11

God is Elohim Shophtim Ba-arets
God that Judgeth in the Earth
Verily there is a reward for the righteous: verily
he is a God that judgeth in the earth
Psalm 58:11b

God is Elohim Tsedeq
God my Righteousness
Hear me when I call, God of my righteousness: thou hast enlarged
me when I was in distress; have mercy upon me, and hear my prayer
Psalm 4:1

In the Beginning ...

God is Elohim Yakol
God, the Most Able
If it be so, God whom we serve is able to deliver us from the burning
fiery furnace, and he will deliver us out of thine hand, O king
Dan. 3:17

God is El Elohe Israel
God the God of Israel
And he erected there an altar, and called it El-elohe-Israel
Gen. 33:20

God is Eloi
And at the ninth hour Jesus cried with a loud voice, saying,
Eloi, Eloi, lama sabachthani? Which is being interpreted,
My God, my God, why hast thou forsaken me?
Mark 15:34

God is El Elyon
The Most High God
And he blessed him, and said Blessed be Abram of the
most high God, possessor of heaven and earth
Gen. 14:19

God is Elohei Yishi
The Lord liveth; and blessed be my rock; and let the
God of my salvation be exalted
Psalm 18:46

God is Eloah Ya'akov
The God of Jacob
Tremble, thou earth, at the presence of the Lord,
at the presence of the God of Jacob
Psalm 114:7

God is Elohay Amen
God of Truth
That he who blesseth himself in the earth shall bless
himself in the God of truth; and he that sweareth
in the earth shall swear by the God of truth
Isaiah 65:16a

God is Elohay Marom
God of Heights
Wherewith shall I come before the LORD, and
bow myself before the high God?
Micah 6:6a

God is Elohay Tishuati
God of my Salvation
Deliver me from bloodguiltiness, O God, thou God of my
salvation: and my tongue shall sing aloud of thy righteousness
Psalm 51: 14

God is Elohay Yakob
God of Jacob
The LORD hear thee in the day of trouble; the
name of the God of Jacob defend thee
Psalm 20:1

God is Elyon
I will cry unto God most high; unto God
that performeth all things for me
Psalm 57:2

God is Elect and Precious
Behold, I lay in Zion a chief corner stone, elect, precious:
and he that believeth on him shall not be confounded
1 Peter 2:6

God is Eli
And about the ninth hour Jesus cried with a loud voice,
saying, Eli, Eli, lama sabachthani? that is to say, My
God, my God, why hast thou forsaken me?
Matt. 27:46

God is Emmanuel
God with us
Behold, a virgin shall be with child, and shall bring
forth a son, and they shall call his name Emmanuel,
which being interpreted is God with us
Matt. 1:23

God is the End of the Law
For Christ is the end of the law for righteousness
to every one that believeth
Rom. 10:4

God is Endless
And it is yet far more evident: for that after the similtude of
Melchisedec there ariseth another priest, who is made, not after the
law of a carnal commandment, but after the power of an endless life
Heb. 7:15-16

God is the Enemy of the Enemies of Israel
And the fear of God was on all the kingdoms of those countries, when
they had heard that the LORD fought against the enemies of Israel
2 Chron. 20:29

God is Eternal
But thou, O LORD, shalt endure for ever; and
thy remembrance unto all generations
Psalm 102:12

God is the Eternal Glory
But the God of all grace who hath called us unto his eternal
glory by Christ Jesus, after that ye have suffered awhile,
make you perfect, stablish, strengthen, settle you. To him
be glory and dominion for ever and ever. Amen
1 Peter 5:10-11

God is the Eternal Judge
Grudge not one against another, brethren, lest ye be
condemned: behold, the judge standeth before the door
James 5:9

God is Eternal Judge of the Quick and the Dead
I charge thee therefore before God and the Lord Jesus Christ, who
shall judge the quick and the dead at his appearing and his kingdom
2 Tim. 4:1

God is the Eternal Power and God Head
For the invisible things of him from the creation of the world are
clearly seen, being understood by the things that are made, even
his eternal power and Godhead; so that they are without excuse
Romans 1:20

God is the Eternity of Israel
And also the Strength of Israel will not lie nor repent:
for he is not a man, that he should repent
1 Sam. 15:29

God is Eved ha Kadosh
And now Lord, behold their threatenings: and grant unto
thy servants, that with all boldness they may speak thy word,
by stretching forth thine hand to heal; and that signs and
wonders may be done by the name of thy holy child Jesus
Acts 4:29-30

God has an Everlasting Kingdom
How great are his signs! And how mighty are his
wonders! His kingdom is an everlasting kingdom, and
his dominion is from generation to generation
Dan. 4:3

God is the Everlasting Light
The sun shall be no more thy light by day; neither for brightness
shall the moon give light unto thee: but the LORD shall be
unto thee an everlasting light, and thy God thy glory
Isaiah 60:19

God is our Exceedingly Great Reward
Fear not, Abram: I am thy shield, and thy exceeding great reward
Gen. 15:1b

The Excellent Glory
For he receiver from God the Father honour and glory, when
there came such a voice to him from the excellent glory,
This is my beloved Son, in whom I am well pleased
2 Peter 1:17

The Exemplar
For I have given you an example, that ye
should do as I have done to you
John 13:15

God is Eyaluth Chyahlooth
my Strength
But be not thou far from me, O LORD; O
my strength, haste thee to help me
Psalm 22:19

God's Eyes are on All
The eyes of the LORD are in every place,
beholding the evil and the good
Prov. 15:3

God's Eyes are Like a Flame of Fire

And in the midst of the seven candlesticks one like unto the Son of man, clothed with a garment down to the foot, and girt about the paps with a golden girdle. His head and his hairs were white like wool, as white as snow; and his eyes were as a flame of fire; and his feet like unto fine brass, as if they burned in a furnace; and his voice as the sound of man waters
Rev. 1:13-15

The face of God
Pni El

And Jacob called the name of the place Peniel: for I have seen God face to face, and my life is preserved
Gen. 32:30

God is Faithful
El Aman, El Emunah, God of Truth

Know therefore that the Lord thy God, he is God, the faithful God, which keepeth covenant and mercy with them that love him and keep his commandments to a thousand generations
Deut. 7:9

God is Faithful and True

And I saw heaven opened, and behold a white horse; and he that sat upon him was called Faithful and True, and in righteousness he doth judge and make war
Rev. 19:11

God is the Faithful and True Witness

These things saith the Amen, the faithful and true witness, the beginning of the creation of God
Rev. 3:14b

Hallowed be Thy Name

God is the Father of Lights
Avi HaMe'orot
Every good gift and every perfect gift is from above,
and cometh down from the Father of lights, with whom
is no variableness, neither shadow of turning
James 1:17

Christ at the Father's Right Hand

And Jesus said, I am: and ye shall see the Son of man sitting on
the right hand of power, and coming in the clouds of heaven
Mark 14:62

God is Holy Father

Our Father which art in heaven, Hallowed be thy name
Matt. 6:9

God is the Father of Heaven and Earth

O give thanks unto the God of heaven: for his mercy endureth for ever
Psalm 136:26

God is the Finisher of our Faith

Looking unto Jesus the author and finisher of our faith
Heb. 12:2a

God is the First and Last

I am Alpha and Omega, the first and the last
Rev. 1:11a

God is the First begotten of the dead

And again, when he bringeth in the first begotten into the
world, he saith, And let all the angels of God worship him
Heb. 1:6

God is the Firstborn of Every Creature

..Who is the image of the invisible God, the firstborn of every creature
Col. 1:15

God is the First Fruits

But every man in his own order: Christ the firstfruits;
afterward they that are Christ"s at his coming
1 Cor. 15:23

God's Followers are Good

Beloved, follow not that which is evil, but that which is good. He
that doeth good is of God: but he that doeth evil hath not seen God
3 John 11

God's Footstool

Thus saith the LORD. The heaven is my throne, and
the earth is my footstool: where is the house that ye
build unto me? And where is the place of my rest?
Isaiah 66:1

God is the Forerunner

Whither the forerunner is for us entered, even Jesus, made
an high priest for ever after the order of Melchisedec
Heb. 6:20

God Forgets our Sins

And their sins and iniquities will I remember no more
Heb. 10:17

God is Forgiveness

And be ye kind one to another, tenderhearted, forgiving one
another, even as God for Christ's sake hath forgiven you
Eph.4:32

God is Forgiver of Iniquity

Bless the LORD, O my soul, and forget not all his benefits: Who
forgiveth all thine iniquities; who healeth all thy diseases
Psalm 103:2-3

God is Forgiving

To the Lord our God belong mercies and forgiveness,
though we have rebelled against him
Daniel 9:9

God is Found in His Appointed Feasts
Also, in the day of your gladness, and in your solemn days, and in
the beginnings of your months, ye shall blow with the trumpets
over your burnt offerings, and over the sacrifices of your peace
offerings; that they may be to you for a memorial before your God:
I am the LORD your God
Numbers 10:10

God is Found by Those who Seek Him
But if from thence thou shalt seek the LORD thy God, thou shalt
find him, if thou seek him with all thy heart and with all thy soul
Deut. 4:29

God is the Foundation
Therefore thus said the Lord God, Behold, I lay in Zion for
a foundation stone, a tried stone, a precious cornerstone, a
sure foundation: he that believeth shall not make haste
Isaiah 28:16

God is the Fountain of Life
The fear of the LORD is a fountain of life,
to depart from the snares of death
Prov.14:27

God is a Friend
And the scripture was fulfilled which saith, Abraham
believed God, and it was imputed to him for
righteousness: and he was called the friend of God
James 2:23

God is the Friend of Sinners
Philos
The Son of man came eating and drinking, and
they say, behold a friend of sinners
Matt. 11:19

God is a Friend that Sticks Closer than a Brother

A man that hath friends must show himself friendly: and
there is a friend that sticketh closer than a brother
Prov.18:24

God is from Above

And he said unto them, Ye are from beneath; I am from
above: ye are of this world; I am not of this world
John 8:23

The Gate for the Sheep

Enter ye in at the strait gate: for wide is the gate and broad is the way
that leadeth to destruction, and many there be which go in thereat
Matt.7:13

God is Gelah Raz

Revealer of mysteries
But there is a God in heaven that revealeth secrets
Dan. 2:28a

Known as the Gift of God

Thanks be unto God for his indescribable gift
2 Cor. 9:15

God is Giver of Abundant Life

I am come that they may have life, and they
may have it more abundantly
John 10:10b

God is the Giver of Good Gifts

Every good gift and every perfect gift is from above,
and cometh down from the Father of lights, with whom
is no variableness, neither shadow of turning
James 1:17

God is One Who Gives Freely

He that spared not his own Son but delivered him up for us
all, how shall he not with him also freely give us all things?
Rom. 8:32

God is the Giver of Hope

But the Lord will be the hope of his people, and
the strength of the children of Israel
Joel 3:16b

God is the Giver of Joy

For his anger endureth but for a moment; in his favour is life:
weeping may endure for a night, but joy cometh in the morning
Psalm 30:5

God Gives Joy and Strength

Yet I will rejoice in the LORD, I will joy in the God of my salvation.
The LORD God is my strength, and he will make my feet like
hinds' feet, and he will make me to walk upon mine high places
Hab. 3:18-19

God Gives Liberally

If any of you lack wisdom, let him ask of God, that giveth to all
men liberally, and upbraideth not; and it shall be given him
James 1:5

God is Glorified

Therefore, when he was gone out, Jesus said, Now is the
Son of man glorified, and God is glorified in him
John 13:31

God is Glorious

Looking for that blessed hope, and the glorious appearing
of the great God and our Saviour Jesus Christ
Titus 2:13

God is the Glory of Israel

Arise, shine; for thy light is come, and the
glory of the Lord is risen upon thee
Isaiah 60:1

God

In the beginning was the Word, and the Word was with God, and
the Word was God. The same was in the beginning with God
John 1:1,2

Known as God's Anointed

How God anointed Jesus of Nazareth with
the Holy Ghost and with power
Acts 10:38a

God's Glory Thunders

Give unto the LORD the glory due unto his name; worship the
LORD in the beauty of holiness. The voice of the LORD is upon the
waters: the God of glory thundereth: the LORD is upon many waters
Psalm 29: 2-3

God's Holy Child is Jesus

The kings of the earth stood up, and the rulers were gathered together
against the Lord and against his Christ. For of a truth against thy holy
child Jesus, whom thou hast anointed, both Herod, and Pontius Pilate,
with the Gentiles, and the people of Israel were gathered together
Acts 4:26-27

God is the God of gods

The Lord God of gods, the Lord God of gods,
he knoweth, and Israel he shall know
Joshua 22:22a

God is the God of Holiness

HOLINESS TO THE LORD
Ex. 28:36b

God is the God of Hosts

For, lo, he that formeth the mountains, and createth the wind,
and declareth unto man what is his thought, that maketh
the morning darkness, and treadeth upon the high places of
the earth, The LORD, the God of hosts, is his name
Amos 4:13

God is the God of Israel

Blessed be the Lord God of Israel; for he hath
visited and redeemed his people
Luke 1:68

God is the God of thy Father

Thou, O LORD art our Father, our redeemer;
thy name is from everlasting
Isaiah 63:16b

God is Go'el

Kinsman-Redeemer
Thou in thy mercy hast led forth the people which thou hast redeemed:
thou hast guided them in thy strength unto thy holy habitation
Exodus 15:13

God is Good

The LORD is gracious and full of compassion; slow to
anger, and of great mercy. The LORD is good to all:
and his tender mercies are over all his works
Psalm 145:8-9

The Good Shepherd

I am the Good Shepherd: the Good Shepherd
giveth his life for the sheep
John 10:11

God is Governor
And thou Bethlehem, in the land of Judah, art not least
among the princes of Judah: for out of thee shall come
a Governor, that shall rule my people Israel
Matt. 2:6

God is the God Most High
For the LORD most high is terrible; he is a great King over all the earth
Psalm 47:2

God is the God of the Whole Earth
For thy Maker is thine husband; the LORD of hosts
is his name; and thy redeemer the Holy One of Israel;
The God of the whole earth shall he be called
Isaiah 54:5

God is the God of Wonders
And I will show wonders in heaven above, and signs in the
earth beneath; blood, and fire, and vapour of smoke
Acts 2:19

God is Gracious
And the LORD passed by before him, and proclaimed,
the LORD, the LORD God merciful and gracious,
longsuffering, and abundant in goodness and truth
Ex. 34:6

God Grants Favour
For I am merciful, saith the LORD, and I will not keep anger for ever
Jer. 3:12b

God is Great, to be Feared; Revered
For great is the LORD, and greatly to be praised:
he also is to be feared above all gods
1 Chron. 16:25

Great High Priest
Having therefore, brethren, boldness to enter into the holiest
by the blood of Jesus, by a new and living way, which he hath
consecrated for us, through the veil, that is to say, his flesh; and
having an high priest over the house of God; let us draw near with
a true heart in full assurance of faith, having our hearts sprinkled
from an evil conscience, and our bodies washed with pure water
Heb. 10:19-22

The Great Shepherd
Now the God of peace, that brought again from the dead our Lord
Jesus, that great Shepherd of the sheep, through the blood of the
everlasting covenant, make you perfect in every good work to do his will
Heb. 13:20-21a

God is our Guide
I will instruct thee and teach thee in the way which
thou shalt go: I will guide thee with mine eye
Psalm 32:8

God is Ha Adonai
The Lord God
Three times in the year all thy males shall appear before the Lord God
Ex. 23:17

God is Ha'Av L'Yeshua HaMashiach
The God and Father of our Lord Jesus Christ
2 Cor. 11:31a

God is Ha Kadosh Barukh Hu
The Supreme King of kings, the Holy One
Meaning "The Holy One; Blessed be He" often used by Jewish people

God is Hallowed

Avinu Shebashamayim
And he said unto them, when ye pray, say, Our Father
which art in heaven, Hallowed be thy name. Thy kingdom
come. Thy will be done, as in heaven, so in earth
Luke 11:2

God is Hashem

The Name
If thou wilt not observe to do all the words of this law that are written
in this book, that thou mayest fear this glorious and fearful name,
THE LORD THY GOD
Deut. 28:58

God Hates Iniquity

These six things doth the LORD hate: yea, seven are an abomination
unto him: A proud look, a lying tongue, and hands that shed
innocent blood, an heart that deviseth wicked imaginations,
feet that be swift in running to mischief, a false witness that
speaketh lies, and he that soweth discord among brethren
Prov. 6:16-19

God is He that filleth all in all

And hath put all things under his feet, and gave him
to be the head over all things to the church, which is
his body, the fulness of him that filleth all in all
Eph. 1:22-23

God is Head of All Things

But speaking the truth in love, may grow up into him
in all things, which is the head, even Christ
Eph. 4:15

The Head of the Church

And he is the head of the body, the church: who is the beginning, the
firstborn from the dead; that in all things he may have the preeminence
Col. 1:18

God is Healer

When the even was come, they brought unto him many
that were possessed with devils: and he cast out the
spirits with his word and healed all that were sick
Matt. 8:16

God is Healer of the Broken-hearted

The Spirit of the LORD God is upon me; because the LORD
hath anointed me to preach good tidings unto the meek; he hath
sent me to bind up the brokenhearted, to proclaim liberty to the
captives, and the opening of the prison to them that are bound
Isaiah 61:1

God is the Health of my Countenance

Why art thou cast down, O my soul? And why art thou
disquieted within me? Hope in God: for I shall yet praise
him, who is the health of my countenance, and my God
Psalm 43:5

God Hears Prayer

The LORD is far from the wicked: but he
heareth the prayer of the righteous
Prov. 15;29

The Heir of all Things

God, who at sundry times and in divers manners spake in
time past unto the fathers by the prophets, hath in these last
days spoken unto us by his Son, whom he hath appointed
heir of all things, by whom also he made the worlds
Heb.1:1-2

God is our Helper

So that we may boldly say, the Lord is my helper, and
I will not fear what man shall do unto me
Heb. 13:6

God is One Who Hides Himself
Verily thou art a God that hidest thyself, O God of Israel, the Saviour
Isaiah 45:15

God is our Hiding Place
Thou art my hiding place and my shield: I hope in thy word
Psalm 119:114

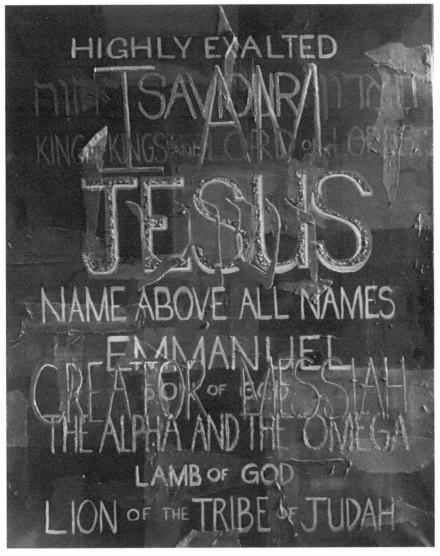

Highly Exalted – Names of God

The High Priest

Seeing then that we have a great High Priest, that is passed into the
heavens, Jesus the Son of God, let us hold fast our profession
Heb. 4:14

God is our High Tower

Metsuda
My goodness, and my fortress; my high tower, and my deliverer; my
shield, and he in whom I trust; who subdueth my people under me
Psalm 144:2

God is Highly Exalted

Wherefore God also hath highly exalted him, and
given him a name which is above every name: that
at the name of Jesus every knee should bow
Phil. 2:9-10a

God Holds the Key of David

And to the angel of the church in Philadelphia write; These things saith
he that is holy, he that is true, he that hath the key of David, he that
openeth and no man shutteth, and shutteth, and no man openeth
Rev. 3:7

God is Holy

Because It is written, Be ye holy; for I am holy
1 Peter 1:16

The Holy One of God

And in the synagogue there was a man, which had a spirit of an
unclean devil, and cried out with a loud voice, saying, Let us alone;
what have we to do with thee, thou Jesus of Nazareth? Art thou come
to destroy us? I know thee who thou art; the Holy One of God
Luke 4:33-34

Known as God's Holy Child Jesus

For of a truth against thy holy child Jesus, whom thou hast anointed...
Acts 4:27

God is the Holy One of Israel

I will help thee, saith the LORD, and thy
redeemer, the Holy One of Israel
Isaiah 41:14b

The Holy Spirit

And grieve not the holy Spirit of God, whereby
ye are sealed unto the day of redemption
Eph.4:30

God is the Holy and True Avenger

That no man go beyond and defraud his brother in
any matter: because the Lord is the avenger of all such,
as we also have forewarned you and testified
1 Thess. 4:6

God is to be Honoured

For the Father judgeth no man, but hath committed all
judgment unto the Son; That all men should honour the
Son, even as they honour the Father. He that hounoureth not
the Son honoureth not the Father which hath sent him
John 5:22-23

God is Honourable

His work is honourable and glorious: and
his righteousness endureth forever
Psalm 111:3

God is the Hope of the World

Now the God of hope fill you with all joy and peace in believing,
that ye may abound in hope, through the power of the Holy Ghost
Rom. 15:13

God's Horn is Exalted

He hath dispersed, he hath given to the poor; his trighteousness
endureth for ever; his horn shall be exalted with honour
Psalm 112:9

God is the Horn of Salvation

And hath raised up an horn of salvation for us
in the house of his servant David
Luke 1:69

God is One Who Humbles and Tests us

And thou shalt remember all the way which the LORD thy
God led thee these forty years in the wilderness, to humble
thee, and to prove thee, to know what was in thine heart,
whether thou wouldest keep his commandments, or no
Deut. 8:2

God is Hupistos

The Highest
And the multitudes that went before, and that followed,
cried, saying, Hosanna to the son of David: Blessed is he that
cometh in the name of the Lord; Hosanna in the highest
Matt.21:9

The Image of the Invisible God

Who being the brightness of his glory,
and the express image of his person, and upholding all things
by the word of his power, when he had by himself purged our
sins, sat down at the right hand of the majesty on high
Heb.1:3

God is Immanent

Elohay Mikarov
Am I a God at hand, saith the LORD, and not a God afar
off? Can any hide himself in secret places that I shall not see
him? Saith the LORD. Do not I fill heaven and earth?
Saith the LORD
Jer. 23:23-24

God is Immutable

Before the mountains were brought forth, or ever thou hadst formed the earth and the world, even from everlasting to everlasting, thou art God
Psalm 90:2

God is Impartial

Then Peter opened his mouth, and said, Of a truth I perceive that God is no respecter of persons: But in every nation he that feareth him, and worketh righteousness, is accepted with him
Acts 10:34-35

God is in our Midst

For where two or three are gathered together in my name, there am I in the midst of them
Matt.18:20

God is Infinite

Great is our Lord, and of great power: his understanding is infinite
Psalm 147:5

God is Infinite in Strength

With him is wisdom and strength, he has counsel and understanding
Job 12:13

God is He Who Inhabits Eternity

For thus saith the high and lofty One that inhabiteth eternity, whose name is Holy; I dwell in the high and holy place, with him also that is of a humble and contrite spirit , to revive the spirit of the humble, and to revive the heart of the contrite ones
Isaiah 57:15

God Inhabits the Praises of His People

But thou art holy, O thou that inhabitest the praises of Israel
Psalm 22:3

God's Inspired Word

All scripture is given by inspiration of God, and is
profitable for doctrine, for reproof, for correction, for
instruction in righteousness: that the man of God may be
perfect, thoroughly furnished unto all good works
2 Tim. 3:16-17

God is the Intercessor

If there be a messenger with him, an interpreter, one among
a thousand, to show unto man his uprightness
Job 33:23

God is Intimate

The secret things belong unto the LORD our God: but
those things which are revealed belong unto us and to our
children for ever, that we may do all the words of this law
Deut. 29:29

God is Invisible

By faith he (Moses) forsook Egypt, not fearing the wrath of
the king: for he endured, as seeing him who is invisible
Heb. 11:27

God is Ishi - my Husband

And it shall be at that day, saith the LORD, that thou
shalt call me Ishi; and shalt call me no more Baali
Hosea 2:16

God is Israel's Living Star

There shall come a Star out of Jacob, and a Sceptre shall rise out of Israel
Num.24:17

God is JAH

Yahweh, the LORD
Sing unto God, sing praises to his name: extol him that rideth
upon the heavens by his name JAH, and rejoice before him
Psalm 68:4

God is Jealous over us
Thou shalt not bow down thyself to them, nor serve
them: for I the LORD thy God am a jealous God
Exodus 20:5a

God is JEHOVAH
Trust ye in the LORD forever: for in the
LORD JEHOVAH is everlasting strength
Isaiah 26:4

God is Jehovah-aman
The Lord who is Faithful
Thus saith the LORD, the Redeemer of Israel, and his Holy
One, to him whom man despiseth, to him whom the nations
abhoreth, to a servant of rulers, Kings shall see and arise,
princes also shall worship, because of the LORD that is faithful,
and the Holy one of Israel, and he shall choose thee
Isaiah 49:7

God is Jehovah-azar
The LORD my helper
Hear, O LORD, and have mercy upon me: LORD be thou my helper
Psalm 30:10

God is Jehovah-bore
The LORD Creator
Hast thou not known? hast thou not heard, that the everlasting
God, the LORD, the Creator of the ends of the earth, fainteth
not, neither is weary? there is no searching of his understanding.
Isaiah 40:28

God is Jehovah Elohim Ab
The LORD God of your Forefathers
And Joshua said unto the children of Israel, How
long are ye slack to go to possess the land, which the
LORD God of your fathers hath given you?
Joshua 18:3

God is Jehovah Gmoolah, El Gemuwal
The God of recompense
For this is the time of the LORD'S vengeance;
he will render unto her a recompense
Jer. 51:6

God is Jehovah ha-Melech
The LORD my King
With trumpets and sound of cornet make a
joyful noise before the LORD, the King
Psalm 98:6

God is Jehovah-hoshiah
O LORD save
Save, LORD: Let the king hear us when we call
Psalm 20:9

God is Jehovah-jireh
Our Gracious Provider
And Abraham called the name of that place Jehovah-jireh: as it
is said to this day, in the mount of the LORD it shall be seen
Gen. 22:14

God is Jehovah-maginnenu
The LORD our Defense
For the LORD is our defense; and the Holy One of Israel is our king
Psalm 89:18

God is Jehovah Moshiekh
The LORD your Saviour
And I will feed all them that oppress thee with their own
flesh; and they shall be drunken with their own blood, as with
sweet wine: and all flesh shall know that I the LORD am thy
Saviour and thy Redeemer, the mighty One of Jacob
Isaiah 49:26

God is Jehovah-nissi
The Lord our Banner
And Moses built an altar, and called the name of it Jehovah- nissi
Ex. 17:15

God is Jehovah-ori
The LORD is my Light
The LORD is my light and my salvation; whom shall I fear? the
LORD is the strength of my life; of whom shall I be afraid?
Psalm 27:1

God is Jehovah-rohi
The LORD my Shepherd
The LORD is my shepherd; I shall not want
Psalm 23:1

God is Jehovah-rophe, Adonay Rof"echah
The LORD our Healer
I am the LORD that healeth thee
Ex. 15:26b

God is Jehovah-sabaoth
The LORD of Hosts
Holy, holy, holy is the LORD of hosts: the
whole earth is full of his glory
Isaiah 6:3b

God is Jehovah-shalom
The LORD is Peace
Then Gideon built an altar there unto the
LORD, and called it Jehovah -Shalom
Judges 6:24

God is Jehovah-shammah
The Lord Who is Present: is There
And the name of the city from that day shall be, The LORD is there
Ezek. 48:35

God is Jehovah-shaphat
The LORD our Judge
For the LORD is our judge, the LORD is our lawgiver,
the LORD is our king; he will save us
Isaiah 33:22

God is Jehovah-tzidkenu
The LORD our Righteousness
In his days Judah shall be saved, and Israel shall dwell
safely: and this is his name whereby he shall be called,
THE LORD OUR RIGHTEOUSNESS
Jer. 23:6

God is Jehovah-tzur
The LORD my Strength
Blessed be the LORD my strength, which teacheth
my hands to war, and my fingers to fight.
Psalm 144:1

God is Jehovah -, the LORD
God's Divine Salvation
These are the generations of the heavens and of the
earth when they were created, in the day that the
LORD God made the earth and the heavens
Gen. 2:4

JESUS
Jehovah is Salvation
And she shall bring forth a son, and thou shalt call his name
JESUS: for he shall save his people from their sins
Matt. 1:21

Jesus Christ
Messiah, Anointed One
Be it known unto you all, and to all the people of Israel, that by the name of Jesus Christ of Nazareth, whom ye crucified, whom God raised from the dead, even by him doth this man stand here before you whole. Neither is there salvation in any other: for there is none other name under heaven given among men, whereby we must be saved
Acts 4:10-12

Jesus of Galilee
And it came to pass in those days, that Jesus came from Nazareth of Galilee, and was baptized of John in Jordan
Mark 1:9

Jesus of Nazareth
Philip findeth Nathanael, and saith unto him, We have found him, of whom Moses in the lae, and in the prophets, did write, Jesus of Nazareth, son of Joseph
John 1:45

Jesus Son of Joseph
And they said, is this not Jesus, the son of Joseph, whose father and mother we know? How is it then that he saith, I came down from heaven?
John 6:42

God is Jezreel
God will sow
And the earth shall hear the corn, and the wine, and the oil; and they shall hear Jezreel
Hosea 2:22

Judge of the Living and the Dead
And he commanded us to preach unto the people, and to testify that it is he which was ordained of God to be the judge of quick and dead
Acts 10:42

God's Judgments are Made Manifest

Who shall not fear thee, O Lord, and glorify thy name? for
thou only art holy: for all nations shall come and worship
before thee; for thy judgments are made manifest
Rev. 15:4

God Judges All

Let us hear the conclusion of the whole matter; fear God, and
keep his commandments: for this is the whole duty of man.
For God shall bring every work into judgment, with every
secret thing, whether it be good, or whether it be evil
Eccl. 12:13-14

God Judges the Motives

For the word of God is quick and powerful, and sharper
than any two-edged sword, piercing even to the dividing
asunder of soul and spirit, and of the joints and marrow, and
is a discerner of the thoughts and intents of the heart
Heb. 4:12

God is the God of Justice

For true and righteous are his judgments
Rev. 19:2a

God is the Just One

Which of the prophets have not your fathers persecuted? and they
have slain them which shewed before of the coming of the Just One
Acts 7:52 a

God is Kadosh

Holy One
To whom then will ye liken me, or shall I be equal? saith the Holy One
Isaiah 40:25

God Keeps Silent

Unto thee will I cry, O LORD my rock; be not silent to me: lest, if
thou be silent to me, I become like those that go down into the pit
Psalm 28:1

God is Kind

But love ye your enemies, and do good, and lend, hoping for nothing
again; and your reward shall be great, and ye shall be the children
of the Highest: for he is kind unto the unthankful and to the evil
Luke 6:35

God is King

Saying, Blessed be the King that cometh in the name of
the Lord: peace in heaven and glory in the highest
Luke 19:38

God is King Eternal, Immortal, Invisible

Now unto the King eternal, immortal, invisible, the only
wise God, be honour and glory for ever and ever. Amen
1 Tim.1:17

God is the King of Glory

Lift up your heads, O ye gates; even lift them up, ye
everlasting doors; and the King of glory shall come in
Psalm 24:9

God is King of Israel

Blessed is the King of Israel that cometh in the name of the Lord
John 12:13b

The King of the Jews

And Pilate wrote a title, and put it on the cross. And the writing
was, JESUS OF NAZARETH THE KING OF THE JEWS
John 19:19

God is the King of kings
Basileus Basileon
These shall make war with the Lamb, and the Lamb shall
overcome them: for he is LORD of lords, and King of kings
Rev. 17:14a

God is King of Nations
Who would not fear thee, O King of nations? for to thee doth it
appertain: forasmuch as among all the wise men of the nations,
and in all their kingdoms, there is none like unto thee
Jer. 10:7

God is King of Peace
First being by interpretation King of righteousness, and
after that also King of Salem, which is King of peace
Heb. 7:2

God is the King of Saints
Great and marvelous are thy works, Lord God Almighty;
just and true are thy ways, thou King of saints
Rev. 15:3b

God is Kurios
LORD
That if thou shalt confess with thy mouth the Lord
Jesus, and shalt believe in thine heart that God hath
raised him from the dead, thou shalt be saved
Rom. 10:9

The Lamb
Arnion
And He showed me a pure river of water of life, clear as crystal,
proceeding out of the throne of God and of the Lamb
Rev. 22:1

The Lamb of God

Amnostou Theou

Behold the Lamb of God, which taketh away the sin of the world

John 1:29b

The Lamb Who Was Slain

Saying with a loud voice, Worthy is the Lamb that was
slain to receive power, and riches, and wisdom, and
strength, and honour, and glory, and blessing

Rev.5:12

Lamb upon the Throne

And every creature which is in heaven, and on the earth, and under
the earth, and such as are in the sea, and all that are in them, heard
I saying, blessing, and honour, and glory, and power, be unto him
that sitteth upon the throne, and unto the lamb for ever and ever

Rev.5:13

God is the Lamp

For thou art my lamp, O LORD: and the
LORD will lighten my darkness

2 Sam. 22:29

The Last Adam

And so it is written, The first man Adam was made a living
soul; the last Adam was made a quickening spirit

1 Cor. 15:45

God Laughs

He that sitteth in the heavens shall laugh: the
Lord shall have them in derision

Psalm 2:4

God is Life

In him was life; and the life was the light of men

John 1:4

God is Life's Guarantor of Joy and Health
Behold, I will bring it health and cure, and I will cure them,
and reveal unto them the abundance of peace and truth
Jer. 33:6

God is the Lifter of my Head
But thou, O LORD, art a shield for me; my
glory, and the lifter of mine head
Psalm 3:3

God is Light
To Phos tou Kosmou – Light of the world
Then spake Jesus again unto them, saying, I am the
light of the world: he that followeth me shall not walk
in darkness, but shall have the light of life
John 8:12

God is the Light of the Gentiles
A light to lighten the Gentiles, and the glory of thy people Israel
Luke 2:32

God is the Light of Israel
And the light of Israel shall be for a fire, and his Holy One for a flame
Isaiah 10:17a

The Light of the World
That was the true Light, which lighteth every
man that cometh into the world
John 1:9

God is the Lily of the Valleys, Rose of Sharon
I am the Rose of Sharon, and the lily of the valleys
Song of Solomon 2:1

Lion of the Tribe of Judah

God is the Lion of the Tribe of Judah
Aryeh Lammatteh Yehudah
And one of the elders saith unto me, Weep not: behold, the
Lion of the tribe of Judah, the Root of David, hath prevailed
to open the book, and to loose the seven seals thereof
Rev. 5:5

God Listens and Hears
If my people, which are called by my name, shall humble themselves, and pray, and seek my face, and turn from their wicked ways; then will I hear from heaven, and will forgive their sin, and will heal their land
2 Chron.7:14

God Lives for Ever
The four and twenty elders fall down before him that sat on the throne, and worship him that liveth for ever and ever, and cast their crowns before the throne, saying, Thou are worthy, O Lord, to receive glory and honour and power: for thou hast created all things, and for thy pleasure they are and were created
Rev.4:10-11

God is Living
It is a fearful thing to fall into the hands of the living God
Heb.10:31

God is the Living Bread
I am the living bread which came down from heaven: if any man eat of this bread he shall live forever: and the bread that I will give is my flesh, which I will give for the life of the world
John 6:51

The Living Stone
To whom coming, as unto a living stone, disallowed indeed of men, but chosen of God, and precious
1 Peter 2:4

The Living Water of Life
But whosoever shall drink of the water that I shall give him shall never thirst; but the water that I shall give him shall be in him a well of water springing up into everlasting life
John 4:14

God is Lo Ammi

And I will sow her unto me in the earth; and I will have mercy upon her that had not obtained mercy; and I will say to them which were not my people, Thou art my people; and they shall say, Thou art my God
Hosea 2:23

God is Longsuffering

The LORD is longsuffering, and of great mercy,
forgiving iniquity and transgression
Num.14:18a

God is the LORD

Praise ye the LORD. O give thanks unto the LORD;
for he is good: for his mercy endureth for ever
Psalm 106:1

God is LORD of all

The word which God sent unto the children of Israel,
preaching peace by Jesus Christ: (he is Lord of all)
Acts 10:36

God is LORD of the Dead

For to this end Christ both died, and rose, and revived,
that he might be Lord both of the dead and living
Rom. 14:9

God is LORD of the Earth

And the LORD shall be king over all the earth: in that
day shall there be one LORD and his name one
Zech. 14:9

God is the LORD from Heaven

Then the fire of the LORD fell...And when all the
people saw it, they fell on their faces: and thy said, The
LORD, he is the God; the LORD, he is God
1 Kings 18:38-39

God is LORD of Glory

Even as the testimony of Christ was confirmed in you: so that
ye come behind in no gift; waiting for the coming of our Lord
Jesus Christ: who shall also confirm you unto the end, that
ye may be blameless in the day of our Lord Jesus Christ
1 Cor. 1:6-8

God is the LORD Jehovah

Therefore, behold, I will this once cause them to know mine hand
and my might; and they shall know that my name is the LORD
Jer. 16:21

God is our LORD
Kyrios

For the wages of sin is death; but the gift of God is
eternal life through Jesus Christ our Lord
Romans 6:23

God is the LORD Adon
LORD

For the oppression of the poor, for the sighing of the
needy, now will I arise, saith the Lord; I will set him
in safety from him that would ensnare him
Psalm 12:5

God is The LORD God
Adonai

The LORD is my strength and song, and he is become
my salvation: he is my God, and I will prepare him an
habitation; my father's God, and I will exalt him
Ex. 15:2

God is The LORD of Hosts

Let it even be established that thy name be magnified for ever, saying
The LORD of hosts is the God of Israel, even a God to Israel: and
let the house of David thy servant be established before thee
1 Chronicles 17:24

God is the LORD God of Hosts
O LORD of hosts, blessed is the man that trusteth in thee
Psalm 84:12

The LORD Jesus
Grace be unto you, and peace, from God our
father and the Lord Jesus Christ
Col. 1:2b

The LORD's Christ
And it was revealed unto him by the Holy Ghost, that he
should not see death, before he had seen the Lord's Christ
Luke 2:26

God is LORD of the Living
I am the God of Abraham, and the God of Isaac, and the God
of Jacob? God is not the God of the dead, but of the living
Matt. 22:32

God is LORD of lords
O give thanks to the LORD of lords: for his mercy endureth for ever
Psalm 136:3

God is my LORD and my God
And Thomas answered and said unto him, My Lord and my God
John 20:28

LORD of the Sabbath
And he said unto them, That the Son of man is Lord also of the sabbath
Luke 6:5

God is Love
He that loveth not knoweth not God; for God is love
1 John 4:8

God Exercises Lovingkindness
Because thy lovingkindness is better than life, my lips shall praise thee
Psalm 63:3

God is Machaceh
Shelter
For thou hast been a shelter for me, and a strong tower from the enemy
Psalm 61:3

God is Machseh
Fortress, Shelter, Refuge
I will say of the LORD, he is my refuge and my
fortress: my God; in him I will trust
Psalm 91:2

God is Majestic
I will speak of the glorious honour of thy
majesty, and of thy wondrous works
Psalm 145: 5

God is The Majesty
We have such a high priest, who is set on the right
hand of the throne of the Majesty in the heavens
Heb.8:1b

God Makes Everything Beautiful
He hath made everything beautiful in his time: also he hath
set the world in their heart, so that no man can find out the
work that God maketh from the beginning to the end
Eccl. 3:11

God Makes Known His Salvation
The LORD hath made known his salvation: his righteousness
hath he openly shown in the sight of the heathen
Psalm 98:2

God Makes Wise the Simple

The law of the LORD is perfect, converting the soul: the
testimony of the LORD is sure, making wise the simple
Psalm 19:7

God is Malakh Adonai

Behold, I send an Angel before thee, to keep thee in the way,
and to bring thee into the place which I have prepared
Ex. 23:20

God is Manifest in the Flesh

And without controversy, great is the mystery of godliness: God was
manifest in the flesh, justified in the spirit, seen of angels, preached
unto the Gentiles, believed on in the world, received up into glory
1 Tim. 3:16

The Man of Sorrows

He is despised and rejected of men; a man of sorrows, and
acquainted with grief: and we hid as it were our faces from
him; he was despised, and we esteemed him not
Isaiah 53:3

God is the Manna

To him that overcometh will I give to eat of the hidden manna,
and will give him a white stone, and in the stone a new name
written, which no man knoweth saving he that receiveth it
Rev. 2:17

God is Ma'on

Refuge, Dwelling Place
LORD, thou hast been our dwelling place in all generations
Psalm 90:1

God is Maowz Dal
A Defence for the Helpless
For thou hast been a strength to the poor, a strength to the needy
in his distress, a refuge from the storm, a shadow from the heat,
when the blast of the terrible ones is as a storm against the wall
Isaiah 25:4

God is Marvelous
Remember his marvelous works that he hath done,
his wonders, and the judgments of his mouth
1 Chron. 16:12

God is Mashiach
Messiah
Rejoice greatly, O daughter of Zion; shout, O daughter of Jerusalem:
behold, thy King cometh unto thee: he is just, and having salvation;
lowly, and riding upon an ass, and upon a colt the foal of an ass
Zech. 9:9

God is Mashiach Ha Elohim
He said unto them, But whom say ye that I am?
Peter answering said, The Christ of god
Luke 9:20

God is Master
But be not ye called Rabbi: for one is your Master,
even Christ, and all ye are brethren
Matt.23:8

The Mediator
For there is one God, and one mediator between
God and men, the man Christ Jesus
1 Tim. 2:5

God is Meek and Lowly in Heart

Take my yoke upon you, and learn of me; for I am meek and
lowly in heart: and ye shall find rest unto your souls
Matt. 11:29

God Meets Every Need

But my God shall supply all your need according
to his riches in glory by Christ Jesus
Phil. 4:19

God is Melekh Ha Melachim

King of Kings
And he hath on his vesture and on his thigh a name written,
KING OF KINGS, AND LORD OF LORDS
Rev.19:16

God is Melekh

The LORD is King for ever and ever
Psalm 10:16a

God's Mercies are Great

It is of the LORD's mercies that we are not consumed,
because his compassions fail not They are new
every morning: great is thy faithfulness
Lam. 3:22-23

God is Merciful

Be ye therefore merciful, as your Father also is merciful
Luke 6:36

God is Merciful and Gracious

The LORD is merciful and gracious, slow
to anger, and plenteous in mercy
Psalm 103:8

God is Messenger

Behold, I will send my messenger, and he shall prepare the way
before me: and the Lord, whom ye seek, shall suddenly come
to his temple, even the messenger of the covenant, whom ye
delight in: behold, he shall come, saith the Lord of hosts
Mal.3:1

God is Messiah

The Great Deliverer of Israel, Mashiach
We have found the Messias, which is being interpreted, the Christ
John 1:41b

God is the Mighty God

Thou showest lovingkindness to thousands, and recompensest the
iniquity of the fathers into the bosom of their children after them:
the Great, the Mighty God, the LORD of hosts, is his name
Jer. 32:18

God is Mighty in Battle

Gibbor Milchamah
Who is this King of glory? The LORD strong
and mighty, the LORD mighty in battle
Psalm 24:8

God is Mighty in Power

Now unto him that is able to do exceeding abundantly
above all that we ask or think, according to the power that
worketh in us, unto him be glory in the church by Christ
Jesus throughout all ages, world without end. Amen
Eph. 3:20-21

God is the Mighty One of Israel

And thou shalt know that I the LORD am thy Saviour
and thy Redeemer, the mighty one of Jacob
Isaiah 60:16b

God is the Mighty Warrior

The LORD shall go forth as a mighty man, he shall stir up jealousy like a man of war: he shall cry, yea, roar; he shall prevail against his enemies

Isaiah 42:13

God is Miqweh Y'Israel

The Hope of Israel

O LORD, the hope of Israel, all that forsake thee shall be ashamed, and they that depart from me shall be written in the earth, because they have forsaken the LORD, the fountain of living waters

Jer. 17:13

God is my God and my Lord

Stir up thyself, and awake to my judgment, even unto my cause, my God and my Lord

Psalm 35:23

The Mystery of God

That their hearts might be comforted, being knit together in love, and unto all riches of the full understanding, to the acknowledgement of the mystery of God, and of the father, and of Christ

Col. 2:2

God is the Name

Thy name, O LORD, endureth for ever; and thy memorial, O LORD, throughout all generations

Psalm 135:13

God is the Name Above Every Name

Far above all principality, and power, and might, and dominion, and every name that is named, not only in this world, but also in that which is to come

Eph. 1:21

God's Name Endures for Ever

His name shall endure for ever: his name shall be
continued as long as the sun: and men shall be blessed
in him: all nations shall call him blessed
Psalm 72:17

God's Name is Excellent

Let them praise the name of the LORD: for his name alone
is excellent; his glory is above the earth and heaven
Psalm 148:13

God's Name is Pleasant

Praise the LORD; for the LORD is good: sing
praises unto his name; for it is pleasant
Psalm 135:3

The Nazarene

And he came and dwelt in a city called Nazareth:
that it might be fulfilled which was spoken by the
prophets, He shall be called a Nazarene
Matt. 2:23

God is One Who Never Leaves us

I will never leave thee, not forsake thee
Heb. 13:5b

God is One Who Never Sleeps

Behold, he that keepeth Israel shall neither slumber nor sleep
Psalm 121:4

God has a New Name

Him that overcometh will I make a pillar in the temple of my
God, and he shall go no more out: and I will write upon him
the name of my God, and the name of the city of my God,
which is new Jerusalem, which cometh down out of heaven
from my God: and I will write upon him my new name
Rev. 3:12

God is Not Mocked
Be not deceived; God is not mocked: for whatsoever
a man soweth, that shall he also reap
Gal. 6:7

God is Not Religious
Pure religion undefiled before God and the father is this,
To visit the fatherless and the widows in their affliction,
and to keep himself unspotted from the world
James 1:27

God is Olam Zerowa
The Everlasting Arms
The eternal God is thy refuge, and underneath are the
everlasting arms: and he shall thrust out the enemy
from before thee; and shall say, Destroy them.
Deut. 33:27

God is Omnipotent
All-powerful
Alleluia: for the Lord God omnipotent reigneth
Rev. 19:6b

God is Omniscient
All-knowing
Shall not God search this out? for he knoweth the secrets of the heart
Psalm 44:21

God is Omnipresent
God is everywhere
Whither shall I go from thy spirit? or whither
shall I flee from thy presence?
Psalm 139:7

God is One
Avi Khol
One Lord, one faith, one baptism, One God and Father of
all, who is above all, and through all, and in you all
Eph. 4:5-

God is the One Who Is, and Who Was, and Who Is to Be

And I heard the angel of the waters say, Thou art righteous, O Lord,
which art, and wast, and shall be, because thou hast judged thus
Rev. 16:5

The Only Begotten of the Father
For God so loved the world, that he gave his only begotten Son, that
whosoever believeth in him should not perish, but have everlasting life
John 3:16

God is 'Or Goyim
Light of the nations
I the LORD have called thee in righteousness, and will
hold thine hand, and will keep thee, and give thee for a
covenant of the people, for a light of the Gentiles
Isaiah 42:6

God is Pantokrator
Almighty
And (I) will be a Father unto you, and ye shall be my
sons and daughters, saith the Lord Almighty
2 Cor. 6:18

Paraclete
If ye then, being evil, know how to give good gifts unto
your children: how much more shall your heavenly
Father give the Holy Spirit to them that ask him?
Luke 11:13

God Pardons

If we confess our sins, he is faithful and just to forgive us
our sins, and to cleanse us from all unrighteousness
1 John 1:9

The Passover Lamb

For even Christ our Passover is sacrificed for us
1 Cor.5:7

God is Patient

Now the God of patience and consolation grant you to be like-
minded one toward another according to Christ Jesus
Rom. 15:5

God is Peace

For he is our peace, who hath made both one, and hath
broken down the middle wall of partition between us
Eph. 2:14

God is Perfect

Be ye therefore perfect, even as your Father which is in heaven is perfect
Matt. 5:48

God is Perfect in Knowledge

Dost thou know the balancings of the cloud, the wondrous
works of him which is perfect in knowledge?
Job 37:16

God is Personal

For whosoever shall call upon the name of the Lord shall be saved
Rom. 10:13

The Physician
Iatros
When Jesus heard it he saith unto them, They that are whole
have no need of the physician, but they that are sick: I came
not to call the righteous, but sinners to repentance
Mark 2:17

The Pierced Messiah
They pierced my hands and my feet
Psalm 22:16b

God's Pleasure
The LORD taketh pleasure in them that fear
him, in those that hope in his mercy
Psalm 147:11

God is my Portion in the Land of the Living
I cried unto thee, O LORD: I said, Thou art my
refuge and my portion in the land of the living
Psalm 142:5

God is the Portion of my Inheritance
The LORD is the portion of mine inheritance
and of my cup: thou maintainest my lot
Psalm 16:5

God is Potentate
...Which in his times he shall show, who is the blessed and
only Potentate, the King of kings and Lord of lords
1 Tim.6:15

God is the Potter
But now, O LORD, thou art our Father; we are the clay,
and thou our potter; and are all the work of thy hand
Isaiah 64:8

God is the Power

And the temple was filled with smoke from the
glory of God, and from his power
Rev. 15:8a

God is Powerful

The voice of the LORD is powerful; the voice
of the LORD is full of majesty
Psalm 29:4

God is Preeminent and Supreme

For it pleased the Father that in him should all fulness dwell;
And having made peace through the blood of his cross,
by him to reconcile all things unto himself; by him, I say,
whether they be things in earth, or things in heaven
Col. 1:19-20

God is Preparing His Bride

Let us be glad and rejoice, and give honour to him: for the marriage
of the Lamb is come, and his wife hath made herself ready
Rev. 19:7

God is Preparing a Home

In my father's house are many mansions: if it were not so I
would have told you. I go to prepare a place for you. And if I
go and prepare a place for you, I will come again, and receive
you unto myself; that where I am, there ye may be also
John 14:2-3

Priest

For he testifieth, Thou art a priest for ever after the order of Melchisedec
Heb. 7:17

Prince

Him hath God exalted with his right hand to be a Prince and a
Savior, for to give repentance to Israel, and forgiveness of sins
Acts 5:31

The Prince of the Kings of the Earth

And from Jesus Christ, who is the faithful witness, and the first begotten of the dead, and the prince of the kings of the earth. Unto him that loved us, and washed us from our sins in his own blood, and hath made us kings and priests unto God and his Father; to him be glory and dominion for ever and ever. Amen
Rev.1:5-6

The Prince of Life

And killed the Prince of life, whom God hath raised from the dead; whereof we are witnesses
Acts 3:15

God is the Prince of Peace

Sar Shalom
And his name shall be called Wonderful, Counsellor, The Mighty God, The Everlasting Father, The Prince of Peace
Isaiah 9:6

God is Prophecy Fulfilled

And he said unto them, These are the words which I spake unto you, while I was yet with you, that all things must be fulfilled, which were written in the law of Moses, and in the prophets, and in the psalms, concerning me
Luke 24:44

God is Prophet

For Moses truly said unto the fathers, A prophet shall the Lord your God raise up unto you of your brethren, like unto me; him shall ye hear in all things whatsoever he shall say unto you
Acts 3:22

God is the Propitiation of the sins of the Whole World

And he is the propitiation for our sins: and not for ours
only, but also for the sins of the whole world
1 John 2:2

God is our Protector

Oh how great is thy goodness, which thou hast laid up for
them that fear thee; which thou hast wrought for them that
trust in thee before the sons of men! Thou shalt hide them in
the secret of thy presence from the pride of man: thou shalt
keep them secretly in a pavilion from the strife of tongues
Psalm 31:19-20

God is our Provider

God having provided some better thing for us, that
they without us should not be made perfect
Heb. 11:40

God is Pure and Undefiled

For I am the LORD your God: ye shall therefore sanctify
yourselves, and ye shall be holy; for I am holy
Lev.11 44a

God is Purifier

Who gave himself for us, that he might redeem us from all iniquity,
and purify unto himself a peculiar people, zealous of good works
Titus 2:14

Rabbi

Rabbi, thou art the Son of God; thou art the King of Israel
John 1:49b

Rabboni

Jesus saith unto her, Mary. She turned herself, and saith
unto him, Rabboni; which is to say, Master
John 20:16

God is the Radiant One

This then is the message which we have heard of him, and declare
unto you, that God is light, and in him is no darkness at all
1 John 1:5

God is the Ransom

Who gave himself a ransom for all, to be testified in due time
1 Tim.2:6

God Reasons with man

Come now, and let us reason together, saith the Lord:
though your sins be as scarlet, they shall be as white as snow;
though they be red like crimson, they shall be as wool
Isaiah 1:18

God is Redeemer

And they sung a new song, saying, Thou art worthy to take the book,
and to open the seals thereof: for thou wast slain,and hast
redeemed us to God by thy blood out of every kindred, and
tongue, and people, and nation; And hast made us unto our
God kings and priests: and we shall reign on the earth
Rev 5:9-10

God is Refiner

Behold, I have refined thee, but not with silver;
I have chosen thee in the furnace of affliction
Isaiah 48:10

God is a Refuge

God is our refuge and strength, a very present help in trouble
Psalm 46:1

Be still and know that I AM God

God is the Refuge of the poor
Ye have shamed the counsel of the poor, because the LORD is his refuge
Psalm 14:6

God is the Rejected Stone
The stone which the builders refused is become
the head stone of the corner
Psalm 118:22

God Rejoices
The LORD thy God in the midst of thee is mighty; he
will save, he will rejoice over thee with joy; he will rest
in his love, he will joy over thee with singing
Zeph. 3:17

God is One Who Remembers
And I will remember my covenant, which is between me
and you and every living creature of all flesh; and the waters
shall no more become a flood to destroy all flesh
Gen.9:15

God's Reproofs are Life
For the commandment is a lamp; and the law is light;
and reproofs of instruction are the way of life
Prov. 6:23

God Restores Losses
And the women said unto Naomi, Blessed be the LORD,
whish hath not left thee this day without a kinsman, that
his name may be famous in Israel. And he shall be unto thee
a restorer of thy life, and a nourisher of thine old age
Ruth 4:14:15a

God Restores the Soul
He retoreth my soul: he leadeth me in the paths
of righteousness for his name's sake
Psalm 23:3

God is One Who Rests
For he that is entered into his rest, he also hath ceased
from his own works, as God did from his
Heb. 4:10

The Resurrection
Jesus said unto her, I am the resurrection, and the life: he that
believeth in me, though he were dead, yet shall he live
John 11:25

The Returning King
The kingdoms of this world are become the kingdoms of our
Lord and of his Christ; and he shall reign for ever and ever
Rev. 11:15

God is Rewarder
And, behold, I come quickly, and my reward is with me,
to give every man according as his work shall be
Rev. 22:12

God is Righteous
The fear of the LORD is clean, enduring for ever: the
judgments of the LORD are true and righteous altogether
Psalm 19:9

God is the Righteous Judge
But with righteousness shall he judge the poor, and
reprove with equity for the meek of the earth
Isaiah 11:4a

The Risen Son of man
He is not here: for he is risen, as he said. Come,
see the place where the Lord lay.
Matt.28:6

God is the Rock
And I also say unto thee, That thou art Peter, and upon this rock I will build my church; and the gates of hell shall not prevail against it
Matt. 16:18

God is the Rock of Ages
He only is my rock and my salvation: he is my defense; I shall not be moved. In God is my salvation and my glory: the rock of my strength, and my refuge, is in God
Psalm 62:6-7

God is the Root of Jesse
And in that day there shall be a root of Jesse, which shall stand for an ensign of the people; to it shall the Gentiles seek: and his rest shall be glorious
Isaiah 11:10

God is the Root and the Offspring of David
I Jesus have sent mine angel to testify unto you these things in the churches. I am the root and the offspring of David, and the bright and morning star
Rev. 22:16

Ruach Adonai
Then Peter said unto her, How is it that ye have agreed together to tempt the Spirit of the Lord?
Acts 5:9a

God is Ruach Ha Kodesh
But the Comforter, which is the Holy Ghost, whom the Father will send in my name, he shall teach you all things, and bring all things to your remembrance, whatsoever I have said unto you
John 14:26

Ruach haKodesh u vaesh

Wherefore we receiving a kingdom which cannot be moved,
let us have grace, whereby we may serve God acceptably with
reverence and godly fear: For our God is a consuming fire
Heb. 12:28b-29

Ruach haMashiach

But ye are not in the flesh but in the Spirit, if so be
that the Spirit of God dwell in you.Now if any man
have not the Spirit of Christ he is none of his
Rom. 8:9

Ruach Hechazon

That the God of our Lord Jesus Christ, the Father of glory, may give
unto you the spirit of wisdom and revelation in the knowledge of him
Eph. 1:17

Ruach Olam

How much more shall the blood of Christ, who through the
eternal Spirit offered himself without spot to God, purge your
conscience from dead works to serve the living God?
Heb.9:14

Ruach Yeshua

After they were come to Mysia, they assayed to go
into Bithynia: but the Spirit suffered them not
Acts 16:7

God is Ruler

He ruleth by his power for ever; his eyes behold the
nations: let not the rebellious exalt themselves. Selah
Psalm 66:7

God is Ruler of His Creation
That I should preach among the Gentiles the unsearchable riches of Christ; and to make all men see what is the fellowship of the mystery, which from the beginning of the world hath been hid in God, who created all things by Jesus Christ
Eph. 3:8b-9

God is Ruler of Night and Day
Yea, the darkness hideth not from thee; but the night shineth as the day: the darkness and the light are both alike to thee
Psalm 139:12

God is Sacred
Speak unto all the congregation of the children of Israel, and say unto them, Ye shall be holy: for I the LORD your God am holy
Lev. 19:2

God is the Sacrifice
For even Christ our Passover is sacrificed for us
1 Cor. 5:7b

God is our Safety
I will both lay me down in peace, and sleep: for thou, LORD, only makest me dwell in safety
Psalm 4:8

God is Salvation
And after these things I heard a great voice of much people in heaven, saying, Alleluia; salvation, and glory and honour, and power, unto the Lord our God
Rev. 19:1

God is the Same
Jesus Christ the same yesterday, and today, and for ever
Heb. 13:8

God is Sanctifier

Elect according to the foreknowledge of God the Father, through
sanctification of the Spirit, unto obedience and sprinkling of the
blood of Jesus Christ: Grace unto you, and peace, be multiplied
1 Pet. 1:2

God Saves the Jewish People

Foe if thou altogether holdest thy peace at this time, then shall there
enlargement and deliverance arise to the Jews from another place;
but thou and thy father's house shall be destroyed: and who knowest
whether thou art come to the kingdom for such a time as this?
Esther 4:14

God is One Who Saves the Needy

He shall spare the poor and needy, and shall save the souls of the needy
Psalm 72:13

God is the Saving Refuge of His Anointed

The LORD is their strength, and he is the
saving strength of his anointed
Psalm 28:8

Saviour

For we have heard him ourselves, and know that this
is indeed the Christ, the Saviour of the world
John 4:42b

God is Saviour of All Men

For therefore we both labour and suffer reproach,
because we trust in the living God, who is the Saviour
of all men, specially of those that believe
1 Tim. 4:10

Saviour of both Jew and Gentile

For I am not ashamed of the gospel of Christ: for it
is the power of God unto salvation to every one that
believeth; to the Jew first, and also to the Greek
Rom.1:16

The Saviour of the World

And we have seen and do testify that the Father
sent the Son to be the Saviour of the world
1 John 4:14

The Scandalon

Stumbling stone
As it is written, Behold, I lay in Zion a stumblingstone and a rock
of offense: and whosoever believeth on him shall not be ashamed
Rom.9:33

The Second Adam

The first man is of the earth, earthy: the second
man is the Lord from heaven
1 Cor. 15:47

God is the Seed of Abraham

Now to Abraham and his seed were the promises
made. He saith not, And to seeds, as of many; but
as of one, And to thy seed, which is Christ
Gal. 3:16

The Seed of David

Remember that Jesus Christ of the seed of David was
raised from the dead according to my gospel
2 Tim. 2:8

God is the Seed of the Woman

And I will put enmity between thee and the woman, and between thy
seed and her seed. It shall bruise thy head, and thou shalt bruise his heel
Gen. 3:15

The Servant is God

Behold My servant, whom I uphold; mine elect, in
whom my soul delighteth; I have put my spirit upon
him: he shall bring forth judgment to the Gentiles
Isaiah 42:1

The Servant of the LORD

Behold my servant who I have chosen; my
beloved, in whom my soul is well pleased
Matt. 12:18a

God is the Seven Spirits

And out of the throne proceeded lightnings and thunderings
and voices: and there were seven lamps of fire burning
before the throne, which are the seven Spirits of God
Rev. 4:5

God is Shaddai

Almighty God

And when Abram was ninety years old and nine, the
LORD appeared to Abram, and said unto him, I am the
Almighty God; walk before me, and be thou perfect
Gen 17:1

God is the Shade and Keeper

The LORD is thy keeper: the LORD is thy shade upon thy right hand
Psalm 121:5

God's Shekinah Glory

Absolute Rest

And the priests could not enter in to the house of the LORD;
because the glory of the LORD had filled the LORD's house
2 Chron. 7:2

God is our Shield
Every word of God is pure: he is a shield unto
them that put their trust in him
Prov. 30:5

God is Shiloh
The sceptre shall not depart from Judah, nor a lawgiver
from between his feet, until Shiloh come; and unto
him shall the gathering of the people be
Gen. 49:10

God is Shophet
Judge, Ruler
O LORD God, to whom vengeance belongeth; O
God, to whom vengeance belongeth, show thyself.
Lift up thyself, thou judge of the earth
Psalm 94:1-2a

God is Slow to Anger
The LORD is slow to anger, and great in power, and will not at
all acquit the wicked: the LORD hath his way in the whirlwind
and in the storm, and the clouds are the dust of his feet.
Nahum 1:3

God is He that Smiteth
And mine eye shall not spare, neither will I have pity: I will recompense
thee according to thy ways, and thin abominations that are in the
midst of thee; and ye shall know that I am the LORD that smiteth
Ezek. 7:9

God is the Son of Abraham
The book of the generation of Jesus Christ, the
son of David, the son of Abraham
Matt. 1:1

God is the Son of David
Have mercy on me, O Lord, thou son of David
Matt. 15:22b

The Son of God
He that hath the Son hath life; and he that hath
not the Son of God hath not life
1 John 5:12

Son of the Father
Grace be with you, mercy, and peace, from God the Father, and
from the Lord Jesus Christ, the Son of the Father, in truth and love
2 John 3

The Son of the Living God
And we believe and are sure that thou art that
Christ, the Son of the living God
John 6:69

The Son of Man
For the Son of man is come to save that which was lost
Matt. 18:11

The Son of Mary
Now the birth of Jesus Christ was on this wise: When as
his mother Mary was espoused to Joseph, before they came
together, she was found with child of the Holy Ghost
Matt. 1:18

The Son of the Most High
He shall be great, and shall be called the Son of the Highest: and
the Lord God shall give unto him the throne of his Father David
Luke 1:32

The Soon Coming King

For the Lord himself shall descend from heaven with a shout,
with the voice of the archangel, and with the trump of God: and
the dead in Christ shall rise first: Then we which are alive and
remain shall be caught up together with them in the clouds, to
meet the Lord in the air: and so shall we ever be with the Lord
1 Thess. 4:16-17

God is Sophia

The Wisdom of God
The LORD by wisdom hath founded the earth; by
understanding hath he established the heavens
Prov. 3:19

God is Soter

Saviour, Deliverer, Preserver
For unto you is born this day in the City of David
a Saviour, which is Christ the Lord
Luke 2:11

God is Sovereign

The LORD hath prepared his throne in the
heavens; and his kingdom ruleth over all
Psalm 103:19

God is the Sovereign Ruler over all Creation

Thine O LORD, is the greatness, and the power, and the glory,
and the victory, and the majesty: for all that is in the heaven and
in the earth is thine; thine is the kingdom, O LORD, and thou art
exalted as head above all. Both riches and honour come of thee, and
thou reignest over all; and in thine hand is power and might; and
in thine hand it is to make great, and to give strength unto all
1 Chron. 29:11-12

God is a Spirit

God is a Spirit: and they that worship him
must worship him in spirit and truth
John 4:24

God is the Spirit of Adoption

For ye have not received the spirit of bondage again to fear; but ye
have received the Spirit of adoption, whereby we cry, Abba, Father
Rom. 8:15

The Spirit of Christ

Now if any man have not the Spirit of Christ, he is none of his
Rom. 8:9

The Spirit of Glory is God

If ye be reproached for the name of Christ, happy are ye;
for the spirit of glory and of God resteth upon you
1 Peter 4:14a

The Spirit of God

And the earth was without form, and void; and
darkness was upon the face of the deep. And the spirit
of God moved upon the face of the waters
Gen. 1:2

God is the Spirit of Grace and Supplication

And I will pour upon the house of David, and upon the inhabitants
of Jerusalem, the spirit of grace and of supplications: and they
shall look upon me whom they have pierced, and they shall
mourn for him, as one mourneth for his only son, and shall be in
bitterness for him, as one that is in bitterness for his firstborn
Zech. 12:10

God is the Spirit of Knowledge and understanding
And the spirit of the LORD shall rest upon him, the spirit of
wisdom and understanding, the spirit of counsel and might,
the spirit of knowledge and of the fear of the LORD
Isaiah 11:2

God is the Spirit of Liberty
Now the Lord is that Spirit: and where the
Spirit of the Lord is, there is liberty
2 Cor. 3:17

Spirit of Life
For the law of the Spirit of life in Christ Jesus hath
made me free from the law of sin and death
Rom. 8:2

God is the Spirit of the Living God
Forasmuch as ye are manifestly declared to be the epistle of Christ
ministered by us, written not with ink, but with the Spirit of the
living God; not in tables of stone, but in fleshly tables of the heart
2 Cor. 3:3

God is the Spirit of the Lord
The Spirit of the Lord is upon me, because he hath anointed
me to preach the gospel to the poor; he hath sent me to heal
the brokenhearted, to preach deliverance to the captives, and
recovering of sight to the blind, to set at liberty them that
are bruised. To reach the acceptable year of the Lord
Luke 4:18,19

God is the Spirit of Peace
But the fruit of the Spirit is love, joy, peace, longsuffering, gentleness,
goodness, faith, meekness, temperance: against such there is no law
Gal. 5:22-23

God is the Spirit of Promise
That we should be to the praise of his glory, who first trusted
in Christ. In whom ye also trusted, after that ye heard the word
of truth, the gospel of your salvation: in whom also after that
ye believed, ye were sealed with that holy Spirit of promise
Eph. 1:12-13

The Spiritual Rock is God
For they drank of that spiritual Rock that followed
them: and that Rock was Christ
1 Cor. 10:4

God is the Spirit of Truth
And I will pray the Father, and he shall give you another Comforter,
that he may abide with you for ever; Even the Spirit of truth
John 14:16-17a

God is the Stem of Jesse
And there shall come forth a rod out of the stem of
Jesse, and a branch shall grow out of his roots
Isaiah 11:1

God is the Stone
And he beheld them, and said, What is this then that is written,
The stone which the builders rejected, th same is become the head
of the corner? Whoever shall fall upon that stone shall be broken;
but on whomsoever it shall fall, it will grind him to powder
Luke 20:17-18

God is the Strength of His People
The way of the LORD is strength to the upright: but
destruction shall be to the workers of iniquity
Prov. 10:29

Unto you who revere my name shall the Sun of righteousness arise with healing in his wings

Malachi 4:2

Sun of Righteousness

God is our Strengthener
I can do all things through Christ which strengtheneth me
Phil. 4:13

God is a Strong Tower

Migdal Oz

The name of the LORD is a strong tower: the
righteous runneth into it, and is safe

Prov. 18:10

The Suffering Servant

Surely he hath borne our griefs, and carried our sorrows: yet we
did esteem him stricken, smitten of God and afflicted.
Bur he was wounded for our transgressions, he was
bruised for our iniquities: the chastisement or our peace
was upon him; and with his stripes we are healed

Isaiah 53:4-5

God is the Sun of Righteousness

But unto you that fear my name shall the Sun of
righteousness arise with healing in his wings; and ye
shall go forth, and grow up as calves of the stall

Mal.4:2

God is a Sun and Shield

For the LORD God is a sun and shield: the LORD will give grace and
glory: no good thing will he withhold from them that walk uprightly

Psalm 84:11

God is Supreme

But out God is in the heavens: he hath done whatsoever he hath pleased

Psalm 115:3

God is a Sure Foundation

Nevertheless the foundation of God standeth sure, having
this seal, The Lord knoweth them that are his

2 Tim 2:19a

God is the Sword of thy Excellency
Jehovah Chereb

Happy art thou, O Israel: who is like unto thee, O people saved by the
LORD, the shield of thy help, and who is the sword of thy excellency!
Deut. 33:29a

God Takes Away
..And said, Naked came I out of my mother's womb, and
naked shall I return thither: the LORD gave, and the
LORD hath taken away; blessed be the name of the
LORD Job 1:21

Teacher Come From God is God
Rhabbi, Rhabbouni, *Didaskalos*

The same came to Jesus by night, and said unto him, Rabbi, we
know that thou art a teacher come from God: for no man can
do these miracles that thou doest, except God be with him
John 3:2

God puts our Tears in His Bottle
Thou tellest my wanderings: put thou my tears
into thy bottle: are they not in thy book?
Psalm 56:8

God is the Temple
And I saw no temple therein: for the Lord God
Almighty and the Lamb are the temple of it
Rev. 21:22

God Tempts no one
Let no man say when he is tempted, I am tempted of God: for
God cannot be tempted with evil, neither tempteth he any man
James 1:13

God is Testator

For where a testament is, there must also of
necessity be the death of the testator
Heb. 9:16

God Tests the Hearts

Every way of a man is right in his own eyes:
but the LORD pondereth the hearts
Prov.21:2

God is Theos

Grace unto you, and peace, from God our
Father and the Lord Jesus Christ
2 Thess. 1:2

God is Theotes

Godhead, Fulness
For in him dwelleth all the fulness of the Godhead bodily
Col.2:9

God's Thoughts Toward us are Manifold

Many, O LORD my God, are thy wonderful works which
thou hast done, and thy thoughts which are to us-ward: they
cannot be reckoned up in order unto thee: if I would declare
and speak of them, they are more than can be numbered
Psalm 40:5

God is Three in One, Equal and Eternal

For there are three that bear record in heaven, the Father,
the Word, and the Holy Ghost: and these three are one
1 John 5:7

God is on His Throne

To him that overcometh will I grant to sit with me in my throne even
as I also overcame, and am set down with my Father in his throne
Rev.3:21

God's Throne is For Ever

Thy throne, O God, is for ever and ever:
the scepter of thy kingdom is a right sceptre
Psalm 45:6

God is the Transcendent One

Now I know that the LORD is greater than all gods
Ex.18:11a

God Transforms us

And be not conformed to this world: but be ye transformed
by the renewing of your mind, that ye may prove what is
that good, and acceptable, and perfect, will of God
Rom. 12:2

God's Treasure - Israel

For the LORD hath chosen Jacob unto himself,
and Israel for his peculiar treasure
Psalm 135:4

God is a Tree of Life

To him that overcometh will I give to eat of the tree of
life, which is in the midst of the paradise of God
Rev. 2:7b

God is Triumphant

And having spoiled principalities and powers, he made a
show of them openly, triumphing over them in it
Col.2:15

The True God

And this is life eternal, that they might know thee the only
true God, and Jesus Christ, whom thou hast sent
John 17:3

God is Trustworthy

The LORD is my strength and my shield; my heart
trusted in him, and I am helped: therefore my heart
greatly rejoiceth; and with my song will I praise him
Psalm 28:7

God is Tsemach Tsedahah

In those days, and at that time, will I cause the Branch
of righteousness to grow up into David; and he shall
execute judgment and righteousness in the land
Jer. 33:15

God is Tsur Yeshuato

Rock of Salvation
O come, let us sing unto the LORD: let us make
a joyful noise to the rock of our salvation
Psalm 95:1

God is The Unchangeable One

But this man, because he continueth ever,
hath an unchangeable priesthood
Heb. 7:24

God is Unchanging

For I am the LORD, I change not
Mal.3:6a

God is Undefiled

For such an high priest became us, who is holy, harmless, undefiled,
separate from sinners, and made higher than the heavens
Heb. 7:26

God is Understanding

But there is a spirit in man: and the inspiration of
the Almighty giveth them understanding
Job 32:8

God is Unfathomable
Great is the LORD, and greatly to be praised;
and his greatness is unsearchable
Psalm 145:3

God is Unsearchable in His Ways
O the depth of the riches both of the wisdom and knowledge of God!
How unsearchable are his judgments, and his ways past finding out!
Rom.11:33

God is Upright
Righteous art thou, O LORD, and upright are thy judgments
Psalm 119:137

God of Vengeance
God is jealous, and the LORD revengeth; the LORD
revengeth, and is furious; The LORD will take vengeance on
his adversaries, and he reserveth wrath for his enemies. The
LORD is slow to anger, and great in power, and will not at all
acquit the wicked: the LORD hath his way in the whirlwind
and in the storm, and the clouds are the dust of his feet
Nahum 1:2-3

God Vindicates
Therefore being justified by faith, we have peace
with God through our Lord Jesus Christ
Rom. 5:1

God is the Vine and Husbandman
I AM the true vine, and my Father is the husbandman
John 15:1

The Vine and branches

God is Very Pitiful and of Tender Mercy
Behold, we count them happy which endure. Ye have heard
of the patience of Job, and have seen the end of the Lord;
that the lord is very pitiful, and of tender mercy
James 5:11

God is the Watcher of our Souls
And Laban said, This heap is a witness between me and
thee this day. Therefore was the name of it called Galeed
and Mizpah; for he said, The LORD watch between me
and htee, when we are absent one from another
Gen. 31:48-49

The Way, the Truth and the Life
Jesus saith unto him, I am the way, the truth, and the
life: no man cometh unto the Father, but by me.
John 14:6

God Weeps
Jesus wept
John 11:35

God Weighs the Spirits
All the ways of a man are clean in his own eyes;
but the LORD weigheth the spirits
Prov. 16:2

God is Wholly Matchless and Indescribable
Hast thou heard the secret of God? and dost
thou restrain wisdom to thyself?
Job 15:8

The Will of God
For this is the will of God, even your sanctification,
that ye should abstain from fornication
1 Thess. 4:3

The Wisdom of God

But unto them which are called, both Jews and Greeks, Christ the power of God, and the wisdom of God. Because the foolishness of God is wiser than men; and the weakness of God is stronger than men

1 Cor. 1:24-25

God is the Word

Logos

In the beginning was the Word, and the Word was with God, and the Word was God

John 1:1

God's Word is Eternal

For ever, O LORD, thy word is settled in heaven

Psalm 119:89

God is the Word of God

And he was clothed with a vesture dipped in blood: and his name is called The Word of God

Rev. 19:13

God's Word is a Lamp

Thy word is a lamp unto my feet, and a light unto my path

Psalm 119:105

God is the Word of Life

That which was from the beginning, which we have heard, which we have seen with our eyes, which we have looked upon, and our hands have handled, of the Word of life

1 John 1:1

The Word Made Flesh

Hereby know ye the Spirit of God: Every spirit that confesseth
that Jesus Christ is come in the flesh is of God
1 John 4:2

God's Word Never Fails

For as the rain cometh down, and the snow from heaven, and
returneth not thither, but watereth the earth, and maketh it bring
forth and bud, that it may give seed to the sower, and bread to the
eater: So shall my word be that goeth forth out of my mouth: it
shall not return unto me void, but it shall accomplish that which
I please, and it shall prosper in the thing whereto I sent it
Isaiah 55:10-11

God is Worthy

Thou art worthy, O Lord, to receive glory and honour
and power: for thou hast created all things, and
for thy pleasure they are and were created
Rev. 4:11

God is Worthy of Thanksgiving

Be careful for nothing: but n everything by prayer and supplication
with thanksgiving let your requests be made known unto God
Phil 4:6

God is Worthy of Worship

Give unto the LORD the glory due unto his name: bring an offering,
and come before him: worship the LORD in the beauty of holiness
1 Chron. 16:29

God is Yashar

Just One
The way of the just is uprightness: thou,
most upright, dost weigh the path of the just
Isaiah 26:7

God is YHWH
Shem HaMeforash – The Ineffible Name
The One who is, the Existent One
And God said unto Moses, I AM that I AM: and he said, Thus shalt
thou say unto the children of Israel, I AM hath sent me unto you
Ex. 3:15

God is YHWH Sabaoth
LORD of Hosts
Thus saith the LORD the King of Israel, and his redeemer the LORD
of hosts; I am the first and I am the last; and beside me there is no God
Isaiah 44:6

God is YHWH Tzva'ot
God of Hosts, Armies or Powers The LORD of hosts
is with us; the God of Jacob is our refuge. Selah
Psalm 46:7

Yesua Habibi *(Arabic)*
I charge you, O ye daughters of Jerusalem, by the roes, and
by the hinds of the field, that ye stir not up, nor awaken
my love, till he please. The voice of my beloved! Behold, he
cometh leaping upon the mountains, skipping upon the hills
Song of Solomon 2:7-8

YESHUA is God
Saviour, "He will save"
For I am the LORD thy God the Holy One of Israel, thy Saviour
Isaiah 43:3a

PART TWO

THE ETERNALITY AND
INFINITUDE OF GOD

God's kingdom and His mercy are everlasting. In the Lord Jehovah is everlasting strength. He is the author of eternal salvation and His kingdom is for ever and ever. Before the creation of the world God existed as the eternal one. Isaiah 57:15 speaks of the High and lofty One that inhabits eternity. "For thus saith the high and lofty One that inhabits eternity, whose name is Holy; I dwell in the high and holy place, with him also that is of a contrite and humble spirit, to revive the spirit of the humble, and to revive the heart of the contrite ones." He is the One who has called us to His eternal glory and we are granted eternal life through believing. Jesus Christ says in John 17:3: "And this is life eternal, that they might know thee the only true God, and Jesus Christ, whom thou hast sent." When Jesus asked the twelve disciples: "Will you also go away?" Simon Peter answers Jesus: "Lord, to whom shall we go? Thou hast the words of eternal life." John says in 1John 5:11-20: "And this is the record, that God has given to us eternal life, and this life is in his Son." These words, says John, are written so that we may know we have eternal life, and believe in the name of the Son of God.

To know Jesus and believe in Him is eternal life, reiterates John in verse 20. Eternity -for ever and ever! This is what we are promised through believing in Christ Jesus. Eternal fire, judgment and damnation is also mentioned in Mark 3:29; Hebrews 6:2 and Jude 7, as the destiny of the devil and his angels and those whose names are not found written in the book of life (Rev.20:15; 21:8). Revelation 20:10 speaks of the devil and his angels being cast into the lake of fire to be tormented day and night for ever and ever. But for those who believe there will be unending peace, world without end (Eph. 3:21). Revelation 22:13 says that God is the beginning and the end. Hebrews tells us that Jesus is our High Priest, who is made a priest for ever after the power of an endless life; a priest for ever with an unchangeable priesthood, who ever lives to make intercession for His people, and is consecrated for evermore. Who, by the shedding of His precious blood has obtained for us eternal redemption (Heb.9:12) by the eternal Spirit, whereby we receive the promise of eternal inheritance through the blood of the everlasting covenant (Heb.13:20-21).

God is infinite and eternal. A.W. Pink says in his book, "*The Attributes of God*": "There was a time, if time is what it could be called, when God, in the unity of His nature, though subsisting equally in three Divine Persons, dwelt all alone. There was no heaven, where His glory is now particularly manifested. There was no earth to engage His attention. There were no angels to uphold His praises; no universe to be upheld by the word of His power. There was nothing, no one, but God; and that, not for a day, a year, or an age, but from "everlasting." During a past eternity, God was alone: self-contained, self-sufficient, self-satisfied; in need of nothing. Had a universe, had angels, had human beings been necessary to Him in any way, they also had been called into existence from all eternity. The creating of them when He did added nothing to God essentially. He changes not (Mal.3:6) therefore His essential glory can be neither augmented nor diminished. God was under no constraint, no obligations, no necessity to create. That He chose to do was purely a sovereign act on His part, caused by nothing outside Himself, determined by nothing but His own mere good pleasure. for He "worketh all things after the counsel of His own will (Eph. 1:11). That He did create was simply for His manifestative glory."

GOD IS THE AUTHOR OF
ETERNAL SALVATION

Jesus Christ, being made perfect through the things which He suffered, became the author of eternal salvation to all them that obey Him. He is the author and the finisher of our faith, well able to perfect us according to the righteousness of God. His desire is for us to be holy and He is perfecting holiness within His people. As the author of eternal salvation God initiates the plan of salvation; His plan is to redeem mankind, and He wills for all to be saved and to come to the knowledge of the truth (1 Tim.2:4). Good works follow a holy life. Romans 14:17 tells us that the kingdom of God is in righteousness, peace and joy in the Holy Ghost, and in Ephesians 5:9 that the fruit of the Spirit is in all goodness and righteousness and truth. 1 Timothy 6:11 says to follow after righteousness, goodness, faith, love, patience and meekness and that the fruit of righteousness is sown in peace by those who make peace (James 3:18). 1 John says that the one who does righteousness is righteous, even as God is righteous. Salvation is our eternal security. When we repent of our sins and turn to Christ our past sins are forgiven and we are saved from eternal damnation. The covering of the blood of Jesus secures us for eternity.

The Word of God says to repent and be converted so that our sins may be blotted out. It was no mean feat for the King of glory to send His Son in human form, the blessed Son of God, Jesus, to suffer and die on Calvary's tree. Through this, God has made a way, the only way, for mankind to come to Himself, upon repentance. The cry of the prophet, John the Baptist in preparing the way for the Messiah was "Repent – for the kingdom of heaven is at hand" (Matt.3:2). He came to "give knowledge of salvation unto his people by the remission of their sins" (Luke 1:77). Salvation is the state of being saved from sin, brought about by having faith in Christ. The word "salvation" also implies protecting someone from harm or loss. It is of Latin origin, and includes restoration, preservation, deliverance and liberation as well as divine function, propitiation, atonement and redemption.

As the redeemed of God, we are Christ's purchased possession, bought by His blood. He is Saviour, both Saviour of Jew and Gentile alike, and Saviour of the world, the Redeemer of mankind. Romans 3:25 says that He has declared our righteousness, by the remission of sins through the propitiation of His blood, also in 1 John 2:2 that He is the propitiation for our sins and for the sins of the whole world, because of His love (1 John 4:10), and that we are thus reconciled to God (2 Corinthians 5:18) so that we may be made the righteousness of God in Christ. Romans 10:4 tells us that Christ is the "end of the law" for righteousness to everyone that believes, and that the just shall live by faith – by believing unto righteousness (Rom.10:10). No matter whether we are Jew or Greek, there is no difference; the atonement is through Jesus Christ says the Apostle Paul in Romans 5:11. Ephesians 1:7 says we have redemption through His blood, the forgiveness of sins, according to the riches of His grace, also Col.1:14.

It is through hearing the Gospel of salvation, the Word of truth, that we are reconciled to God, having believed. Hebrews 9:12-15 says that we receive the promise of eternal inheritance because Christ obtained eternal redemption for us by offering Himself in our place, when He redeemed us by His blood (1 Pet. 1:18-19). Verse 23 goes on to say that we are thus born again by the incorruptible seed of the Word of God, which is the very Word of truth spoken of in James 1:18, causing us to be God's first fruits. We are justified freely by His grace through Christ Jesus, and one day our bodies will be redeemed according to Romans 8:23. Until then we are sealed by the Holy Spirit of God (Ephesians 4:30). Fruit bearing is of great value to God. He is pleased when we are bringing forth fruit for His glory.

THE HOLINESS OF GOD

The name of God is matchless and His ways unfathomable as the Word of God tells us. The aspect of God's holiness is a part of His nature revealing who He is. He is also love, in essence. There are numerable attributes and characteristics of God descriptive of His supreme nature. Holiness and love are but two of these attributes listed on the following pages. I will speak of His holiness which is expressly important, for the Word of God tells us: "Without holiness no man shall see the Lord" in Hebrews. God is so holy that His glory He will not give to another, which is where we read that He is a jealous God.

Because of who He is, He deserves all the glory attributed to His name. In the Bible, the writer says; "Be ye holy, for I am holy." He wants His people to be partakers of His divine nature, to live holy lives. Leviticus 11:45 says: "Ye shall therefore be holy, for I am holy" and Paul the Apostle writes in Romans 12:1: "I beseech you therefore, brethren, by the mercies of God, that ye present your bodies a living sacrifice, holy, acceptable to God, which is your reasonable service. And be not conformed to this world: but be ye transformed by the renewing of your mind, that ye may prove what is that good, and acceptable, and perfect, will of God." It is clear that God's will, His perfect will, is for us to be transformed to be like Him, holy. This is done in the power and enablement of the Holy Spirit and through the Word of God. It is the application of God's Word which renews the mind and transforms it. God empowers that which He first makes holy.

God's holiness is seen in a detailed account of the life of Moses as in Exodus chapter 3. The LORD instructed Moses to remove the sandals from his feet in approaching the Almighty God, for the ground even where he stood was holy. In Psalm 99:5 the Psalmist says to worship at His footstool, for He is holy, also in Revelation 4:8 the angels in heaven cry "Holy, holy. Holy, Lord God Almighty."

There is an account in the Bible of a man called Uzzah who approached the ark of the covenant of God, and whilst expressly forbidden, he touched the ark, and died as a result (2 Sam. 6:6-7). This action cost him his life. Thus, when we approach God in prayer, we need to approach Him with the reverence He is due.

Approaching God requires humility. The sin of pride is probably the worst known sin. It is the antithesis to humility. For the sin of pride Lucifer fell from heaven. Human pride is at the root of all sin.

Holiness is a characteristic of God describing and expressing the perfection of all that He is. It is the basis of all his actions. For everything He does is right and good. If we have a true understanding of God's holiness, we will also realize how awful sin is, and detest it. God's righteousness and justice are a direct result of his holiness. Holiness as a quality of the Christian life is far more than not doing what is wrong. It is also doing what is right. In our desire to know God, we must discern this about the Almighty; He resists the proud, but His grace is drawn to the humble. Humility brings grace to our need, and grace alone can change our hearts. Ezekiel 39:7 says: "So will I make my holy name known in the midst of my people Israel; and I will not let them pollute my holy name any more: and the heathen shall know that I am the LORD, the Holy One in Israel."

THE HOLY ONE OF ISRAEL

God is known as the Holy One of Israel and the Scriptures tell us that He is the enemy of the enemies of Israel. Whether it is the Jew under attack for their faith or race, or another, we would be responsible to them and ought to defend them, if we have any sense of human rights and fear of God. Where other nations and Israel are concerned, I'd rather stand with Israel than against. God's favour is upon His people. That's not to say she has not faced difficult times, but that God blesses those who bless Israel. His Word says so. He has the final word, and it is everlasting. Ezekiel says: "Therefore say, Thus saith the Lord God, I will even gather you from the people, and assemble you out of the countries where ye have been scattered, and I will give you the land of Israel." Jesus said: "Heaven and earth will pass away, but my words will not pass away" and the Psalmist says: "Forever, O Lord, Thy word is settled in heaven." God is a good Father and he is also Holy Father. Matthew 6:9 says: "Our Father, which art in heaven, hallowed be thy name." God's name is all too often used with irreverence as people declare his name flippantly or even more sadly, with disrespect. God's name is to be revered and used in honour, it is special and is to be glorified and magnified. God is sometimes referred to as the Top Man, the Man upstairs, or the Big Guy, but all such references are a disrespect to Him whose name is worthy of all praise and glory. Psalm 99:3 says: "God's name is holy" as does Psalm 103:1: "Bless the Lord, O my soul: and all that is within me, bless his holy name." Zeroah Kodesh is Holy arm in Hebrew, from Isaiah 52:10 and 53:1.

THE GLORY OF GOD

God is surrounded by glory and clothed in majesty. In Psalm 19:1 the writer says: "The heavens declare the glory of God and the firmament showeth His handiwork." Psalm 104:31 says: "The glory of the Lord shall endure forever." When Jesus, the long-awaited Messiah came into the world and the angels announced His birth, Luke says: "The glory of the Lord shone around and they declared: "Glory to God in the highest." The Word tells us, the redeemed of God: "Christ, in you, the hope of glory" Col. 1:27. Revelation 4:11 and 5:12 says: "You are worthy, O Lord, to receive glory and power and honour and blessing." The Word of God also tells us that the glory of the Lord is to be revealed in Isaiah 4:5, Romans 5:2 and 1 Peter 4:13. And we, His people are to do all we do for the glory of God in I Cor. 10:31.

Matthew records in the Lord's prayer: "Thine is the kingdom, the power and the glory." Jesus was glorified when He arose to be at the Father's right hand following His death on the cross. Ephesians 5:12 speaks of the church, the body of believers, being presented to God, a glorious church. God is manifested in glory. God's glory is revealed in His Son, Jesus, as well as in creation. God's glory may be expressed as his tangible presence or manifest power. Adjectives like "weight," "heavy," "thick," and "Shekinah" are connected to the glory of God. Under the Old Covenant it was necessary for the priests to be prepared for service to minister to the Lord, there was much preparation to enter the holy place in the tabernacle. No one dared approach the Holy Presence of God without perfectly fulfilling the law. Now God has provided the Lamb, His own Son, Jesus, as access to Himself.

Solomon dedicated the temple, in 2 Chronicles 7:1-3, the Bible says the glory of the Lord descended and filled His house. This was the radiant holiness of God eternal, the light bursting forth into man's world. Psalm 108:5 says: "Be thou exalted, O God, above the heavens: and thy glory above all the earth."

Revelation 21:23 tells us the holy city has no need of the sun, neither of the moon, to shine in it, for the glory of God did lighten it, and the

Lamb is the light thereof. God wants His bride to be righteous and holy, Rev.22:11. Jesus is described in Rev.22:16 as the "bright and morning star." In Hebrew this is Ko chav nogah hashachar. God is clothed in light. Jonathan Edwards, the eighteenth-century revivalist said:" Grace is but glory begun, and glory is but grace perfected."

It is vain to glory in ourselves and detract from the true glory. "Praise be Thy name, not mine; magnified be Thy work, not mine; blessed be thy holy name, but to me let no part of men's praises be given thou art my glory; Thou art the joy of my heart. In Thee will I glory and rejoice all the day, but yet of myself I will not glory, but in my infirmities. (Psalm113:3; 115:1; 2 Cor.12:5) from *"The Imitation of Christ,"* Thomas á Kempis, page 171. "God protects the humble and delivers him (James 4:6; Job 5:11). He loves and comforts the humble; unto the humble man He inclines Himself; unto the humble he gives great grace; and after his humiliation he receives him to glory. Unto the humble He reveals His secrets; (Matt.11:25), and sweetly draws and invites him unto Himself. The humble man, though he suffer confusion, is yet perfectly in peace; for he rests on God and not on the world." (*The Imitation of Christ*, page 67).

There are many beautiful worship songs ascribing glory to God and declaring His greatness. The words of one of these are as follows: "You deserve the glory and the honour. I lift my hands in worship and I bless your holy name You are great, you do miracles so great, there is no one else like you, there is no one else like you, for you are great, you do miracles so great, there is no one else like you..." One of my poems follows, entitled "All Hail":

The longing in my heart to know my Savior's love
Can only be fulfilled by power from above
The holiness and glory that my soul desires to see
Will then one day be satisfied when He returns for me
To give Him room today by drawing near in prayer
I'll find my heart's desire – naught else to Him compare
Oh! fill my heart, Thy will be done, restore my soul I pray
I long to see Your lovely face, all hail that glorious day!

If we are displaying our spirituality to impress men, still seeking honour from others, still living to appear special or "anointed" before people, can we honestly say we have been walking near to the Living God? We know we are relating correctly to God when our hunger for His glory causes us to forsake the praise of men. It is only the pure in heart who will perceive God, according to the words of Jesus. His desire is that we become truly Christ-like. This must be our singular goal. Indeed, we seek holiness, but holiness arises in the hidden places of our hearts, through truthfulness.

In 1 Chronicles 16 King David's psalm of praise and gratitude may be compared to his psalm of praise in 2 Samuel 22 when he was delivered out of the hand of all his enemies. David exalts the Lord and extols His virtues. He acknowledges the Lord as his rock, his fortress and deliverer, 2 Sam.22: 2, his shield, and the horn of his salvation, his high tower, refuge, saviour, and the one who saves him from violence, verse 3, the one who is worthy to be praised, verse 4, He says that God heard him in his distress, verses 8-17, describes the majestic power of God through the elements – a powerful picture of vivid imagery displaying the strength and wonder of the Almighty. Verse 20 tells us that the Lord brought David into a large place and delivered him, that He rewarded him according to his righteousness and the cleanness of his hands and the keeping of His Word. Verse 26 interestingly points out that God shows Himself merciful with the merciful and upright with the upright, pure with the pure and even unsavoury with the froward. David describes God as his lamp who lightens his darkness. It is not that he did not experience dark times, but that God illumined them, bringing him victory. David describes God's way as perfect, His Word is tried, He is a buckler to those who trust Him. A Rock – unlike any other, his strength and power. The One who makes his way perfect, setting him on high, teaching his hands to war, and giving him the shield of salvation, even declaring that God's gentleness has made him great, verse 36. God protects him from his enemies and made him strong in battle, helping him to overpower his enemies, to the extent that not even God answered when David's enemies called for help. God helped David to maintain his authority, verse 44, and delivered him from the violent man. This causes David to give thanks to the Lord and sing praises, declaring Him to be the tower of his salvation, showing him mercy, and to his offspring for evermore. David's view of the Lord was one of a big, big God, from whom all his ability, strength and wisdom ensued; a magnanimous God of great power and majesty.

THE MAJESTY OF GOD

The majesty of God is extolled in the Psalms especially. Majesty is indicative of power and royalty. In the book of the prophet Isaiah, it is the majestic nature of God that is described as the cause for the humbling of man; "The glory of His majesty" causing the very earth to shake. Psalm 93:1 declares "the Lord reigns, He is clothed with majesty; the Lord is clothed with strength." This describes His might. Psalm 145 declares that His works shall praise Him and His saints shall bless Him, speaking of the glory of His kingdom, and talk of His power, verses 10-11. "To make known to the sons of men his mighty acts, and the glorious majesty of His kingdom, which is an everlasting kingdom." This resounds with greatness.

The writer of Hebrews describes the Son, Jesus, as having been set on high, as high priest, set at the right hand of the throne of the Majesty in the heavens. Here, the word Majesty is used as a title of God, not just an attribute, as His being majestic in nature, but as a title. Holy One is similar, in this respect, for just as God is holy in nature, He also has the title Holy One of Israel. 2 Peter 1:16-17 says they were "eye-witnesses of his majesty," speaking of Jesus, for "he received from God the Father honour and glory, when there came such a voice from the excellent glory: "This is my beloved Son, in whom I am well pleased." YHWH Kodesh means God is holy in Hebrew, see Ex. 15:11. Holy and Righteous One is Kadosh uvatsadik (Acts 3:14), Holy One of God is Kedosh haElohim (Mark 1:24).

The doxology in Jude verses 24-25 is especially life-giving: "Now unto Him that is able to keep you from falling, and to present you faultless before the presence of His glory with exceeding joy, to the only wise God, our Saviour, be glory and majesty, dominion and power, both now, and for ever, Amen." The book of Revelation likewise has much to say regarding the majesty of God, initially in the description of Jesus, in chapter one verses 12-16, saying His countenance was as the sun shines in his strength. It must have been a fearsome sight, enough to make the apostle quake with fear as he fell at His feet as dead.

Revelation 4:2 to 5:14 describes the throne room in heaven. Likewise, here the twenty-four elders fall down and worship Him. Isaiah's vision of the Lord in Isaiah 6 caused him to prostrate himself and to cry out: "Woe is me for I am undone, I am a man of unclean lips!" It is evident that in the presence of such awesome majesty and holiness, the only response is to fall prostrate in worship and adoration. Frequently, throughout Scriptures, where there is the presence of God, the place is filled with smoke such as in the Old Testament temple and in Revelation 15:8. There is further description of the temple in Revelation 19:4-9. In chapter 21 verse 11 is described the holy Jerusalem as "having the glory of God and her light was like unto a stone most precious, even like a jasper stone, clear as crystal." Verse 8 tells us of those who will not live in the presence of the Almighty God; the fearful and unbelieving, the abominable and murderers, whoremongers, idolaters and all liars, the following chapter includes "dogs and sorcerers." This is harsh warning and an urgent call to obey God's commandments and live a righteous and holy life. Psalm 93:1 says: "The LORD reigneth, He is clothed with majesty; the LORD is clothed with strength, wherewith He hath girded Himself." Isaiah 2:10 speaks of the fear of the Lord and the glory of His majesty. The following poem "Glory" is one I wrote several years ago to exalt God:

Lord, I want to praise Your Name
You are the only One, always the same
I give You thanks, You are so good
Your love so great, Your Word - my food

Lord God my heart will sing Your praise
My lips rejoice, sweet anthems raise
I bless You Lord with joyful song
For all the mighty deeds You've done

Lord God be glorified in me
Your grace and wondrous majesty
Be worshipped and exalted now
And one day every knee will bow

Lord God, all praise and glory be
To You for all eternity
Be magnified for evermore
You are the one all saints adore

Lord God, we lift Your glory high
And in Your presence, "Holy" cry
All praise to Him upon the throne
All glory be to You alone.

Glorifying God is to build him up and exalt Him. Deprecating one's self does not do the same thing. That would be false humility. To put ourselves down does not have the adverse effect of lifting God up. It does not make Him any greater. Only exalting Him glorifies Him. There is no need to have a low opinion of ourselves; we are made in His image. John the Baptist did say, however, of Jesus: "He must increase, I must decrease." In the book, "*The Greatest Thing in The World*", (page 27), the writer, Henry Drummond states: "It is so much the more our duty, not like the advocate of the evil spirit, always to keep our eyes fixed upon the nakedness and weakness of our nature, but rather to seek out all those perfections through which we can make good our claims to a likeness to God."

God's will is our holiness. 1 Thessalonians 4:3 says: "For this is the will of God, even your sanctification." and Paul continues to say in 5:23 "And the very God of peace sanctify you wholly; and I pray your whole spirit and soul and body be preserved blameless unto the coming of our Lord Jesus Christ." Further, in Jesus' high priestly prayer to the Father, He prayed: "Sanctify them through thy truth: thy word is truth." Here we are instructed that it is not only God's will for our lives to be sanctified and made holy in every way, but that the very means to do so is provided through the Word of God. We are made holy through the shed blood of Jesus Christ, through Christ himself. Hudson Taylor, the Missionary said: "God's work, done in God's way, will never lack God's supply." This applies not only to missionary work, but to the very work God is intending to do in our lives in terms of personal holiness. God never leaves anything unprovided for.

The Scripture says: "But we all with unveiled face reflecting as a mirror the glory of the Lord are transformed into the same image from glory to glory even as from the Lord the Spirit." It is the Divine obligation that we be holy, the reason being that God himself is holy. It is necessary that we should be holy for our own sakes, it is an absolutely necessary virtue, for a holy life like that of the life of Christ. 1 Corinthians 1:30 says: "But of him are ye in Christ Jesus, who of God is made unto us wisdom, and righteousness, and sanctification, and redemption." 2 Corinthians 7:1 says: "Having therefore these promises, dearly beloved, let us cleanse ourselves from all filthiness of the flesh and spirit, perfecting holiness in the fear of God." Jesus prayed in the ideal prayer that God's will be done in earth as it is in heaven. God gives us the divine call to keep His words, and the strength to obey. For this is the love of God – that we keep his commandments. And His will is for the character of Christ to be formed in each of His children.

GOD IS WORTHY AND
WORTHY OF WORSHIP

"Worship the Lord in the beauty of holiness" says 1 Chronicles 16:29 and in Psalm 96:9. Jesus responded to Satan in the desert with the words: "Thou shalt worship the Lord thy God and Him only shalt thou serve." In Revelation we are told "Worship God" (22:9). In Revelation 5:14 the twenty-four elders fell down and worshipped Him that lives for ever and ever. Jesus spoke of true worship when speaking with the woman at the well in John 4:24, saying: "They that worship Him must worship Him in spirit and truth." She believed that Jerusalem was the place where one ought to worship, but Jesus revealed to her the manner of worship that God requires. Philippians 3:3 says that "we are the circumcision, which worship God in the spirit, and rejoice in Christ Jesus, and have no confidence in the flesh." Spirit worship is from the heart, not in ritualistic or legalistic tradition, nor with vain repetitions, said Jesus, in Matthew 6:7, as the heathen do. It is not about the amount of words we say in our prayers, because God already knows what we need before we ask Him. It is best to let our words be few according to Solomon. "Let not thine heart be hasty to utter anything before God: for God is in heaven, and thou upon earth: therefore, let thy words be few." And "A fool's voice is known by a multitude of words." The fear of God ought to keep us from speaking many words. Psalm 51:15 says: "O Lord, open thou my lips, and my mouth shall show forth thy praise, and in Psalm 51:17 when King David prayed a prayer of repentance he said: "A broken spirit and a contrite heart God will not despise." This is not to say that we should limit our words in prayer. I believe King David poured out his heart to God.

"Sing unto God, sing praises to His name: extol Him that rideth upon the heavens by His name JAH, and rejoice before Him" says Psalm 68:4. "O worship the Lord in the beauty of holiness: fear before him, all the earth (Psalm 96:9). "The Lord is high above all the earth, exalted far above all gods" (Psalm 97:9)."Let them praise thy great and terrible name for it is holy" (Psalm 99:3). To worship God is to exalt him (Psalm 108:5; 118:28; 145:1). There is none of self where God is being exalted and extolled. The Scriptures speak often of worshipping God with the whole heart; He desires for us to give him first place. In 2 Chronicles it is recorded that King Jehoshaphat worshipped God by bowing his head with his face to the ground (2 Chronicles 20:18). Daniel prayed and worshipped the Lord by kneeling and facing Jerusalem, giving God thanks (Dan.6:10). Daniel 9:3-19 records one of Daniel's prayers, full of contrition and humility, whereby he seeks the Lord by prayer and supplications, fasting, sackcloth and ashes, confessing iniquities, trespasses and sins, and imploring the mercies and forgiveness of God. He extols God's virtues and righteousness, and asks Him to hear and bless, to incline His ear and hear – for His mercies, sake. God heard Daniel's prayer and sent an angel. Daniel feared the Lord.

THE FEAR OF THE LORD

The "fear of the LORD" is mentioned frequently in the Holy Scriptures. This is not the same as servile fear or of being fearful in the negative sense. Rather, this fear is a holy fear and an awesome respect as is mentioned in Malachi 4:2: "Unto you who fear My name shall the Sun of righteousness arise with healing in His wings." The fear of the Lord is often mentioned in the book of Proverbs. Chapter 1 verse 7 says: "The fear of the Lord is the beginning of knowledge, but fools despise wisdom and instruction. Verse 29 goes on to say that those who hated knowledge did not choose the fear of the Lord. The fear of the Lord is to receive Gods counsel, and not to despise His reproof. Whereas hearkening unto wisdom will cause one to dwell safely and to be quiet from fear of evil. To receive the Word of the Lord and keep His commandments, to incline one's ear to wisdom and apply one's heart to understanding, to cry out after knowledge and understanding and seek wisdom as hidden treasure – this will bring the understanding of the fear of the Lord, according to Proverbs 2:1-5. This further tells us that it is the Lord who gives wisdom, verse 6, and out of His mouth come knowledge and understanding. The Spirit of the fear of the Lord in Hebrew is Ruach Yirat Adonai, Isaiah 11:2.

In Psalm 111:10 David says: "The fear of the Lord is the beginning of wisdom: a good understanding have all they that do His commandments, and "Blessed is the man that feareth the Lord, that delights greatly in His commandments" in Psalm 112:1, which goes on to share the blessings of such obedience, for it is obedience that characterizes the life of one who fears the Lord, one whose life is obedient to God's Word, applying its timeless truths to our lives.

The Scriptures also tell us some of the specific aspects or characteristics of the fear of the Lord in Proverbs 8:13 which is to hate evil – pride, arrogance and the evil way and the froward mouth. Froward means perverse, difficult to deal with, or moving away from. Proverbs 9:10 says that the fear of the Lord is the beginning of wisdom and that the knowledge of the Holy is understanding. The following verse says that this will increase one's life span, verse 11, and that it prolongs one's days. Proverbs 14:26 says it is a strong confidence providing safety and refuge and that it is a fountain of life -to depart from the snares of death (10:27). It is valuable (Prov. 15:16). "Better is a little with the fear of the Lord than great treasure and trouble therewith." Proverbs 16:6 says that by the fear of the Lord men depart from evil and in 19:23 that it tends to life, and he that has it shall be satisfied; he shall not be visited with evil. By humility and the fear of the Lord are riches, and honour, and life. The Scriptures encourage us to be in the fear of the Lord all the day long, 23:17. In Ecclesiastes the writer says also: "But thou fear God" (5:7), and in 12:13: "Fear God and keep the commandments is the end of the whole matter." Psalm 89:7 says that God is greatly to be feared, and in Psalm 96:4 that He is to be feared above all gods.

Conversely, the fear of man brings a snare, as Solomon says in Proverbs 29:25. Jesus says in Matthew 10:28: "But rather fear Him which is able to cast into hell." And about men, in verse 26, to "fear them not therefore." Frequently Jesus tells us not to fear as in Luke 12:32: "Fear not, little flock." This fear is not the same as the fear of God, as in Romans 3:18, this fear brings bondage, Romans 8:15. 2 Corinthians 7:1 describes the fear of God which is a holy thing. Ephesians 5:21 says to submit to one another in the fear of God. Hebrews 12:28 describes this as reverence or godly fear. I Peter 1:17 says to conduct our lives of sojourning here in fear, as in 1 Peter 2:18, to serve our masters with all fear meaning to respect our employers. 1 John 4:18 describes the type of fear that has torment.

The "fear of man" is an expression often used in biblical terminology to describe the trap of being ensnared with popular opinion. The fear of man causes double mindedness, it causes people to bend or sway to popular opinion rather than to seek God's wisdom; it operates from a level of moral weakness so there is little or no strength of character where there is the fear of man. It is often the cause of the flattering tongue and it also hinders one from complete obedience to the Lord, as in Saul's case, who was one of the kings of Israel. This is why Jesus must have first place if we are to be true worshippers and followers. God will not give his glory to another. To develop this healthy awesome respect for the Lord we pray, as well as devote ourselves to the reading and study of God's Word, and a life of obedience, and develop intimacy with God through a life of praise and worship.

Revelation 11:18 speaks of a reward being given to those who fear God's name. Revelation 14:7 says: "Fear God, and give glory to Him; for the hour of His judgment is come: and worship Him that made heaven, and earth, and the sea, and the fountains of waters." In chapter 15:3-4 it says: "Great and marvelous are thy works, Lord God Almighty; just and true are thy ways, thou King of saints. Who shall not fear thee, O Lord, and glorify thy name? For thou only art holy: for all nations shall come and worship before thee; for thy judgments are made manifest." This is called the song of Moses the servant of God and the song of the Lamb. Additionally, in chapter 19:5 we read of the bride of Christ, the Church: "And a voice came out of the throne, saying, "Praise our God, all ye his servants, and ye that fear him, both small and great."

There are various accounts of people in the Scriptures who both feared God or who feared man. One is recorded in Matthew of King Herod who had put John the Baptist in prison. Chapter 14 verse 5 says that Herod would have put John to death but he feared the multitude because they counted John as a prophet. Herod feared John, it is recorded in Mark 6:20, because he was a just man and holy. Also, in Mark 11:32 it is recorded: "they feared the people." The same is mentioned in Matthew 21:46 of Jesus, where the Pharisees sought to lay hands on him, but they feared the multitude because they took Jesus for a Prophet. Also, in Mark 11:18 the scribes and chief priests feared Jesus and sought how they might destroy Him. Luke 19:21 records the parable of Jesus where a certain nobleman leaves tasks for his servants to occupy until he comes. The first servant proves faithful and is rewarded with authority as he has increased the money entrusted to him, likewise, the second man, even though the amount was less. But the third man hid the money and said: "For I feared thee…" and he was considered a "wicked servant," and even an enemy, since he would not have the Lord reign over him. Jesus' arrest was near at the feast of Passover, it is written in Luke 22:2 and "the chief priests and scribes sought how they might kill him; for they feared the people." Also, in the story about the blind man, his parents feared the Jews and didn't even testify to their son's healing since, if any confessed that Jesus was the Christ, they would have been put out of the synagogue. In the book of Acts, the captain and the officers feared the people, but the apostles were fearless and said: "We ought to obey God rather than men" (Acts 5:29).

Unfortunately, in today's world, to be regarded as "God-fearing" is no longer an attribute we would see on a resume or a letter of character reference.

Growing up in a close-knit Italian family, we had friendship with a local Jewish man who happened to be a heart surgeon and an artist who became a close friend over the years. In my later teen years I asked him to write a letter of referral for assistance in securing employment. It wasn't until decades later that I fully appreciated his comment written – "From God-fearing stock." Initially those words didn't seem to mean so much to me, possibly even causing a measure of embarrassment since I was not at the time aware of their value. Now, forty years later, and especially since his passing away, I am very moved by this man's observations.

In J.M. Pendleton's work *"Christian Theology,"* (page 42) he states: "God's attributes are his perfections, inseparable from his nature and constituting his character. All faith is based upon the knowledge of God, and the more we know of his character the more we will be capable of having faith in Him, for all true knowledge of God contributes to faith in Him."

GOD IS CREATOR

The Bible begins by referring to God as Creator and introducing Him as the strong Creator of the whole universe (Elohim). After which the Scriptures go on to use the more personal name, Jehovah. Elohim is used more than 2,000 times in the Scriptures. Psalm 58:11 says: "Surely there is a God (Elohim) who judges the earth." "For this is what the Lord (Jehovah) says -He who created the heavens, He is God (Elohim). Isaiah 45:18. "In the beginning God created the heaven and the earth" says Genesis 1:1. It has been said that this is the most profound statement in the whole of the Bible. The Word of God sets forth no argument for the existence of God. This is the beginning of time, the absolute beginning of all created things. God's existence is a self-evident fact, seen in every aspect of His creation.

The Gospel of John, chapter one, also tells us: "In the beginning was the Word." This is a direct reference to Jesus as Creator, who was present with the Father in the beginning. "And the Word was with God, and the Word was God" says the writer. "The same was in the beginning with God." Then verse three tells us: "All things were made by him, and without him was not anything made that was made." Clearly, we see reference to Jesus being fully present and involved in the Creation of the world. Jesus is Creator. The Holy Spirit moved (hovered) over the face of the waters, says Genesis 1:2. And goes on to say in Genesis 1:26: "And God (Elohim) said, "Let us make man in our image, after our likeness... so God created man in his own image, in the image of God created he him; male and female created he them" (verse 27). Colossians 1:16 adds: "All things were created by him."John 17:5 makes reference to Jesus being present before the creation, when He speaks of "the glory which I had with thee before the world was" and again in verse 24: "For thou lovest me before the foundation of the world." "All is appointed by the great Work-master, who has left nothing in His creation without due order," says, Thomas á Kempis in *"The Imitation of Christ,"* page 167.

The Word of God says in 2 Corinthians 4:18: "We look not at the things which are seen, but at the things which are not seen: for the things which are seen are temporal; but the things which are not seen are eternal." This is somewhat paradoxical. We are intended to look at the things which are seen. God made the world and all that is in it. He made it and declared it "good" and his work has been crafted exquisitely and beautifully, with loving thought, skill, beauty and purpose. "Nature is never silent. The Creator has determined that, whether He be seen or not, no living soul shall tread this earth without being spoken to by the works of His hands." Says Henry Drummond in *"The Greatest Thing in the World"* (page 183). "Our whole conception of the eternal is derived from the temporal." The Bible tells us that since the beginning His attributes are clearly seen (Rom. 1:20). The works of God are clearly made known through His creation. The heavens declare the glory of God says Psalm 19:1. In John 1, Colossians 1, and Hebrews 1, Jesus is seen as the Creator. In John, the writer says that Jesus was present in the beginning with the Father God, verses 1-3 and in verse 10 that the world was made by Him. In Hebrews it says that God has spoken unto us in these last days by His Son, by whom also He made the worlds and in Colossians 1:16-17: "For by him were all things created, that are in heaven, and that are in earth, visible and invisible, whether they be thrones, or dominions, or principalities, or powers: all things were created by him, and for him: and he is before all things, and by him all things consist."

In George Di Palma's book: *Darwin – God's Ambassador* the author speaks of the Divine Intelligence that breathed life into earth and universe. He describes the divine ingenuity that brought this world into existence in a chapter entitled:

The Divine Architect (page 28), saying that the concept that the order and perfection of the solar system with earthly life and nature somehow emerging from an explosion out of nothing defies all scientific assessment (page 32).

From the video footage: "God of Wonders" host Dr. John C. Whitcomb, produced by Eternal productions 2008, I have adapted the following: The Lord is truly the God of Wonders; His wonders surround us; these marvels reveal much about our Creator. There is nothing irrational about an eternal Being. Mass energy wears out but God does not; He endures for ever. Who hasn't felt the rumble of an approaching storm and not considered God's might? A bolt of lightning may reach over 5 miles in length, contain over 1 million electrical volts and soar to temperatures of over 50,000 degrees Fahrenheit in a split second, hotter than the surface of the sun. This is one manifestation of our Creator's majestic power. In Scripture lightening is often used as a symbol of God's wrath against His rebellious people. Job says: "The thunder of His power who can understand." This should cause us to stand in awe of our great God. The sun is 93 million miles from our earth. The sun gives off incredible energy; It drives all the energy on earth. The nitrogen and hydrogen released by a thunderstorm fertilizes the ground. Over one million earths would fit inside the sun. He made the stars also. Without the light of the sun all life on earth would soon perish. Psalm 147:4-5 says: "He telleth the number of the stars; he calleth them all by their names. Great is our Lord. And of great power: his understanding is infinite.

The visible universe contains over 100 billion galaxies. Each of these galaxies has a diameter millions of trillions of miles wide and each contains hundreds of billions of stars. All men can do is marvel. God stretches out the heavens like a curtain it says in Isaiah. It is as if the universe is truly being stretched out. "The heavens declare the glory of God; and the firmament showeth his handiwork" says Psalm 19:1.

This should invoke a sense of reverence and awe in our hearts. From elegant to complex the Creator's works declare His wisdom. Each snowflake is a reflection of Gods creativity. Surely there is a treasury of snow, as God has declared. God has designed each one, making it unique as He has designed each person – to reflect His glory. It is an unmistakable mark of His care. Consider the design behind the complex molecules such as DNA which makes up our genes. This indicates a supremely intelligent Designer. The DNA molecule has even been designed so that it is self-correcting. It is not something that comes about through natural selection.

The Sequoia tree has been designed from a humble seed to reach a height of 300 feet and weighing many tons. Each seed always produces after its own kind. The Creator made life to reproduce this way – with the seed in itself. Life itself is within the unassuming seed. The guiding hand of our all-loving Creator can be seen in the growth of plants which yield a harvest of blessings for mankind. Flowers reflect a picture of God's splendor; they even have their own perfume. Some even know what time it is; opening and closing with clockwork precision. Every green leaf receives its energy from the sun releasing oxygen which every creature needs for survival. They are an awesome testimony to the Creator's provision. The insects also need the plants, which absorb carbon dioxide. All fits together in an intricate pattern reflecting His glory. This all points to a wise and compassionate Creator. The unlimited ingenuity of our Creator is seen in the sea animals with a variety of shapes and colours. Underwater symbiotic relationships are also seen. Different species of fish have been relegated to dwell at different depths of the sea providing a great quantity of food for mankind. They are a marvelous testimony to God's creativity. The sophistication, variety and beauty declare how God created all things for His good pleasure.

We have all watched birds flying. Only birds have been created with the lightweight bones, tailored feathers and bellow-like lungs necessary for flight. As a result, bird have the remarkable ability to fly and soar with grace and ease. Each bird species has a specific function, and some have the capability to migrate long distances. Birds are a testimony to God's wisdom and love, and yet Jesus said that we are of more value than many sparrows (Luke 12:7). In Hebrew the God of heaven and earth is known as Elah Sh'maya v'Arah (Ezra 5:11; 7:23).

The metamorphosis of the butterfly is yet another marvel of creation. The evidence points to the reality that the Creator has made all things. All creation reflects aspects of God's character. God says He has written His law in every human conscience so that men are without excuse.

YAH, YAHWEH OR YHWH - JEHOVAH

Jehovah or YHWH is a sacred word for LORD and is considered the only proper name for God. It was considered so sacred that Jews would not utter it, which is why the abbreviation is used. This is called the Tetragrammaton. Some Bibles make the distinction between Adonai and YHWH by putting LORD in all capitals when translated from YHWH. Rabbinical Judaism teaches that the name is forbidden to all except the High Priest, who should only speak it in the Holy of Holies of the Temple in Jerusalem on Yom Kippur. He then pronounces the name "just as it is written." In Hebrew it is pronounced Yehovah, in English Jehovah. As each blessing was made, the people in the courtyard were to prostrate themselves completely as they heard it spoken aloud. As the Temple has been destroyed since CE 70, most modern Jews never pronounce YHWH but instead read Adonai ("My Lord") during prayer and while reading the Torah and as HaShem ("The Name") at other times. Similarly, the Vulgate used *Dominus* ("The Lord") and most English translations of the Bible write "the LORD" for YHWH and "the LORD GOD" for Adonai YHWH instead of transcribing the name. (The Septuagint apparently originally used the Hebrew letters themselves amid its Greek text but all surviving editions instead write either *Kyrios* [Κυριος, "Lord") or *Theos* (Θεος, "God") for occurrences of the name.)YHWH has many forms that describe the character of God: -

	Pronunciation
Jehovah Elohim -the Lord God	El-o-heem
Jehovah Elohim Israel – The Lord, the	
God of Israel	El-o-heem Ees-ray-el
Jehovah-jireh – the Lord will provide	yi-reh
Jehovah-rophe – the Lord who heals	ro-feh
Jehovah-nissi – the Lord is my banner	nee-see
Jehovah-m'kaddesh – The Lord who sanctifies	m-ka-desh

Jehovah-shalom – the Lord is peace	sha-lom
Jehovah-tsidkenu – The Lord Our Righteousness	tsid-kay-noo
Jehovah-rohi – the Lord Our Shepherd	ro-hee
Jehovah- shammah – the Lord is there	sha-mar

The name YHWH or Jehovah appears 6,823 times in the Old Testament. It appears the first time in Genesis 2:4 with Elohim, as Jehovah-Elohim. Sometimes the names Jehovah and Elohim appear together in the same sentence. In his book, *"Names of God,"* Nathan Stone says:"The name Jehovah is derived from the Hebrew word Havah, to be, or being. This is very close to the Hebrew verb Chavah, meaning to live, or life. Most of these compound names of God arise out of some historic incident, and portray Jehovah in some aspect of His character as meeting human need,"

EL

When El is used in the Bible as a name for God it is almost always connected with another word to form a compound name. El is a root word that meant "strength, might or power" and could also refer to false deities or even an individual. For example, the following are some of the compound names of God using the El form:-

	Pronunciation
El Abir (Deut. 10:17) Mighty One	El A-beer
El Chaiyai (Psalm 42:8) The God of my life	El Kay-ai
El Channun (Jonah 4:2) The Gracious God	El Ka-noon
El De'ot (1 Sam. 2;3) Omniscient God	El Day-ot
Eloah (Job 42:12) God	El-o-ay
Elohim (Gen.1:1) God of Power and Might	El-o-heem
Eloi (Mark 15:34) My God	Ee-loy
El Elyon (Gen. 14:19-20) The God Most High	El El-yon
El Gaol (Job 19:25) God is Redeemer	El Ga-ol
El Gibor (Isaiah 10:21) The Mighty God	El Gee-boor
El Hakkadosh (Isaiah 5:16) The Holy God	El Ha-ka-dosh
El Kadosh (1 Sam. 6:20) HolyGod	El Ka-doash
El Hanne'eman (Deut. 7:9) The Faithful God	El Ha-nay-man
El Qanna (Ex. 34:14) The Jealous God	El Ka-na
El Mishpat (Isaiah 30:18) God of Justice	El Mish-pat
El Olam (Isaiah 40:28) The Everlasting God	El O-lam
El Palet (Psalm 18:2) Deliverer	El Pa-let
El Ro'i (Gen. 16:13) The Strong One Who Sees	El Ro-hee
El Shaddai (Psalm 91:1) The All-sufficient God, Almighty	El Sha-daiy
El Tsaddik (Psalm 7:9) The Righteous One	El Tza-deek
El Tzur (Isaiah 30:29) God our Rock	El Ts-oor

| El Yehuati (Isaiah 12:2) The God of my Salvation | El ye-hoo-a-tee |
| El Yeshurun (Deut. 33:26) The Righteous God | El ye-shoo-roon |

Throughout the Bible there are many unique words and phrases to describe God and they are used in very specific situation, yet they all describe the same Being and Deity, God.

The use of the plural word Adonai reveals that God is LORD or Master of the universe, being in complete control and in charge of everything He has made. The various names of God describe different aspects of His character and emphasize His role in the stories of our lives. Due to YHWH being more sacred to believers of the time, Adonai was the name often used when God dealt with the Gentiles. This name also infers that God is Lord over all of us, both collectively and individually. Despotes translates as Master, reminding us He is Master of our lives.

Elohim occurs in the Bible 2,570 times and El, 250 times. It is used in instances which indicate the power of God. Elohim expresses greatness and glory, containing the idea of creative and governing power, of omnipotence and sovereignty. Elohim is the plural. It has the usual Hebrew ending for all masculine nouns in the plural. This name is seen as the Godhead covenant within itself. It is, however, accompanied by verbs in the singular tense. "I am Elohim, and there is no Elohim beside me." Deut. 32:39 and Isaiah 45:5,22. These verses declare that there is no other God besides the LORD.

JEHOVAH-JIREH

Jehovah-jireh is the King James Version translation of YHWH-jireh meaning "The Lord will provide" Genesis 22:14. It is the name given when God provided the ram to be sacrificed instead of Isaac. God had commanded Abraham to offer his "son of promise," Isaac, as a burnt offering on Mount Moriah. Isaac questions Abraham regarding the intended offering: "Where is the lamb?" Abraham responds in faith: "God Himself will provide the lamb for the burnt offering, my son" Genesis 22:1-8. Hebrews 11:19 tells us that Abraham believed God would raise Isaac from the dead. Genesis 22:13 says that Abraham saw a ram in the thicket caught by its horns. Here, God had provided a substitute for Isaac. Jehovah-jireh provided a sacrifice to save Isaac, which was a foreshadowing of the provision of God's Son, Jesus, for the salvation of the whole world. Jehovah-jireh means literally: "The Lord will see to it." The Latin roots of the word "provide" come from "pro", meaning "before" and "video" meaning "to see" meaning "in advance" or before the need is known. God is preparing us an answer before we know that it is a need. Genesis 22:1-14. God knows in advance everything that is going to transpire and has already made provision for us. The Lord will provide.

When Jesus Christ taught about our heavenly Father's provision in Matthew chapter 6 He said: "Take no thought for your life, what ye shall eat, or what ye shall drink; nor yet for your body, what ye shall put on" verse 25. He goes on to say in verse 28: "And why take ye thought for raiment? Consider the lilies of the field, how they grow; they toil not, neither do they spin: And yet I say unto you, that even Solomon in all his glory was not arrayed like one of these. Wherefore, if God so clothes the grass of the field, which today is, and tomorrow is cast into the oven, shall he not much more clothe you, O ye of little faith?" verse 30. He then goes on to tell us in verse 33 to seek first His kingdom and His righteousness. For the kingdom of God is in righteousness, peace and joy in the Holy Ghost. It is said that the "lilies of the field" Jesus was referring to were not the cultivated lilies we see today in the florist stores and gardens. When speaking of worry Jesus was referring to wild flowers – "the grass of the field" verse 29, He was speaking of a flower that grew wild and in abundance in the fields. It was colourful and known to most people in the crowd. And even King Solomon in all his splendour of beautifully-coloured rich garb, was not dressed like one of these "lilies" - a simple wild flower! Seeking first God's kingdom and righteousness is key. Then God will give us all we need – including clothes. "The lily of the field" was possibly Anemone Coronaria "Crown Anemone", which grows in every part of Israel. "This flower has been associated with the tri-unity of God, with sorrow and death. God tells us not to worry as all our needs will be met. Christ assures us that we are more valuable than birds, flowers, clothes, food and water. And teaches us of the care of our Heavenly Father for His children as something infinitely more valuable. He is providing all things for us. God's manner of creation is diverse even in the reproductive aspects of a simple lily, he has taken such measures to array the flowers with such beauty and mystery and is intimately acquainted with us in every detail and every respect." (*A Puritan's Mind.com*).

JEHOVAH-ROPHE

The name Jehovah-rophe means Jehovah heals. The word rophe appears some sixty or seventy times in Scripture, always meaning to restore, to heal or to cure, not only in a physical sense but in the moral and spiritual sense also. God healed people in Old Testament times, as he does today. He is a God who restores. God does whatever He pleases. King Hezekiah was not only healed but granted additional years to live. "The Hebrew word *rophe* means "heal," "cure," "restore," or "make whole." Shortly after his people left Egypt for the Promised Land, God revealed himself as Jehovah-rophe, "the LORD who heals." The Hebrew Scriptures indicate that God is the source of all healing. Ann Spangler, author of the book, "*The Names of God*" says: "As you pray to Jehovah- rophe, ask him to search your heart. Take time to let him show you what it contains. If he uncovers any sin, ask for his forgiveness and then pray for healing. The New Testament reveals Jesus as the Great Physician, the healer of body and soul, whose miracles point to the kingdom of God" Exodus 15:26 speaks of Jehovah-rophe, saying "...I am the LORD that healeth thee."

JEHOVAH-NISSI

Jehovah-nissi means Jehovah my banner (Ex. 17:15). "In ancient times, a banner was not necessarily a flag such as we have today. It is translated pole, standard, ensign, often a pole with a bright shining ornament which glittered in the sun. The word here for banner means to glisten among other things," says Nathan Stone, in his book, *"Names of God."* It is translated variously pole, standard, ensign, and among the Jews it is also a word for miracle. Ann Spangler says in her book, *"Praying the names of God."* "Ancient armies carried standards or banners that served as marks of identification and as symbols that embodied the ideals of a people. A banner, like a flag, was something that could be seen from afar, serving as a rallying point for troops before a battle. Though banners were first used in Egypt, Babylonia, Assyria, and Persia, the Israelites carried them on their march through the desert. When you pray to Jehovah-nissi, you are praying to the God who is powerful enough to overcome any foe." Moses built an altar and called it The LORD is my Banner. He said, "For hands were lifted up to the throne of the LORD. The LORD will be at war against the Amalekites from generation to generation" (Exodus 17:15-16).

JEHOVAH-M'KADDESH

This means Jehovah who sanctifies. The Lord is the one who sanctifies or makes holy. He calls us to be a holy people. The Bible says in 1 Corinthians 1:30 that it is Jesus Christ who has been made for us sanctification. Also, in the high priestly prayer of Jesus, He says: "Sanctify them through thy truth: thy word is truth…and for their sakes I sanctify myself, that they also might be sanctified through the truth." John 17: 17 and 19. Peter spoke of God purifying our hearts by faith in Acts 15:9, and Paul spoke of the sanctifying work of the Church in Ephesians: "That he might sanctify and cleanse it with the washing of the water by the word, that he might present it to himself a glorious church not having spot, or wrinkle, or any such thing; but that it should be holy and without blemish." The name Jehovah M'Kaddesh is found in Leviticus 20:8: "And ye shall keep my statutes, and do them: I am the LORD which sanctify you."

JEHOVAH-SHALOM

The name Jehovah-shalom means the Lord is peace. "Shalom" is a Hebrew word, so much richer in its range of meanings than the English word "peace," which usually refers to the absence of outward conflict or to a state of inner calm. The concept of shalom includes these ideas but goes beyond them, meaning "wholeness," "completeness," "finished work," "perfection," "safety," or "wellness." Shalom comes from living in harmony with God. The fruit of that harmony is harmony with others, prosperity, health, satisfaction, soundness, wholeness, and well-being. When you pray to Jehovah-shalom, you are praying to the source of all peace. No wonder his Son is called the Prince of Peace." Says Ann Spangler, adding, "To live in the presence of God through the power of the Holy Spirit is to be at peace - at peace with God, with others, with ourselves. He is the source of true shalom, of prosperity, harmony, safety, health, and fulfillment. No matter how turbulent our world becomes, we can be at peace, showing forth his presence regardless of circumstances."

JEHOVAH TSIDKENU

Jehovah Tsidkenu means: "The Lord our righteousness." The Lord is righteous in all His acts and in all He does. We can depend on Him to act righteously on our behalf. He Himself is our righteousness through the person of Jesus Christ. When we come to God, we do so not in our own righteousness or right standing, but on Christ's merits, and through His righteousness. As believers we have the breastplate of righteousness to protect us in spiritual battle from the fiery darts of the wicked one. This breastplate is the armour of Christ's righteousness and not our own. Isaiah chapter 11 describes the reign of Christ and verse 5 says that "righteousness shall be the girdle of his loins." Verse 4 also says: "With righteousness shall he judge the poor." Psalm 50:6 says that the heavens declare his righteousness. Jeremiah 23:6 calls Him: "THE LORD OUR RIGHTEOUSNESS" as one of His titles, and in Malachi 4:2 the Lord is referred to as: "The Sun of righteousness." Hosea 14:9 tells us that the ways of the Lord are right. In Romans 3:21 we read that: "Now the righteousness of God without the law is manifested... even the righteousness of God which is by faith of Jesus Christ unto all and upon all them that believe" (verse 22). Through the Gospel of Christ, the righteousness of God is revealed. To be righteous is to be in right relationship with God and displaying His character in terms of His faithful love, His mercy, humility, integrity and justice. God is the only One who is completely righteous.

THE LORD'S NAME

I believe we are to exalt the Lord. Even in Scripture there's a difference in meaning between Lord and LORD. In Judaism the "ineffable name" is what is referred to as the name of YHWH which in Judaism is too holy to utter. They have no problem with the name G-d, though most use it as I have written with a dash between the "G" and "d," so as to preserve its sanctity, they do the same with L-rd. This is based upon tradition. Messianic Jews do this in practice, if one looks at the Messianic literature. Some write the Name with a capital "N", but this is not biblical according to the King James authorized version. It is not even grammatically correct to use a lower case "G" for God, although it is not a proper name. Yet, would express reverence when using a capital "G." It is probably more a matter of "grammatical laziness" as is common with the modern use of cell phone texting. Further, with several well-known televangelists calling themselves "little gods" one just cannot help but wonder, how do we distinguish to whom, or Whom, we are referring? The Oxford dictionary has "God" with a capital "G" referring to "the creator and supreme ruler of the universe." I noticed that the months of the year are capitalized as well as the days of the week (note their origins). He is our heavenly Father, Abba (Aramaic for Father, not daddy) and deserves to be revered. (Hebrew4Christians.) I agree that we should be directing our attention to the state of the world, but as Jesus said to the Pharisees who were being pedantic "these ought ye to have done, and not to leave the other undone" (Matt. 23:23) Both are extremely relevant matters.

The Bible says to ascribe greatness unto the Lord, and to sing praises to His name. "His name alone is excellent" says the Psalmist in Psalm 148:13 and in Psalm 145:2: "I will praise thy name for ever and ever." Psalm 138:2 says: "I will worship toward thy holy temple and praise thy name for thy lovingkindness and for thy truth: for thou hast magnified thy word above all thy name." Many people today use the expression "Oh, my god." but it is not being used in the same way that King David meant it when he declared it in in worship to the Lord of glory. Those who use it in this way do not actually call on God when it is being used.

It is being taken "in vain." It is being used as a thoughtless expletive. There are many alternatives which could be used, such as "Oh my", or "my word." "heavens above," or "goodness gracious." Even using such expressions are in a sense a means of expressing surprise or shock. Because God is constant, we do not need to live in any such state of alarm or surprise. "OMG" has a sense of alarm or urgency about it, and it is not glorifying to God. He requires reverence and due respect. Even our everyday language has left us with little in terms of adjectives with which to ascribe greatness to our God since so many of the expressions we use are taken up in regular usage there are left few remaining words with which to honour God, our Creator. If that cheesecake is simply divine, and the soccer game was totally awesome, the trip was amazing, and we are at least good, if not great, then what else are we to say about God? We are left with few words that qualify as an apt description of the Majestic Creator God whom we serve.

One morning in a worship meeting a little girl when questioned described God as "nice." Maybe she meant "kind," or "good." To be "nice" many of God's other attributes would be forgone. His justice, Hs wrath, His vengeance. We can say God is awesome, and this can be open to include both His love as well as His justice, whereas "nice" limits the understanding to mere benevolence, that of a caring and sweet-natured being. To that little girl, who is as yet unaware of God's other attributes, such as the severity of God's judgement then His "niceness" may be appropriate. For the rest of us, it is not. For me personally, God is not nice, but He is wonderful. The Word of God declares: "Great is the Lord."

There are references to "the Name" in the NIV Bible (New International Version) with a capitalized letter "N" in the place of the title the Lord Jesus Christ. In other writings, such as the book of Hermes, the Name is referring to the antichrist. However, the Name in Judaism is referring to the ineffable name of God. The NIV as well as many other modern Bible translations have demoted the name of the Lord Jesus Christ many times in their translations. The name of Christ is used 214 fewer times in the NASB (New American Standard Bible) than the King James Version, and 176 times in the NIV. The New King James Bible translation omits the word Lord 66 times, God 51 times, heaven 50 times, repent 44 times, blood 23 times and hell 22 times, replacing it with hades. The word devils has been omitted. In other versions also, demons has been used in the place of the word devils, which is used in the KJV. Webster's dictionary defines a demon as a divinity, whereas devil as a spirit of evil. So already one is reading in the modern versions that the word demon is divine in nature, where the KJV depicts devils as evil creatures. The word damnation has also been omitted, as has New Testament and the name JEHOVAH.

The word holy has been removed very often from the newer versions of the Bible. The NIV and the NASB and other versions omit the word Christ after the Lord Jesus on many occasions. Acts 8:37 is virtually omitted in its entirety in most modern versions. This is a very important verse. "And Philip said, it thou believest with all thine heart, thou mayest. And he answered and said, I believe that Jesus Christ is the Son of God." Servant replaces Son even in the New King James version. Comforter is replaced with Helper when referring to the Holy Spirit. This is the same as the New World translation by the Jehovah's Witness sect. The term the Presence is being used in modern versions. This term is used in Satanism to describe Lucifer but is also being used in the new Bible versions. In Roman Catholic circles, the "host" is often referred to as the Presence. References to the blood of Christ have been removed 41 times from the NIV. Colossians 1:14 has been removed in its entirety from the NIV and other modern translations. "In whom we have redemption through his blood, even the forgiveness of sins."

The phrase "As above, so below" is a phrase used in black magic to conjure up devils. This has been introduced into the Message version in the Lord's prayer in place of "Thy will be done in earth, as it is in heaven." It is worth noting here, that even the term "in earth" has been rendered "on earth" in most Bibles. This gives the impression that the words are referring to a place, such as the planet earth. But I believe the intent of the verse here, is to say literally IN earthen vessels. May God's will be done IN us. This would also be in contextual agreement with Jesus' other high-priestly prayer in John 17, where Jesus prays for His own people, the body of Christ. He is not praying for change *on* the earth as such, but change *within* His people, the body of Christ. My rendition would also refute Dominion Theology which I address later.

The title "Bright and morning star" in Revelation 22:16 is referred to also in 2 Peter 1:19: " Until the day star arise in your hearts." The other reference is in Isaiah 14: 12 a where the name of Lucifer is mentioned. "How art thou fallen from heaven, O Lucifer, son of the morning!" In modern versions, the name of Lucifer has been omitted and this has been translated in the NIV and other new versions as "morning star" leading to the confusion between this and other references where Jesus Christ is clearly the Bright and Morning Star, where it says: "son of the morning." This was precursed in 1881 by the then head of the Theosophical society, Madame Helena Blavatsky. The Roman Catholic Vulgate Bible says the same thing.

The word He in reference to God has in newer translations been translated as the One, to accommodate the he/she notion. E.g. Luke 1:49; 7:20. In the newer translations, quantitative words are used instead of qualitative. These newer versions, besides the NIV and the NASB, are the Good News, the Amplified, the New Jerusalem Bible, the New Century Version, Today's English Version, The Everyday Bible, the Message paraphrase, the Voice, and the New English Bible. There are others that also are not known as translations but paraphrases, as is the Message, which some have said is good for nothing other than kindling. There are severe warnings in Scripture about not adding to, or taking away, from the Word of God (Deut. 4:2 and Rev. 22:18-19).

Many question which is easier to understand, an older version or not. The King James Version actually uses one or two syllable Anglo-Saxon words, where the more modern translations may use words with more syllables. The KJV reads at 5th Grade North American standard of education. In 1 Corinthians 1:10 the Word of God says that we should speak the same thing so that there be no divisions, and Philippians mentions eating the same spiritual food. The King James Version is known to be the preserved, inspired version of Holy Scripture.

Westcott, the Bishop of Durham, changed the Bible in over 8,000 places, such as in Mark 10:24 where it is omitted "…for those who trust in riches." Leaving - "How hard it is to get into heaven" as the text. This presents a different Gospel. In 1881 Wescott and Hort published "The New Testament in the Original Greek." It is also called the "Westcott and Hort text." The very title implies that any other text is based on non-original sources. Whilst it is true that they used original sources, they omitted to tell readers that those sources were considered to be corrupt, by many centuries of biblical theologians, and so were not used for the famed 1611 KJV. In addition, the newer translations are moving away from references to God and heaven. The Scriptures point out that Jesus Christ is the chief corner stone, whereas the NIV refers to Him as the capstone. These are two different things, where the cornerstone is a part of the foundation, the capstone is on the top of the building. The eye of Horus is represented in the capstone, which is the darkened eye of Lucifer, the antichrist. Gail Riplinger adds in her message on the New Age Bible versions that "we are moving from a word-based culture to an image-based culture."

The newer Bible translations preach another Gospel of works-based salvation, to the end that popular Christianity has been infiltrated by wolves in sheep's clothing. The new versions support Theistic Evolution, which is basically turning the truth of God into a lie. Psalms 119:140,160 and 12:6-7 all testify to the preservation of the Word of God. "Thy word is very pure," "Thy word is true from the beginning: and every one of thy righteous judgments endureth forever," "The words of the Lord are pure words: as silver tried in a furnace of earth, purified seven times. Thou shalt keep them, O Lord, thou shalt preserve them from this generation for ever." The newer versions all carry a changing of the reading and omit either a part or all of some verses.

The Bible teaches that God's Word will endure for ever. It is eternal in nature. It is inspired. It says that it has been given by holy men of God who spoke as they were moved by the Holy Spirit. Jesus said that His words would never pass away.

PRAISE GOD!

Throughout history many have given their very lives so that the Word of God would continue. These were martyrs who continued to translate the Holy Scriptures under threat of death. We have much to be thankful for, and we are indebted to these martyrs of the faith for what we have today has come to us with much self-sacrifice.

The Bible speaks of the power of Jesus' name in Acts 4:12, saying: "Neither is there salvation in any other: for there is none other name under heaven given among men, whereby we must be saved." In Romans, it is written: "For whosoever shall call upon the name of the Lord shall be saved" (10:13). When praying to the Father, Jesus mentions asking in His name. This does not mean that we can ask according to our own preferences and tag the name of Jesus on the end to assure ourselves of answered prayer. What this means is to pray in accordance with the will of God.

There are also various names for God as Father in Hebrew beginning with Avi, meaning Father. Avi-ezer, means my Father helps, Avi-nadav means my Father gives freely, Avi-hud means my Father is glorious, Avi-tuv, my father is good, Avi-shalom, my Father is peace, Avi-gayil, my father is joy and Avi-shua, my Father saves.

The Holy Spirit is referred to in Hebrew as Ruach. Ruach haChachmah is the Spirit of Wisdom, Ruach Vinah, the Spirit of Understanding, Ruach Da'ot, Spirit of Knowledge, Ruach Elsah, Spirit of Counsel, Ruach Hanuvah, Spirit of Prophecy, Ruach Avdut, Spirit of Sonship and Ruach Bno, Spirit of His Son.

Zechariah 14:9 speaks of a future day: "And the LORD shall be king over all the earth: in that day shall there be one LORD, and his name one." In addition, Joel 2:32 says: "And it shall come to pass, that whosoever shall call on the name of the LORD shall be delivered: for in mount Zion and in Jerusalem shall be deliverance, as the LORD hath said, and in the remnant whom the LORD shall call." Here, the Scriptures are referring to Jehovah, or Yahovah, in Hebrew.

The name of our Lord Jesus, is in Hebrew Yeshua. The Greek is Iesous. Jesus is spelled as written, Yeshua. Not Yahshua, Yahushua, Yahusha, Yashayahu, Yahuveh, Ahayah, or Yahuah. The correct name would have been Yehoshua, Hebrew for Joshua, but the Hebrew language changes some words where there are vowel sounds together. When the angel appeared to Mary as recorded in Matthew 1:21, the angel said: "And she shall bring forth a son, and thou shall call his name JESUS: for he shall save his people from their sins." The Lord Jesus is written Iesous Christos Kyrios in Greek. In Italian Signore Gesù Christo, in French Seigneur Jesus-Christ, in Spanish Señor Jesucristo and in Portuguese Senior Jesus Cristo.

GOD IS THE LORD OF HOSTS, LORD OF THE ARMIES, LORD OF SABAOTH

Noah built an altar to the Lord and offered burnt offerings on the altar, and God smelled a sweet savour. God made a covenant with Noah and promised there would not be a flood ever again to destroy all flesh; He made this covenant revealed through the rainbow (Gen.9:11-17). In Leviticus God says to the children of Israel to bring an offering, a sheaf of the firstfruits of their harvest to the priest and wave the sheaf before the Lord. The meat offering was for a sweet savour to the Lord. These offerings were to be a statute for ever for Israel (Lev.23:11-14). As Noah built an altar and presented offerings to the Lord, we too, as believers, are required to present our gifts to God. Romans 12:1 says we are to present our bodies to God as living sacrifices which is our reasonable act of service and worship. God does not ask us to offer burnt offerings of sheep and goats; Christ made on end of such offerings, becoming a sacrifice for us, once and for all, by His sacrificial death on the cross, in our stead. But God does require us to give our lives nevertheless. We do this by giving to him all that we are -our utter devotion and complete reverence.

We give back to God in honour and gratitude for all He has given to us. It is our reasonable act of service; our duty. The very least we can do. He longs for our hearts – first place. We are to give Him our gifts; the first fruits of all that comes our way, whether it be time, talents, finances, resources, possessions or gifts. All that we have; Our service. Including any credit or glory that may come to us. This is to be returned to Him. These gifts, given in faith, are a sweet-smelling aroma and savour to the Lord; something beautiful for God. It is out of appreciation that we make our offerings, they are gifts to him for a debt we could never pay; a "Thank You" to our heavenly Father.

Genesis 8:22 says that while the earth remains there will be seed time and harvest. Jesus spoke of seeds and harvest in the gospels and said to pray the Lord of the harvest that He would send forth labourers into His harvest (Luke 10:2). Matthew 13 describes the parable of the sower that Jesus explained to His disciples. He said that by this parable we would be able to understand all parables. It is the parable of the sower. The parable shows that of the seed sown, some fell by the wayside, some on stony places, some among thorns, and some on good ground. The parable explains that the seed is the Word of God. In verse 18 we see the wayside seed is sown and the wicked one snatches the seed which was sown in his heart because the Word of the kingdom which he had heard he did not understand (verse 19). The seed sown on stony places is the one who hears the Word and receives it with joy, but he has no root in himself, and when tribulation and persecution arises because of the word, this person is eventually offended. This type of person actually receives the Word with joy and walks as though a believer for a time but is eventually offended. Jesus warns His followers that there will be persecution, He even promises tribulation, and this causes the weak or shallow person to fall away. This type of believer has had some influence of a Christian walk for a time because Jesus says they receive the Word with joy, except the heart had not been properly prepared. The seed sown on thorny ground is the one who hears the Word, and the cares of this world and the deceitfulness of riches choke the Word and he becomes unfruitful. This type of person is quite complex and confused, since double-mindedness is revealed; a desire for the things the world has to offer. Gradually, cares of this world and the beguilement of the deceit of riches creeps in and crowd out the importance of the Word so that it can no longer grow to fruition. This, too, takes time. Meanwhile steadfast believers are growing and walking alongside these types of people. The seed on good ground is he that hears the Word, understands it, and bears fruit. Fruitfulness may be described in terms of godly character, souls saved and answered prayer. The fruits of the Holy Spirit; love, joy, peace, patience, kindness, gentleness, goodness, faithfulness and self-control as well as humility and grace and other qualities ought to be evident in the life of the professing believer.

Reading into the seed sown by the wayside, we realize that the seed must be received at a heart level and understood. There needs to be preparation. Just as when a farmer plants seed. Secondly, the Word needs a firm foundation in a heart that is prepared for battle. In the Psalms David says: "Great peace have they which love thy law: and nothing shall offend them." (Psalm 119:165.) If a person has a love for the Word of God, they will not be vulnerable to attack in this area. This person gets offended when persecution arises and does not have the inner strength to sustain it. The seed sown on thorny ground reveals that there must be no competition in the heart of a person. God must be Lord of all. This individual has a love of money as well as being a "worry wart" and having concerns about the things of this world. The seed sown on good ground is one who hears, understands the Word, and is fruitful. Fruitfulness makes God glad.

Although we are not meant to judge other people as Jesus says, we are nevertheless meant to be fruit inspectors, and be discerners of character. Judging is akin to assessing the motives of one's heart, which in truth, only God can do. He is the only one who knows the thoughts and intentions of a person's heart and what motivates us to do as we do. Discernment, however, is a God-given gift which enables us to act wisely and righteously. We need to have a measure of this in order to live righteous lives and to make wise choices, especially where relationships are concerned. Our values and morals need to be based on good judgment. Especially where the poor are concerned. Surely the poor beggar on the street is worthy of more than the time it takes us to reach into our pocket for a copper. Acknowledgement, a smile of compassion, and a kind word may do far more good in raising their level of self-respect and human dignity. Quite possibly the cry of the poor reaching the Father's ears may well be heeded by Jehovah Sabaoth as these poor ones are being overwhelmed by their circumstances and cry "out of the depths."

The Lord of Hosts and related names, Lord God of Hosts, and God of Hosts, occur some 270 times in the Old Testament. Again, the word LORD capitalized refers to Jehovah, the self-existent, redemptive God. Sabaoth translates as "armies."

The phrase "host of heaven" refers to every living thing, even angelic, celestial beings as well as the sun, moon, stars, planets, the heavenly bodies, all creatures and all of creation, as being subject to the power of God. We, in turn, as His creation, exist to love and serve His purposes. From the description of Amos (4:13), God's attributes of sovereignty, omniscience and omnipotence are clearly implied by this majestic name as in Isaiah 6:3: "And one cried unto another, and said, Holy, holy, holy, is the Lord of hosts: the whole earth is full of his glory," and Isaiah 44:6: "Thus saith the Lord the King of Israel, and his redeemer the Lord of hosts; I am the first, and I am the last; and beside me there is no God." The revelation of

God by His names is invariably made in connection with some particular need of His people, and there can be no need of man to which these names do not answer as showing that man's true resource is in God. Even human failure and sin but evoke new and fuller revelations of the divine fullness. The NIV Bible version substitutes the name Lord Almighty for the LORD of hosts, whereas Lord Almighty is in actuality El Shaddai which has a different meaning. Lord of hosts is the name to use when we find ourselves most powerless and there is none other to help. Jehovah Sabaoth speaks of God's available power in our time of trouble and which ensures divine victory over every enemy. Martin Luther's great hymn of 1529, expresses the truth found in the name Lord Sabaoth in the second stanza of the hymn where he warns abut striving against the world, the flesh and the devil in our own strength.

"A Mighty Fortress is our God":

A mighty fortress is our God, a bulwark never failing;
Our helper He, amid the flood of mortal ills prevailing:
For still our ancient foe doth seek to work us woe;
His craft and pow'r are great, and, armed with cruel hate,
On earth is not his equal.

Did we in our own strength confide, our striving would be losing,
Were not the right Man on our side, the Man of God's own choosing:
Dost ask who that may be? Christ Jesus, it is He;
Lord Sabaoth, His Name, from age to age the same,
And He must win the battle.

And though this world, with devils filled, should threaten to undo us,
We will not fear, for God hath willed His truth to triumph through us;
The Prince of Darkness grim, we tremble not for him;
His rage we can endure, for lo, his doom is sure,
One little word shall fell him.

That word above all earthly pow'rs, no thanks to them, abideth;
The Spirit and the gifts are ours through Him Who with us sideth;
Let goods and kindred go, this mortal life also;
The body they may kill: God's truth abideth still,
His kingdom is forever.

The Lord of Hosts is the one to be reverenced (Is.8:12-13). Jehovah Sabaoth comes to our aid when we are in a personal crisis. He answers the cries of those who are hopelessly overpowered by circumstances. He is the great Deliverer who can bring you out of every trial. He is Protector, Deliverer and Enforcer of Justice. He fights our wars for us: "Not by might, nor by power, but by My Spirit, says the Lord of Hosts." Says Zechariah 4:7.

A. W. Tozer says: "The flaming desire to be rid of every unholy thing and to put on the likeness of Christ at any cost is not often found among us. We expect to enter the everlasting kingdom of our Father and to sit down around the table with sages, saints and martyrs; and through the grace of God, maybe we shall; yes, maybe we shall. But for the most of us it could prove at first an embarrassing experience. Ours might be the silence of the untried soldier in the presence of the battle-hardened heroes who have fought the fight and won the victory and who have scars to prove that they were present when the battle was joined."

Tozer continues by saying that it is "necessary" for God to use suffering in his holy work of preparing his saints, adding, "It is doubtful whether God can bless a man greatly until he has hurt him deeply." Says Tozer in his book "*The Root of the Righteous.*"

God cannot readily use a person to serve His higher purposes, if they are given to a quick temper, or impatience. In Timothy, Paul describes the office of leaders in the church and the necessary qualities. Patience is developed and learned through trials, for in such circumstances God is refining His servants. In trying times, we learn to wait on the Lord and submit to His higher power. Chastisement is reserved for the sons of God says Hebrews. It is through discipline, which is hardship, that we grow through the seasons of life, only the rebel heart fails the test. Usually the tests come in times of need or want. In Jesus' case He was tempted three times in the wilderness, with food, power and glory. The world, the flesh and the devil are the enemies of our souls, but as we walk in God's ways we are equipped to face such difficulties and come through victoriously. Jesus was tempted in all points as we are, yet without sin. Through these testings, the Word tells us He learned obedience – through the things which He suffered. Usually it is our fleshly desires of food and sex, money and material gain, relationships and power that are the most challenging. The Apostle Paul suffered many things; beatings, abuse, shipwrecks, imprisonment and many other trials. He also had a "thorn in the flesh" to which God said: "My grace is sufficient for you, for My strength is made perfect in weakness." This should tell us something, that God uses weak vessels. Without a "test" there is no testimony. Trials fit us for the kingdom, for loyal service. Without them we are undisciplined. Commonly it is health and financial troubles that try most people to a challenging level. When we are touched by our physical frailty we are prone to either crumble or to look up, financial crises do the same and in both cases we find that God supplies if we yield to His chastening hand.

Where God leads – He meets the needs. God is purifying His people. Jesus endured the cross, despising the shame. He said we are blessed if we are persecuted for righteousness" sake. We are even to take insults joyfully for Christ's sake. This runs counter-culture to the standards of the post-modern society in which we live where human rights are exalted at every turn. People will indeed speak falsehood concerning us if we are walking in the way of righteousness, for we will be going against the grain and this causes friction. In modern society it is the norm for people to demand their rights, to stand up for themselves, not to be submissive or humble, but assertive. To be otherwise is considered weakness.

God's ways are contrary to the world, the flesh and the devil. What is of the flesh cannot please God. Two natures within us are competing for supremacy. We are to first submit to God, then we have the fortitude and grace to resist the devil and all that comes with his dominion. To attempt to resist the devil without first submitting to God is for the most part an exercise in futility, since we require God's strength to enable us for resistance and battle. The devil is a real foe and we must be well-equipped to withstand his onslaughts and assaults, but we can rest assured that with God we are victorious and more than conquerors.

It is God's will for us to rise above circumstances, whether in time of want or fullness – to be content. In Philippians 4:11-12 Paul says: "For I have learned in whatsoever state I am, therewith to be content. I know both how to be abased, and I know how to abound: everywhere and in all things I am instructed both to be full and to be hungry, both to abound and suffer need." Quite probably the apostle is saying that in a spiritual sense, one is not unlike the other state; what matters is our approach to either one or the other. Jesus said to rejoice in sufferings in Matthew 5:12; To rejoice when we are reviled and persecuted, when people speak all manner of falsehood or evil against us. He says: "Rejoice!"; Kick up your holy heels, for even the former prophets of old were so persecuted. Jesus intends for us to die to self. John12:24-25 says: "Except a corn of wheat fall into the ground and die, it abides alone: but if it die, it brings forth much fruit. He that loves his life shall lose it; and he that hates his life in this world shall keep it unto life eternal." He is speaking, I believe, of our worldly ambitions, the things we have a tendency to follow after; the acclaim of man and so on. As He did, we are meant to take on the humble form of a servant, and He humbled Himself, even to the point of death on the cross.

Kingdom values tend to be contrary to worldly ones; the way up is down, and the way down is up, it appears. We are meant to take the lowest place, not to seek after the first place, or to seek honour for ourselves. God will see to it that we are honoured for our sacrifices on His behalf. Nothing escapes His notice.

GOD IS KING

Along with the Psalmist, in Psalm 45, I declare: "My heart is overflowing with a good theme; I write my composition concerning the King: My tongue is the pen of a ready writer." This Psalm speaks of God's awesome Majesty. It is one of the Psalms of the sons of Korah, described as a song of love; Psalms 42 -49 are also written by the sons of Korah. Psalm 47 describes God as the Lord Most High who is awesome; that He is King over all the earth. Psalm 48 says that Mount Zion is the city of the great King. In Revelation, John describes Jesus as King of kings. Jesus came as King of the Jews (Matt. 27:11,29,37; Mark 15:2,9,12,18 and Luke 23:38). Psalm 10:16 says the Lord is King for ever, and in Psalm 47:7 as King of all the earth. Adonai haAdonim, is Lord of lords in Hebrew, Deut, 10:17. The God of all flesh in Hebrew is Elohay Kol Barar, Jer. 32:27, and Sovereign Ruler is Adonai haKadosh va'Amiti.

Psalm 89:18 says: "The Holy One of Israel is our King." And in Psalm 145:12-13 says that his kingdom is of glorious majesty and is an everlasting kingdom. Fixed upon the cross was the inscription: "Jesus of Nazareth, King of the Jews" (John 18:39; 19:3). Jesus often spoke in parables about the kingdom of God. In Mark 4:11 He spoke of the mystery of the kingdom of God and in Luke 18:17 that one must enter the kingdom as a little child. He said that one having riches would have great difficulty entering the kingdom in Mark 10:23-25 and Luke 18:24-25. In John 18:36 Jesus said that His kingdom was not of this world.

In the Acts of the Apostles they preached matters concerning the kingdom of God. In Revelation 11:15 it says that the kingdoms of this world are become the kingdoms of our Lord. Also, in Revelation 19:16 it says that written on Jesus' thigh is the name "King of kings and Lord of lords." One modern song about the King of kings is written by Jarrod Cooper and aptly describes the beauty of our King and the glory He deserves:

King of kings, Majesty, God of heaven living in me;
Gentle Saviour, closest Friend; Strong Deliverer, Beginning and End;
All within me falls at Your throne.

Your Majesty, I can but bow, I lay my all before You now,
In royal robes I don't deserve, I live to serve Your Majesty.

Earth and heaven, worship You, Love eternal, Faithful and True;
Who bought the nations, ransomed souls,
Brought this sinner near to Your throne,
All within me cries out in praise.

Your Majesty, I can but bow, I lay my all before You now;
In royal robes I don't deserve, I live to serve Your Majesty.

GOD IS ONE, I AM

In David Pawson's book "*Unlocking the Bible,*" he says on page 29:

"Genesis 1 depicts a personal God. He has a heart that feels. He has a mind that thinks and can speak His thoughts. He has a will and makes decisions and sticks to them. All this forms what we know as a personality. God is not an it, God is a He. He is a full person with feelings, thoughts and motives like us."

The Scriptures teach that there is one God, and that even the demons believe and tremble. The Old Testament mentions the names of many false gods, also known as foreign gods, or gods of the nations, and declares that these are idols. To believe in many gods as do the Hindus is called Pantheism. However, there are many today who are teaching in the evangelical Church the doctrine of the "little gods" theory; that people being made in the image and likeness of God are actually "little gods."

In the garden of Eden the serpent spoke to Eve saying: "Ye shall not surely die: For God doth know that in the day ye eat thereof, then your eyes shall be opened, and ye shall be as gods, knowing good and evil." (Gen. 3:4-5). To believe that people are little gods is to have fallen for the lie of the serpent, the devil, as they declare "I AM" and make themselves like the Most High in their own eyes. There is one God; He is Supreme, Majestic and Sovereign.

The Bible says in 1 John 4 to test the spirits for many false prophets have gone out into the world, and in Matthew's gospel chapter 24 that many false Christs and false prophets would arise bringing great deception. Jesus also said in Matthew 7 to "Beware of false prophets, which come to you in sheep's clothinginwardly they are ravening wolves. Ye shall know them by their fruits." verses15-16a. 1 Thessalonians 5 says to test all things. Jude 1:4 speaks of ungodly men who crept in unawares and says to earnestly contend for the faith. Jacob Prasch of Moriel Ministries, says ; 'There is always real cheese in a rat trap.'

2 Samuel 7:22 says: "Wherefore thou art great, O LORD God: for there is none like thee, neither is there any God beside thee, according to all that we have heard with our ears." Exodus 20:3 declares: "Thou shalt

have no other gods before me." Isaiah 44:8b says: "Is there a god beside me? Yea, there is no God; I know not any." I Corinthians 8:6 says: "But to us there is but one God, the Father, of whom are all things, and we in him; and one Lord Jesus Christ, by whom are all things, and we by him." Ephesians 4:6: "One God and Father of all, who is above all, and through all, and in you all." And James 2:19 says: "Thou believest that there is one God; thou doest well: the devils also believe, and tremble." The fact that there is one God is further confirmed in other Scriptures; Sam. 22:32; Psalm 50:1; Rom. 16:27; and 1 Tim. 1:17; 2:5. 'Ego eimi is the Greek translation of I AM'.

Jesus Christ said in Matthew 24:24: "For there shall arise false Christs and false prophets and shall show great signs and wonders; insomuch that, if it were possible, they shall deceive the very elect." Peter warns in 2 Peter chapter 2 of false teachers who shall arise from among the body of believers. Paul instructs through Timothy in 1 Timothy 4:1: "Now the Spirit speaketh expressly, that in the latter times some shall depart from the faith, giving heed to seducing spirits and doctrines of devils." We have been warned.

JESUS CHRIST; LAMB OF GOD

"Behold, the Lamb of God which takest away the sins of the world!" cried John the Baptist (John 1:36). Isaiah speaks of the future Messiah as "a lamb to the slaughter" (53:7). The sacrifice of the lamb by Abraham was a foreshadow of Christ (Gen.22). Under the Old Covenant a sacrificial lamb without blemish was necessary to appease God's requirements as a substitute for sin. This was fulfilled through the Lamb of God on Calvary, once for all time. 1 Peter 1:19 describes Jesus as a Lamb without blemish. In Revelation 5:12 it says: "Worthy is the Lamb that was slain." And in Revelation 5:8 we read where the elders fall down before the throne. Chapter 12:11 tells us that we overcome by the blood of the Lamb. The marriage supper of the Lamb is recorded in 19:7-9, the bride is the Lamb's wife – the Church, and in 21:23 we see that in the future kingdom of Christ there will be no need for the sun for the Lamb will be its light. Chapter 22:1-3 describes the throne of the Lamb in the great city, the holy Jerusalem. The Lamb of God in Hebrew is Seh haElohim (John 1:29; Rev. 5:12).

The name of Jesus is the most beautiful name. In the name of Jesus there is power. It is by the confession of His name that man is saved. Jesus is God's very own Son, the Bible says, as well as having come as God in human form. When speaking with Philip in John chapter 14, He says: "…he who has seen me has seen the Father." In John 10:30 Jesus says: "I and my Father are one."

In *"Evidence that Demands a Verdict,"* the author, Josh McDowell says: "Throughout the New Testament the apostles appealed to two areas of the life of Jesus of Nazareth to establish His Messiahship. One was the Resurrection, and the other was fulfilled messianic prophecy. The Old Testament written over a one-thousand-year period, contains nearly three hundred references to the coming Messiah. All of these were fulfilled in Jesus Christ, and they establish a solid confirmation of His credentials as the Messiah." Canon Liddon in his studies has found 332 distinct predictions which were literally fulfilled in Christ. McDowell adds later, in regards to the Resurrection of Christ: "All the millions and millions of Jews, Buddhists and Mohammedans agree that their founders have never come up out of the dust of the earth in resurrection."

JESUS IS THE WAY,
THE TRUTH, AND THE LIFE

Many versions of the Bible have been written. I prefer the Authorized King James Version. However, lately there are some books that are full of error and cannot in truth be termed translations yet are regarded as such by some. Among these are The Message, The Passion Bible and the Queen James. These have all added to or taken away from the Word of God as have the versions published by the various cult groups, the Jehovah's Witness New World Translation, and the Book of Mormon, as well as The Clear Word Bible, from the Seventh Day Adventist's cult. Gail Riplinger has an informative message worth inquiring into regarding various Bible versions, entitled *"New Age Counterfeit Bible Versions."* She has also penned a book entitled "New Age Bible Versions," which also covers extensive information regarding counterfeit Bible Versions. The Passion translation consists of a number of interpretations and additions to the text. The sole purpose of this work by Simmons is to promote the false ideology of the New Apostolic Reformation. It is a movement that has its stronghold in the younger generation."

In the Word of God John 14:6 says: "Jesus saith unto him, I am the way, the truth, and the life: no man cometh unto the Father, but by me." Here, Jesus declares Himself as the way to God, the Father. John 6:63b says: "the words that I speak unto you, they are spirit, and they are life." After Jesus said this, many of His disciples turned away, but Simon Peter said: "Lord, to whom shall we go? Thou hast the words of eternal life. And we believe and are sure that thou art that Christ, the Son of the living God" verses 68-69. It is worth noting that the pre-Incarnate Jesus took on flesh but did not lay aside His deity when He came to earth – only the glory He had previously had with the Father.

GOD IS OUR ROCK

In 1 Corinthians the Apostle Paul speaks of the spiritual Rock as being Christ Himself and in 1 Peter 2:8 the writer says that Christ is a rock of offense, even to them that stumble at His Word. In the Old Testament there are many references to God being our rock. Deuteronomy 32:3-4a says: "Because I will publish the name of the Lord: ascribe greatness unto our God. He is the Rock, His work is perfect."And there is a chastisement in verse 18: "Of the Rock that begot thee thou art unmindful, and hast forgotten God that formed thee.""The God of my rock" is mentioned in 2 Samuel 22:3 and in verse 32..."and who is a rock, save our God?" In verse 47 it says: "The Lord liveth; and blessed be my rock; and exalted be the God of the rock of my salvation." Chapter 23:3 refers to God as the Rock of Israel.

The Psalmist often speaks of God as the rock; "Unto thee will I cry, O Lord my rock." Psalm 28:1a; Psalm 31:2-3: "Be thou my strong rock, for an house of defense to save me. For thou art my rock and my fortress; therefore for thy name's sake lead me, and guide me," "Lead me to the rock that is higher than I." In Psalm 61:2b; "He only is my rock" in Psalm 62:2; and in verse 7 "In God is my salvation and my glory: the rock of my strength, and my refuge, is in God." "For thou art my rock and my fortress." Psalm 71:3; In Psalm 78 where King David describes the guidance and deliverance of God towards His people, he says of God in verse 35: "And they remembered that God was their rock, and the high God their redeemer." Psalm 89: 26 says: "He shall cry unto me, Thou art my Father, and my God, and the rock of my salvation." Psalm 94:22 "But the Lord is my defense; and my God is the rock of my refuge."

In the New Testament Jesus says that the wise man builds his house upon a rock. (Matthew 7:24-25 and Luke 6:48-49) and that if our foundation is built on a rock our house will not fall. He was speaking of hearing His words and doing them. In Matthew 16, Simon Peter says to Jesus that he believes Him to be the Christ, the Son of the living God, to which Jesus replies that God had revealed this to him, and then Jesus says: "And I also say unto thee, That thou art Peter, and upon this rock

I will build my church; and the gates of hell shall not prevail against it." Here Jesus is speaking of Himself as this rock as in Ephesians 2:20 which describes the Church being built on the foundation which has Christ as the chief corner stone. "The stone which the builders refused is become the headstone of the corner" Psalm 118:22. God is solid as a rock, He is strong and mighty, immovable and firm. We can depend upon Him. He is described here as a rock of salvation, a rock of refuge and a rock of strength.

Christ is known as the Rock of the Church. It was a large rock, a stone, that was rolled over the entrance to the tomb where Jesus was buried for three days and nights. The Matthew Henry commentary says: "The sorrows of death surrounded him, in his distress he prayed, Heb. 5:7. God made the earth to shake and tremble, and the rocks to cleave, and brought him out, in his resurrection, because he delighted in him and in his undertaking."

GOD IS THE CORNERSTONE

The Bible speaks of Christ Jesus as being the Chief Cornerstone, and of the Church, having Christ as the Cornerstone, being built on the foundation of the apostles and prophets. (Eph.2:20). In Psalm 118:22 the Psalmist declares that the stone which the builders rejected has become the chief cornerstone, speaking of the Jews and Christ, also in Luke 20:17. In Isaiah 28:16 it says: "Therefore thus saith the Lord God, Behold, I lay in Zion for a foundation a stone, a tried stone, a precious corner stone, a sure foundation: he that believeth shall not make haste." 1 Peter 2:6-8 says : "Wherefore also it is contained in the Scripture, Behold I lay in Zion a chief corner stone, elect, precious: and he that believeth on him is not confounded. Unto you therefore which believe he is precious: but into them which be disobedient, the stone which the builders disallowed, the same is made the head of the corner, and a stone of stumbling, and a rock of offense, even to them which stumble at the Word, being disobedient: whereunto also they were appointed." Some translations render this term, cornerstone, as capstone. It is incorrect. The capstone is at the top of a building, whereas the cornerstone is a part of the foundation. This may seem to be a moot point for some, but with the symbology of the capstone revealed on the one-dollar U.S. currency which shows the eye of Horus as a part of the capstone, it is important to remember here that Jesus is the cornerstone and not the capstone, which could otherwise lead to confusion or misrepresentation.

GOD IS THE MORNING STAR

The Morning Star is a title of Christ used in Scripture to refer to Jesus. In Isaiah 14:12Lucifer is referred to as "son of the morning" - not "bright and morning star," otherwise 2 Peter 1:19; Revelation 2:28 and 22:16 refer to Christ. 2 Peter says "…until the daystar arise in your hearts," the morning star is referenced in both the other Scriptures from Revelation. In Numbers 24;17 the Scriptures tell us that "A Star will come out of Jacob" and in Matthew 2:2: "We saw his star in the east and have come to worship Him." Isaiah 60:1 says; "Arise, shine, for your light has come." and in John 8:12 Jesus describes Himself as the "Light of the world."

THE LILY OF THE VALLEY AND THE ROSE OF SHARON

Commentators suggest writing this metaphor speaks of the allegory of the love between Christ and the Church, His faithful believers. This book is a beautiful love poem describing the passionate love between Solomon and his lover with many agricultural and botanical metaphors. Whether the Lily of the valley and the Rose of Sharon actually refer to Christ or to His bride, it is nevertheless a beautiful picture of passionate, romantic love. Jesus is the greatest beauty and desire of our souls.

GOD IS LOVE

God's goodness, mercy, patience and faithfulness are part of His love. God's love is active. Isaiah 43:1-5 reveals characteristics of God -three natural attributes and two moral attributes. God's love is not a love of emotion, but of action, as expressed in the life of Jesus Christ. His love gives freely to the object of its affection, those who choose to follow His Son, Jesus. God paid the penalty for our evil deeds by going to the cross Himself. His justice needed to be satisfied, but He took care of it for all who will believe in Jesus of Nazareth. Jeremiah says: "The Lord has appeared of old unto me, saying, Yea, I have loved thee with an everlasting love: therefore with lovingkindness I have drawn thee" Jer. 31:3.

Hosea says: "I drew them with cords of a man, with bands of love" (11:4a). In Deuteronomy the Lord speaks of His love for His people, Israel: "For thou art an holy people unto the Lord thy God: the Lord thy God hath chosen thee to be a special people unto himself, above all people that are on the face of the earth. The Lord did not set His love upon you, nor choose you, because ye were more in number than many people; for ye were the fewest of all people: but because the Lord loved you..." (7:6-8a).

God calls His people, beloved. Colossians 3: "Put on therefore, as the elect of God, holy and beloved, bowels of mercies, kindness, humbleness of mind, meekness, longsuffering; forbearing one another and forgiving one another, if any man have a quarrel against any: Even as Christ forgave you, so also do ye. And above all these things put on charity, which is the bond of perfectness" (Colossians 3:12-14).

God instructs us to love fervently, with a pure heart, and to let love be without hypocrisy. In 1 Corinthians 13 we read the beautiful "love chapter" describing the kind of love we are to aspire to, it uses the term "charity" in the King James version of the Bible. "Charity suffereth long, and is kind; charity envieth not; charity vaunteth not itself, is not puffed up, doth not behave itself unseemly, seeketh not her own, is not easily provoked, thinketh no evil; rejoiceth not in iniquity, but rejoiceth in the truth; beareth all things, believeth all things, hopeth all things, endureth all things. Charity never faileth (verses 4-8a). 1 John speaks also of the love of God and tells us that there is no fear in love, but perfect love casts out all fear.

God's love is expressed in Him sending His Son Jesus Christ to die a sacrificial death on our behalf; "For God so loved the world, that He gave His only begotten Son, that whosoever believeth in Him should not perish, but have everlasting life." (John 3:16). What love! He did not condemn us, though we were so unworthy and deserving of judgment, He made a way for us to repent and be forgiven, and to enter into life eternal. What provision! All of grace, and mercy, sinners condemned to die, but God reached down and drew us back to Himself. I wrote the following poem in 1992:

My Jesus, Lord, who died on Calvary
Thou who hung upon the cross for me
Christ, now risen, there is none like thee
My God, my Saviour – blessed be!

One other poem from my personal writings is entitled "He loves me still": -

I am weak, but He is strong, in every need provides,
I stray, my Shepherd draws me back, with lovingkindness guides
I fall, and yet He picks me up, when doubting He is faithful
When troubles rise He speaks to me: "Be still" -for He is able

When I am restless, He's my peace, though lacking faith, I yield
Yet when I fail my Lord forgives; in battle He's my shield
He knows the way I've taken, refining me like gold
I'll never be forsaken by the Ancient One of old

In trouble or in peril, His Spirit sets me free
No matter what may happen, my Saviour He will be
When I am sick, more grace supplies, when lonely comfort gives
When feet are slipping He's my Rock; He loves me still; He lives!

The Bible has much to say about the love of God, especially in the letters of John beginning in verse 5 of the second chapter; "But whoso keepeth his word, in him verily is the love of God perfected: hereby know we that we are in Him." Obedience is the key. Keeping God's Word (1 John). This is what makes us perfect in love. Loving our brother, is mentioned in 1 John 2:10; 3:11, 14, 16-17,23 and 4:7-8,11,21; 5:2. This is imperative, if we say we love God we will love one another. The passage in 2:15 says to not love the world, more specifically "the world" doesn't refer to the beauty of creation, but to the world's value system; one-up-man ship, competition against others and striving for the first place, seeking people's praises and accolades, rewards of this life, materialism and "mammon" or worldly wealth, worldly goods and the world's values and principles and measures. The standards of this world are a far cry from the values taught by Jesus Christ.

The "Sermon on the Mount" where Jesus said things like; "If your enemy hungers, feed him" or "love your enemies" and "bless those who despitefully use you and persecute you", these things truly go against the grain and run counter-culture to the values of the world around us where we are encouraged to stand up for our rights and to assert ourselves, to seek monetary reward for virtually everything, and to value the opinion of man, not doing good in secret, but making sure people know about it. Keeping our good deeds a secret is even a challenge for most of us. However, love makes no fan-fare. It doesn't parade itself. Jesus was really saying to us to take a back seat, to not force ourselves or our opinions upon others. To let it go when we have a difference with another. For the wisdom from above is pure, peaceable, gentle and easy to be entreated, full of mercy and good fruits, without partiality and without hypocrisy, and the fruit of righteousness is sown in peace of them that make peace" says James 3:17-18. We are not conditioned by the world's mold to be submissive and meek, to afford another the last word or to take reproaches, without retaliation, much less – gladly! But Matthew 5:44 says: "Love your enemies." Even to pray for those who use us. At the same time, we are to take a stand against unrighteousness, and to not allow evil to go unchecked, we are meant to hate evil. There is a time to hate, says the writer of Ecclesiastes, as well as a time to love. Love is compassionate, 1 John 3: 17, showing mercy to those without, and sharing our worldly goods.

The love of the Father is mentioned in chapter 3:1 of 1 John. This amazing love -that He has chosen to call us sons of God. Love is of God, says 1 John 4:7, it is a choice, manifested in action led by the Holy Spirit. Verse 18 says there is no fear in love, and that perfect love casts out fear. We can often put another's mind at ease with a simple kind word, or a gentle response to their care. This is the very love that casts out fear, since fear has torment. If something causes fearful ruminations, it is not from God. Jude 21 goes on to say: "Keep yourselves in the love of God", it is something to be attended to and practiced.

In the book of Revelation God reminds the Church that they have left their first love, in Rev. 2:4 and in Rev. 3:15-19 He rebukes the Laodicean Church for her luke-warmness. The Shema is one of only two prayers that are specifically commanded in Torah (the other is Birkat Ha-Mazon -- grace after meals). It is the oldest fixed daily prayer in Judaism, recited morning and night since ancient times. The Shema says: "Hear O Israel: the LORD our God is one LORD: And thou shalt love the LORD thy God with all thine heart, and with all thy soul, and with all thy might." In the Psalms David says: "O love the LORD, all ye his saints." In Psalm 91: "Because he hath set his love upon me, therefore will I deliver him: I will set him on high, because he hath known my name." Proverbs 10:12 tells us that love covers all sins. 1 Timothy 6:10 we are warned that the love of money is a root of all kinds of evil in. In Romans 13:8, God says that we are to love one another and John 13:35 Jesus says if we love him we will keep His words, and that the Father and Son will come and make their abode with us (John13:23), He then goes on to say that there is no greater love than to lay down our lives for our friends, and 1 Corinthians describes the qualities of God's love. Love is a fruit of the Spirit, says Galatians 5:22 and John tells us we love because He first loved us. Christianity is maturity of love more than knowledge. Knowing and loving Jesus Christ, not an increase of the intellect, but a desire to walk as He walked – with holiness and power.

THE GOODNESS AND GREATNESS OF GOD

Another attribute to be considered more deeply is that of God's greatness. Not only is God good, He is the Great I AM, and He is great! Most often in responding to the question from a greeter "How are you?" we reply; "I'm good" or even "Great." This does not reflect the person's moral character however, but rather describes how one is doing. Where God is concerned, His whole being can be regarded as great. In the Gospels when Jesus was speaking to a certain man, the man responded with "Good Teacher, what must I do that I may inherit eternal life?" Here, Jesus replied: "Why do you call me good? There is One who is good, and that is God." Maybe that man employed the term "good" with a flippant manner, without perhaps considering the implications of the word. Something like using a figure of speech, rather than using the word good with reverence, in a holy fashion. Likewise, we too, use phrases or figures of speech without attaching much importance to them. Here, Jesus, was quick to point out that the goodness of God was particular to Him and was no mere flippant adjective but an integral part of the Divine nature. Likewise, God is great, could be further emphasized by considering all that His greatness embodies -the vastness, the boundlessness, the immensity and largeness of His Divine nature, the expanse of His holiness, the depth of His love. To say one is great, must surely in truth only apply to the Majesty in heaven. Psalm 145:3 says: "His greatness is unsearchable." In Ephesians 1:19 we read of the greatness of His power. We call some people good, especially if they are famous. Important historical figures are even considered to be great. We use the expression; "Great men of the faith." There are what we call great musicians or artists, poets, scientists. We regard also many things in life to be good; even pizza or footballers. The beauty of language affords us to be aptly descriptive for the occasion. To be great must be beyond the very best. It supersedes goodness in that greatness is all-encompassing. It is the largesse of good. It is very big and grandiose, as is God.

God is great and greatly to be praised, says the Word of God. His goodness, however, leads man to repentance. This is descriptive of his moral nature, His kindness towards mankind. God's goodness brings to mind the picture of Aslan, the lion, in C. S. Lewis's story, *"The Lion, the Witch and the Wardrobe."* In the final scene, Lucy Pevensey remarks on the nature of Aslan, who is a type of Christ. In the closing words, her brother says; "he's not a tame lion" and Lucy replies with a smile, "No, but he *is* good." The redemptive nature of Christ is revealed through Aslan as the story unfolds and the Pevensey children make their journey through the magical land of Narnia. This portrayal of Aslan reveals much about the goodness of God, and yet His justice comes forth as He reigns as victor over the wicked witch. To say: "God is good" is often used as a mannerism in Christian circles. Whether circumstances be poor or favourable, one might simply say "God is good" (to which the reply is usually "All the time"). Familiar usage, however, can cause terms or words to lose their intended impact. In geographical terms the word great mostly refers to the biggest, such as The Great Lakes, The Great Wall of China, or Great Britain, representing an entire empire. In Genesis 1:25,31 God saw what He had made and called it "good." A declaration. Psalm 34:8 says: "Oh taste and see that the Lord is good."

It is the essence of God's very nature to be good. It is an intrinsic part of who He is. In Jeremiah 29:11 the Word says; "For I know the thoughts that I think towards you, says the Lord, thoughts of peace and not of evil, to give you an expected end." Also rendered as "plans for good, and not for evil, to give you a future and a hope." God's intentions are good. He gives good gifts to His children. "Every good and every perfect gift is from above, and cometh down from the Father of Lights, with whom is no variableness neither shadow of turning" (James 1:17). The gifts and calling of God are without repentance, meaning God doesn't take away what He gives, He doesn't change His mind, is not fickle. The Bible tells us that "the Lord is good to all" (Psalm 145:9), and that "the Lord is good to them that wait for Him" (Lam. 3:25). Psalm 23 tells us that goodness and mercy shall follow us all the days of our lives and in Psalm 33:5 it says: "the earth is full of the goodness of the Lord." Psalm 52:1 says the goodness of God endures continually.

GOD IS KIND AND GIVING

God is a lavish giver. He is magnanimous. He wants His people to be kind in nature. Love is kind. But this does not mean giving from what we do not have. In order to be generous, you do not borrow a sum of money from your unsaved relatives, so you can send it in to a rich televangelist. This is not God's idea of giving. We are to lay aside a portion of our income on a weekly basis according to 1 Corinthians 16:1-2 to give in accordance with our provision. You will always have something to give when you are living by faith. You cannot give what you do not have so begin by giving a bag of groceries to a poor neighbour, or some clothing to a needy friend, or a bag of household goods to a local charity store. It will cost you. When you give it is intended to be a sacrifice. If you practice this kind of giving your life will be simpler. God is a God of order and this follows even in our homes where there need not be lavish wares and clutter. This is not a matter of personal taste, but of principle. Our desires are not designed to be after the things that this world has to offer.

One might say that God intends for all of His children to be wealthy, for if they are poor, they are unable to give to others. But we are meant to give from what we have, and we all have something if we have a roof over our heads. Jesus Christ did not even have that. The Bible says the Son of man had nowhere to lay His head. The Apostle Paul lived in a rented flat for at least two years of his ministry. This is not to glorify a poverty mindset, but to say that earthly wealth in God's eyes is something immaterial versus spiritual wealth. God has saved us by His kindness and love and by pouring out abundantly of His Spirit, says Titus 3:4. And Paul adds, in Ephesians 2 "That in the ages to come He might show the exceeding riches of His grace in His kindness toward us in Christ Jesus." In the Old Testament, Psalm 117 says to praise Him for His merciful kindness. In Isaiah 54 God is speaking to Israel saying: "For a mere moment I have forsaken you, but with great mercies I will gather you and have everlasting kindness on you."

In Jonah 4:2 God is described as a gracious and merciful God, slow to anger and abundant in lovingkindness, also in Joel 2:13, where He is addressed as a God of great kindness, even relenting from doing harm. King Solomon writes that what is desired in a man is kindness. In the Gospels Jesus says that God causes the sun to shine on the just and the unjust alike. And the rain blesses the unrighteous as well as the righteous. God is kind – yet was utterly intolerant of the hypocrisy of the Pharisees, the religious people of the times when Jesus walked this earth. He pulled no punches with the scribes; they would cause men to carry heavy burdens that they could not lift themselves. They would say and not do. They did their works to be seen by people, all show. They loved the best seats in the synagogues and liked to be called "Rabbi." They were proud. The scribes and Pharisees "devoured widows' houses" and for a pretense made lengthy prayers. It was the chief priests and scribes who condemned Jesus. They neglected the weightier matters of the law; justice, mercy and faith. They "majored on minors", they were full of extortion and self-indulgence, "full of dead men's bones," all uncleanness and outwardly clean and righteous yet hypocritical and lawless (Matthew 23).

In Luke's Gospel Jesus explains a story to show what kindness and mercy is all about and said to His followers to "go and do likewise." Putting the Lord first, we are then to go and love our neighbor as ourselves. We read in the Gospels the account of God's care and compassion towards the man who fell among thieves and was left for dead in Luke 10:30-37. The very words of Jesus speak of the compassion of the Samaritan who helped the man who had been injured, and Jesus finishes the story with the injunction: "Go and do thou likewise", showing mercy to others. If we limit our kindness to those we feel deserve our mercies, we are not truly exhibiting the love of God. It is easy to be kind to those we like.

The Word of God says in Micah 6:8: "To do justly, to love mercy and to walk humbly with thy God." We are here to do good to all. Especially to our own families and fellow believers of faith, yet not to limit it to that, but to extend goodness to all. The Samaritan in this story showed compassion toward the injured man who had fallen among thieves and was left half dead. He bandaged his wounds, put him on his own animal, took him to an inn and took care of him and provided for his welfare, Luke 10:34. He behaved as a good neighbor should, according to Jesus.

The man who questioned Jesus was a lawyer, and was trying to justify himself by asking: "Who is my neighbor?" He was testing Jesus who responded with the commandment: "You shall love the Lord your God with all your heart, with all your soul, with all your strength and with all your mind, and your neighbor as yourself." Deuteronomy 6:5. "On these two commandments hang all the law and the prophets." (Matt. 22:40)

In the Old Testament, there is a very interesting account in the life of David. He had defeated Israel's enemies and reigned over all Israel; he administered judgment and justice to all his people it says in 2 Samuel 8:15. David asks if there is anyone left in the house of Saul to whom he could show kindness. Mephibosheth was the son of Jonathan, Saul's son, and he was lame in both feet. David told him not to fear and promised that he would show kindness to him for his father, Jonathan's sake. David then restored to Mephibosheth all the land of his grandfather, Saul, and allowed him to eat at his table like one of his own sons. David also showed kindness to Hanun, the son of Nahash, repaying the kindness of Hanun's father. Nahash was the king of the people of Ammon. They did not trust David's men and treated them shamefully despite David's kindness and vulnerability. Even so, God caused David to prevail and David received the king's crown through the battle of Rabbah. Following this, there was much bloodshed and David was disobedient to God in numbering his people. He was convicted of his sin and repented of his foolishness, but God sent a plague to the land, and there was much destruction. The Lord subsequently relented and David built an altar to the Lord. Even in this, David purchased what was needed at full price, since he did not want to offer to his Lord that which cost him nothing (2 Sam.24:24). Hence the plague was withdrawn when David offered burnt offerings and peace offerings and the Lord heeded his prayers. Due to the bloodshed, however, and David's sin with Bathsheba, David's son, Solomon, was appointed to build the temple in his place (1 Chron. 22:8). David knew God well enough to trust in His mercies, even though His judgment had been very severe and had caused David to fear. Yet David preferred the hand of God to that of falling into the hand of men, which had been the alternative. These records of David's life show that he had a kind heart. He was merciful and compassionate, and indeed "a man after God's heart."

Under the law of the Old Covenant tithing was commanded by God. The tithe is a tenth. This meant that God's people were to give a tenth of their income. In the New Testament no such command is made. If anything, one's giving might supersede that of the lawful requirements, but it is not strictly a tithe. To even call it a tithe is not biblical for believers in Christ Jesus, who came to set us free from the law. He fulfilled the law. Our giving, says the Bible, should be done freely, and cheerfully. It is also to be done with love, says 1 Corinthians. Jesus also said: "it is more blessed to give than to receive," and "give, and it shall be given unto you." As believers, we are meant to give as the Holy Spirit leads. The Bible does say that the early Church believers would set aside a portion of their income on a weekly basis. This would go to the local Church and help the Missionaries. God also wants us to be hospitable as a way of life. When we give it is to be from the heart, not in a legalistic manner, as tithing is. There are numerous televangelists who preach on tithing along with sowing money as seed into their ministries; this teaching is error. In the Proverbs, 22:16 it says: "He that oppresseth the poor to increase his riches, and he that giveth to the rich, shall surely come to want." Many give of their hard-earned cash to these scamsters who live lavish lifestyles. Here, God says clearly to not give to the rich. They will, of course, try to convince you why you should. They live for wealth and materialism and are making merchandise of many people. The people who give to such snake-oil salesmen are just as culpable. It is vital to be discerning. We are meant to give where there is a need and there are many others who are far needier and deserving of a token of kindness.

GOD'S COMFORT,
COMPASSION AND MERCY

The Holy Spirit is known as the Comforter, and the Consolation of Israel. The Bible says in 2 Corinthians 1:4 that God comforts us in all our tribulation, that we may comfort others with the comfort with which we ourselves are comforted of God. Frequently the apostles faced various conflicts and sufferings yet found consolation and hope in God. This happened to the Apostle Paul, to the extent that he even despaired of life but God delivered them (2 Cor. 1:10). The Holy Spirit as Wonderful Counsellor is spoken of in Isaiah 9:6, also referring to Christ, as Messiah. God's comfort is frequently revealed in the Gospels, such as in the account of the death of Lazarus. In John chapter 11, the writer says: "Jesus wept." He comforted Martha, Mary and their family. Clearly Jesus was close to them and empathized with them in their sorrow. When we have suffered along with others we may truly enter into their suffering and pain. And it is often this sharing of their burden which enables them to find the necessary strength to go on. We are enabled to be of comfort to others once we have ourselves been the recipient of God's comfort. In the book of Job there were three men who came alongside Job in his time of sorrow and loss. These men were not the source of blessing that we would want around at such a difficult time. They reprove and accuse Job and seem to be full of their own personal opinions for the most part. In the end God restores Job's losses and Job prays for his three comforters. We use the same expression today, "Job's comforters," to describe a people who have been of little support during a time of difficulty. It happens when another cannot identify with our situation. There is a well-known expression: "Better felt than telt." Often it is better to say less and to convey empathy when another is suffering. Often a person is not seeking answers, but consolation. God consoles. He is gentle, realizing our weaknesses. He remembers our frame, says the Bible, that we are dust, therefore He is compassionate and merciful towards His children.

It is God's nature to be compassionate. He cares for all He has made. Even as a sparrow falling to the ground catches His attention, and the hairs of our heads are numbered, we can be sure that our smallest concern is not overlooked by our Father in heaven, for He is compassionate and kind. Psalm 145:8 tell us that the Lord is gracious and full of compassion. His mercy is within His nature and He cannot be separated from it. It does not diminish nor expand but is constant. As Tozer says: "God's mercy is simply what God is – uncreated and eternal. It never began to be; it always was. Heaven and earth were yet unmade and the stars were yet unformed and all that space men are talking about now was only a thought in the mind of God. God was as merciful as He is now. And did it not only never begin to be, but the mercy of God also has never been any more than it is now." Were it not for the mercies of God, the Bible says, we would all be consumed. "It is of the Lord's mercies that we are not consumed, because His compassions fail not. They are new every morning: great is thy faithfulness" Lamentations 3:22-23. Psalm 145:8-9 says: "The LORD is gracious, and full of compassion; slow to anger, and of great mercy. The LORD is good to all: and his tender mercies are over all his works."

The Bible says to honour all men but to love the brotherhood of believers. To prefer one another, to be kind to one another, tenderhearted and courteous. The "one another's" in the Scriptures are in reference to other believers, those of the household of faith. We are, however to extend that love to others too. "For God so loved the world…" As mentioned we see striking compassion in the story of the Good Samaritan. This kindly man set the injured man on his own donkey after he had been attacked by robbers, he then bathed his wounds and took care of him. Today, we would be hard pressed to find people freely inviting the homeless into their homes and taking care of them. Francis and Edith Schaeffer of L'Abri, Switzerland did so and made a vital impact for Christ throughout their lives. Well-known men and women have started orphanages, George Muller did so, in the last century. But on a daily basis, we do not often make this form of hospitality a common practice. We would be concerned for our own safety, or the cleanliness of our homes. And yet the Scriptures say in Hebrews to practice hospitality for in doing so we might entertain angels unawares. We could invite a few neighbours over along with some disadvantaged people, allowing the homeless to bathe and have a meal and some good company would be a massive witness for the cause of Christ and allow them to enjoy the tranquility of a Christian home, the peaceful environment and the joyful welcome. It may not change the world but it may change a heart. "There but for the grace of God, go you or I." For many homeless people there has been the possibility of a devastating relationship break-up, with ensuing depression, then possibly mental ill-health and substance abuse as a means of coping. Sharing Christian love is our God-given duty, a labour of love, which we are to extend to others.

It seems to me that it is often easier to extend kindness towards an unbeliever who may be poor, someone with whom we may have no further contact after our encounter, than it is to show consistent grace towards a fellow believer with whom we differ on some doctrinal basis. In such cases there seems to be a whimsical parting of ways with a coldness attached to it. One might feel there is more love exhibited towards the non-believer than towards the fellow brother. And in many cases, this is true. The Bible warns about the end times, that the love of many will grow cold. We are to love one another with such a deep reverence and respect for our Maker that He calls us to lay down our lives for one another. So, would we truly give our lives if called to do so, and yet when it comes to matters far short of that, show such intolerance? I doubt it. For love must be sincere. Genuine; to be authentic, Christian character need to be consistent. The love we have for the brethren in the faith would overflow naturally into the lives of others and the compassion and tenderness that we extend toward the unsaved would be the minimum respect we would show to a brother or sister. We would listen to a non-believer for some considerable time in order to then present him with the truth of the Gospel, and yet we are reluctant to give the time of day listening to the views of those who are already saved, unless they fit perfectly within our own frame of reference. This may be a problem with the ego. It may also be that we are so committed to converting the unbeliever that we are willing to go to lengths that otherwise we would not go to in a relationship that may require honesty and risk-taking. There needs to be a drawing together in this area, a willingness to take risks, to be open in communication with one another, and to be transparent. The truth can stand up to testing. We need to be looking for similarities and not points of division. A true sharing in what we agree constitutes fellowship. Dialogue and debate are also healthy except where there is a lack of truth and respect. To be in agreement there needs to be both. Truth is the basis for unity if we read correctly the words of Jesus in John 17. This is known as Jesus' high-priestly prayer. In verses 21-23 He prays that His followers would be one. But Jesus also prayed that we would be sanctified through the truth, and that His Word is truth. See verses 17and 19, as well as verse 6. Here it is evident that true Christian unity means that there needs to be a foundation upon truth, this is the basis for true fellowship. There is no unity without agreement upon the Word of God. We are to extend God's mercy towards our fellow brothers and sisters especially.

GOD IS WISDOM

In Proverbs, chapter eight, God speaks of the contrast between worldly wealth and enduring riches. We are to receive his instruction and not silver, his knowledge rather than gold. Wisdom is better than rubies and is incomparable; riches and honour are with wisdom, knowledge, discretion, understanding and the fear of the Lord. Enduring riches and righteousness. The fruit of God is better than fine gold. His revenue is better than choice silver, and those who inherit his righteousness and justice inherit true wealth which will fill their treasuries (Prov. 8:21). Finding God's riches brings favour through heeding His Word. The Proverbs begins with the injunction to search for wisdom, knowledge and understanding are its companions. The fear of the Lord is the beginning of wisdom says the writer, Solomon. It also says to have sound discretion. Discretion may be likened to wisdom; it is not clamorous or loud. Neither is love (1 Cor. 13). It holds its peace. The Scriptures tell us that "the earth will be filled with the knowledge of the glory of the Lord as the waters cover the seas." Blanketed over. His voice utters knowledge. Wisdom and knowledge are linked, but where knowledge may be an accumulation of information or the ability to do something, or to have acquired information, wisdom is its practical application. Understanding is to appreciate an intended aim; to be able to relate or project without experiencing for one's self. Understanding is having insight as well as the ability to know how things or people tick, in a sense. When a person is wise they know when to keep silent; to not speak out of turn. Knowledge may refer not only to the knowledge of God but to the mechanics of life; how something is made or put together. It may well be accumulation of facts or information, but not limited to the things of God, but also to the science of life. Knowledge is valuable, but without wisdom it is likely to lead to pride, for "knowledge puffeth up, but love edifies," says Paul, in 1 Corinthians.

The fear of the Lord keeps a person from going astray. It guides a person to do what is right in every decision of life, by putting God first. Most often wisdom lets its words be few. It has the quality of being peaceable, able to resolve conflicts amicably according to James the writer of the New Testament Epistle. These characteristics are inextricably linked; wisdom, knowledge, understanding, discretion and the fear of the Lord. Discretion does not reveal all, or speak out in advance regarding a matter. In wisdom the worlds were made. God spoke all of creation into being. Wisdom is the key point of the book of Proverbs and it symbolizes the Lord Jesus. Proverbs says to keep sound wisdom and discretion (3:31b), it keeps us free from worry and concern. Wisdom is the principle thing, says Solomon, therefore get wisdom. It will be an ornament of grace on your head and a crown of glory. Instruction is your life (13b). It keeps us from getting into trouble, and helps preserve discretion, keeps us from stumbling into immorality. Prov. 8:13 tells us that the fear of the Lord is to hate evil and is the beginning of wisdom. And Proverbs 9:10b says. "The knowledge of the Holy is understanding." Diligence, hard work and keeping our tongue are some of the things Solomon addresses, along with honesty and integrity, prudence, discernment and heeding counsel.

Proverbs 13:13 says that fearing or regarding the commandment brings reward and that there is strong confidence with the fear of the Lord (14:26), it is a fountain of life (v 27) and by it one departs from evil (16:6). It is better to get wisdom than gold, and understanding is to be chosen rather than silver says the writer (16:16). Proverbs tells us the name of the Lord is a strong tower, the righteous run to it and are safe. God's very name brings safety. Calling upon the name of the Lord Jesus when in difficulty brings relief. Death and life are in the power of the tongue, and those who love it will eat its fruit. We can speak death or life to ourselves and our circumstances. Proverbs 19:23 says we will not be visited with evil if we have the fear of the Lord. The Bible has something to say about the things God hates; diverse weights and measures, double standards are an abomination to Him (20:23) He also despises haughtiness and shutting our ears to the cry of the poor (21:13) Verse 23 says that guarding our mouth will keep us from trouble. The Word of God says to be zealous of the fear of the Lord all day long (23:17b). Whilst other people are pursuing pleasure we can be sure that if our heart is fixed on righteousness and the pursuit of God we will find favour with Him. The Proverbs gives guidance regarding the company we keep; not to associate with those who have a loose tongue, those given to change, the fickle, troublemakers, not a false witness, the lazy, arrogant or boastful, not to put confidence in an unfaithful person, or the contentious, foolish, deceitful or liars, those who oppress the poor, extortioners, those who cause people to go astray, the covetous, flatterers, scoffers, bloodthirsty, transgressors, angry people, and those who stir up strife. We are instructed to be content, not to strive for riches. With many riches man is inclined to forget God, and to become obsessed with gain, this "fullness" can cause one's heart to stray. When we are in need we tend to lean more closely upon the Lord. We know that we shall not want, as the Psalmist says, as we trust in the Lord to be our Shepherd (Psalm 23:1). We tend to seek God for our every need when there is some area of lack in our lives. It fosters dependency on God, whereas an abundance and plenty can lead to a disinterest of spiritual things. Not many rich will enter onto the kingdom of God, said Jesus. Having an abundance of this world's goods tends to cause a spiritual dullness and insensitivity towards the things of God. It has been said: "Blessedness is the greatest of perils because it tends to dull our keen sense of dependence on God and makes us prone to presumption." Without maturity of character, having too much can lead to ruin. The Apostle Paul warns that those who seek after worldly wealth have pierced themselves through with many sorrows. Contentment and a freedom from covetousness is far more beneficial. Psalm 19:9 says that the fear of the Lord is clean and enduring. Psalm 147:11 David says the Lord takes pleasure in them that fear Him. Isaiah says that the fear of the Lord is his treasure. Job was a man that feared God and eschewed evil. 2 Corinthians speaks of "perfecting holiness in the fear of God (7:1). God's will for us is to have sufficient and for us to have our needs met, if we read the Lord's prayer correctly (Matthew chapter 6). This is for daily provision. Paul speaks of having an abundance for every good work. The Psalmist says that if the Lord is our Shepherd we shall not be in want. So, we may present our requests to God with thanksgiving, and in accordance with His will, He will surely supply. But we must also be consistent with faith-filled words that do not contradict, and our lips must utter knowledge. In our prayers, faith and agreement must be in alignment with the will of God and His purposes for our lives. If we are trusting God in our heart, then the words that come forth from our mouths will be faith-filled. "As a man thinks in his heart, so is he." Jesus said that we will give an account for every idle word on the day of judgment. If we have said some things with our tongue that have been damaging, the best thing we can do is go before God and repent, renounce declarations we have made that have caused harm and declare what God says to be true. Go humble ourselves and ask forgiveness and begin to speak what is right and true. By the words of our mouths we shall be justified and by the words of our mouths we shall be condemned. According to our words it shall be done to us. Jesus spoke to the fig tree, and because it had no fruit on it he cursed it and it withered and died. He said to "speak to the mountain and it shall move, and nothing shall be impossible for you." This does not mean that "words are containers for power" as many would believe, but our words do have an effect upon the very course of our lives. In James' epistle the tongue is likened to the rudder of a ship. The life follows where the tongue goes. There is a saying "It is better to hold your tongue and be thought a fool, than to open your mouth and prove it." Wise people tend to say less, but this should not be a point of debate for those who have "the gift of the gab" – some people are very gifted when it comes to speaking. Choosing what we say, when we say it, to whom and when and where, are all points worthy of consideration.

GOD'S ARM OF STRENGTH

Psalm 89:13 says that God's arm is mighty and His hand is strong; "High is Thy right hand", speaking of God's justice, judgment, mercy and truth. This is metaphorical and doesn't imply that God has a physical arm. God says that even His arm would strengthen David and the Word tells us that God redeemed His people with an "outstretched arm." (Ex.6:6) and Jeremiah 32:17. Psalm 98:1 says that His arm is holy. In Isaiah 40:11 the Word says: "He shall gather the lambs with His arm." The arm speaks of strength, and God gives a warning to those who would trust in their own strength, the arm of flesh, or in another. God's intention is for us to draw our strength from Him. His arm also refers to his saving power (Isaiah 53:1). Deuteronomy 33:27 says: "Underneath are the everlasting arms." We know that God's arms are outstretched toward the poor and needy. To be poor in spirit is to know our need for God. There is little room for a haughty or self-confident attitude when it comes to our position before the Lord of all glory. We are to acknowledge that our strength comes from the Lord, and then we can rejoice in all we do, knowing that it is from the Lord that we are even enabled to do anything, and therefore to give Him all the glory.

GOD IS OUR CONFIDENCE

Proverbs 3:26 tells us the Lord shall be our confidence. The Latin word for "confidence" is "confidentem" meaning "firmly trusting, bold" or "confidere" meaning to have full trust or reliance. "Fidere" means to have trust or faith. God is always faithful. "Semper Fidelis." This is best known as the motto of the United States Marine Corps, though also used by a military unit of the Duke of Beaufort's Regiment of Foot, raised in South-western England in 1685, and as the motto of the French town of Abbeville since 1369. This implies that God is able to be fully trusted. We can rely on Him and depend upon Him. He will give a solid support and a firm footing, so that we will not fall, if we are leaning upon Him in faith. God is Trustworthy. He is a God who is dependable. In our modern-day world, where standards and values are rapidly changing, and fickle, we can be sure that God never changes. His Word is true, and He is true to His Word. What God say He will do in His Word, that He will do. He is reliable, and His promises are firm.

GOD CELEBRATES

God spoke to Israel and instructed them to keep the feasts of the Lord as holy convocations, to observe a Sabbath of solemn rest and not to work on those days. In Leviticus 23: 14-15 is mentioned the Lord's Passover and the Feast of Unleavened bread lasting seven days, also in Exodus chapter 12. The feast of First Fruits is mentioned in Leviticus 23:10 and verse 28 tells of the day of Atonement. The Feast of Tabernacles is in verse 34. Exodus 12 describes the feast of the Lord's Passover where the blood of the sacrificial lamb was sprinkled on the doorposts and the lintel of the household, verse 7. This first took place in Egypt before the people of Israel departed from their sojourn. Exodus 12:42 describes this as a night of solemn observance to the Lord for bringing them out of the land of Egypt. In Exodus 23:14 God says to Israel: "Three times you shall keep the feast to Me in the year." The Feast of Unleavened Bread, the feast of Harvest and the Feast of Ingathering, mentioned also in Exodus 34:22-23, Deuteronomy 16:10,16 and in Ezekiel 45:21-25. The children of Israel were instructed again in Numbers 9 to keep the Passover at its appointed time, verses 2,4,5 and 12, and in 2 Chronicles 35:17.

In Exodus 20:8 in the Ten Commandments the Lord says to observe the Sabbath day and to keep it holy. In 2 Chronicles Hezekiah the king sent letters to all Israel regarding the keeping of the Passover, vv. 1-2. Numbers 28:17 mentions the Passover and this chapter describes the offerings. Ezra 3:5 describes the feasts appointed to Israel and the offerings. In Isaiah 56: 2, 6 the Lord says that man who observes the Sabbath is blessed by doing no evil, keeping justice and righteousness and in not defiling the Sabbath. Isaiah also records those things that are a true and righteous fast to the Lord in chapter 58, not the afflicting of one's soul, finding personal pleasure or exploiting labourers but to loose the bonds of wickedness, undo the heavy burdens, let the oppressed go free, break every yoke, share bread with the hungry, be hospitable to the poor, clothing the naked, to take away the yoke and the pointing finger, speaking wickedness, v.9 to extend one's soul to the hungry and satisfy the afflicted soul, v.10, not to defile the Sabbath by doing what one pleases, v.13, or speaking one's own words. In Hebrew Lord of the Sabbath is Adon haShabbat (Matt. 12:1-8.)

Christians may question whether or not to keep the Sabbaths and holy days, believing these to be a thing of the past, the Old Covenant and under the law, or solely for Israel. We don't dismiss the Ten Commandments because these were the law, yet we regard the superior law of love that Jesus taught us. Jesus observed the feasts of Israel, He was our very Passover Lamb, the ultimate sacrifice. Exodus 31:13-17 says that the Sabbath was given to be observed throughout the generations of Israel as a perpetual covenant, as a sign between the Lord and the children of Israel forever. This was spoken to Moses when God gave the Ten Commandments on Mount Sinai. Zechariah 14:16-17 shows a command for Israel to go up to Jerusalem at the Feast of Tabernacles and worship the Lord. In Matthew 26:17 Jesus' disciples went to Him and asked: "Where do you want us to prepare for You to eat the Passover?" Jesus says: "I will keep the Passover at your house with My disciples, verse 18, and Luke 22:9. Jesus' parents also went up to Jerusalem every year at the Feast of Passover (Luke 2:41). Here Jesus was present with them. It was also called the Feast of Unleavened Bread (Luke 22:1). In John 7:8 Jesus instructs His disciples to go up to the feast. Jesus was also walking in the temple at the Feast of Dedication (John 10:22).

1 Corinthians 5:7-8 says: "Therefore purge out the old leaven, that you may be a new lump, since you truly are unleavened. For indeed Christ, our Passover was sacrificed for us. Therefore let us keep the feast not with old leaven, nor with the leaven of malice and wickedness, but with the unleavened bread of sincerity and truth."

Celebration is a part of life; many believers celebrate with the traditional holidays such as Christmas and Easter. We would be honouring God to celebrate His birth, death and resurrection remembering the reason, and sanctifying the Lord in our hearts.

Whilst the world is becoming increasingly antichristian many believers are rising up in self-righteous revolt about "keeping the "Christ" in Christmas" and offering up other pithy wee jingles like "Jesus is the reason for the season." I have done it myself. And, of course, out comes the Christmas tree, with the tinsel and the gold and silver baubles and every other trapping imaginable. For one thing December 25th is not Jesus' birthday. It is the feast of Saturnalia, a pagan deity. Joseph and

Mary didn't travel through the mountains in Israel's cold winter season, and the shepherds would not have been out tending their sheep at that time of year. The Messiah's birth could have been as early as spring, as He was known as the Lamb of God, but may have been around October, during the Jewish feast of Tabernacles. We simply don't know. So, we celebrate it anyway, just to keep up with the Jones's and not to upset the donkey cart. It may not be wrong at all to celebrate such holidays, as long as we do not fall into idol worship, and that we remember the Lord Jesus, and seek to honour Him.

In the Scriptures, only the heathen celebrated birthdays, Pharaoh and Herod, other than the heralding of the coming Messiah. If we were meant to make a biggie out of this event God would have made sure we knew the day. But conversely the Scriptures condemn the observance of days and months and seasons and years. Galatians 4:10, and says in verse 7 that: "you are no longer a slave, but an heir, but then indeed when you did not know God, you served those things which by nature are not gods..." This wasn't just about immorality, but about observances.

The Scriptures record in the book of the prophet Isaiah the Lord also spoke saying: "The new moons, the Sabbaths and the calling of assemblies, your appointed feasts My soul hates, they are a trouble to Me." God is weary of them and tells us to instead do good in Isaiah 1:13-17 "Cease to do evil, learn to do good, seek justice, rebuke the oppressor, defend the fatherless, plead for the widows." And in verse 18 a call for deep repentance.

About the day; Saturnalia was an ancient Roman festival in honour of the deity Saturn held on December 17th of the Julian calendar and later expanded with festivities through to 23rd December. Saturnalia is a festival of light leading to the winter solstice. The renewal of light and the coming of the new year was celebrated in the later Roman Empire at the Dies Natalis of Sol Invictus, the "birthday of the Unconquerable Sun", on December 25th. This was a week-long period of lawlessness. In the world, not much has changed in that respect.

In the 4th century CE Christianity imported the Saturnalia festival hoping to take the pagan masses in with it, with its leaders promising the pagans that they could continue to celebrate Saturnalia as Christians. The Roman Emperor Justinian made Christmas a Civic holiday in 529 AD. The various civilisations had their own names for Saturn, AKA

Vulcan, Kronos, Tammuz, Molech and Baal, all names for Nimrod, the father of all Babylonian gods. The people would sacrifice their children to these gods (Jer.32:35) to appease these gods and to hopefully purge themselves of sin. Purgatory has its roots here. In Genesis 10:9 Nimrod tries to replace God. Satan was a common name for Nimrod through Asia Minor, the fire god to whom infants were burned and eaten in human sacrifice, even among those who were once God's people.

In Revelation 2:6,15 we read about the doctrine of the Nicolaitans which Christ twice tells the Church He hates. Nikos means conqueror or destroyer, Laos means people. Hence those who follow Nimrod, the conqueror-destroyer. Santa Claus was originally Father Christmas or Father Winter, later Saint Nicholas or St. Nick. So, along with the occasion comes Santa, or St. Nick, the kindly old gentleman on a sleigh who rides through the clouds of heaven and with fatherly affection steals the adoration of little children the world over who wait in anticipation for their dreams and wishes to come true, which parents promise that Santa will fulfil if they are good little boys and girls. This misplaced attention is a prime tack of the enemy if ever I saw one. Just as the devil uses fear to manipulate and control, thereby causing people to erroneously worship him by subscribing to him the fear that only the Lord Almighty is due, only with reverential awe, the devil has likewise cajoled the children and the parents of this world into a lukewarm affection by serving this goodly gentleman who gives lavishly, even though the Scriptures tell us in James's letter that "Every good and perfect gift comes from above, from the Father of lights, with whom there is no variableness nor shadow of turning."

Now, I'm all for celebrations. And the good news is –so is God. He instituted the Sabbath as a rest for His people, it was a covenant, (Ex. 31:16). The feasts of Israel were to be kept by His people for perpetual generations. (Exodus 34 and Lev. 23). Jesus celebrated them. Throughout the Gospels we see where Jesus was keeping the feasts (John 4:45; 5:1; 6:4; 7:2,8,10-11,37; 10:22; 12:20;13:1).

Jesus and the early Church celebrated the Feasts of Unleavened Bread, the Feast of Weeks and the First Fruits or Harvest as well as the feast of Tabernacles. They may have observed Hanukkah which came in later, between the two Testaments.

Interestingly a court in Ohio recently ruled that since Christmas has no Christian roots, they concluded that Christmas-keeping and manger scenes could remain in their schools because they are not really a part of either Christianity or religion. But that prayer and Bible reading, which are, must remain excluded from schools!

These are some of my findings after much research on the subject. I believe in the daily celebration of life. And that kindness and giving should be a way of life for all believers, not reserved for one season of the year. Christmas often brings with it a superficial religiosity, a dressing up for the occasion, when what God wants is for His people to serve Him alone, not with syncretism (the merging of false pagan customs with the worship of the true God), which was punishable by death in ancient Israel ((Lev. 18:21,29). Also note for this study Ex. 34:10-17; 23:23-33; Lev. 20:22-26 and Deut. 20:13-18. The true God knew that serving other gods always led to sacrificing their children to them. Let it not be your children!

The event is pagan (however we dress it up.) And more often than not it leads to a lot of disappointment as hopes for many people are left unfulfilled, and memories awakened of happier days gone by with loved ones who are no longer with us. What is really important is to make the whole of life a celebration, whether or not we use these days to celebrate our Saviour, and to live in the true Spirit of love, kindness, peace and generosity all year round, which indeed we do, if we truly belong to Him. Given the fact that most believers do celebrate the season it would be important to emphasize here that in keeping of the feast, it is worth remembering why we are celebrating, and to use the occasion as a witness to unsaved friends and loved ones, whilst they are most often open to the Good News of the Gospel. There are many creative ways of sharing the love of our Saviour, and this is often a good time to share, whilst people are exposed to the Gospel message throughout the holidays.

THE RESURRECTION

In all of my time as a believer in Christ I have not heard any sermons about the days that Jesus was in the grave, three days and nights, before he rose again according to the Scriptures. I have probably heard 4,000 sermons and Bible studies at weekly church services, heard over 10,000 sermons on Christian radio, attended numerous seminars, conferences and retreats, listened to a multitude of C.D.'s and teaching tapes, read an ample-sized library of books and seen several Christian films and documentaries, as well as hundreds of online videos of teaching, yet this subject has rarely, if ever, been addressed.

The Christian faith world-wide is founded on this doctrine, that Jesus rose again from the dead, and yet is very sketchy about the biblical basis for the whole occasion even though the Christian calendar is based upon it. Christians simply do not want to discuss it, stating that as long as we believe that Jesus rose from the grave it should not really matter too much about the three days and nights, even though Friday to Sunday is not three days and nights, and the Church's teaching of a Good Friday tradition is consistently upheld, even though the Scriptures do not affirm that Jesus died on a Friday. I gather that people assume, (or, theologians have deduced), that it may have been a Friday because they glean from the Scriptures that the body of Jesus had to be put into the tomb for burial "before the Sabbath" and so, since we all agree that the usual Jewish Sabbath day is a Saturday, then Friday must have been the day of Jesus' death. Even if this deduction makes it only three days, only in part, then somehow, the Scriptures appear to be fulfilled.

However, the error is in not examining some points fully. First, the Bible clearly says that Jesus would be *three days and three nights* in the tomb. Matthew 12:38 – 40 Says:

> "Then some of the scribes and Pharisees answered, saying,
> "Teacher, we want to see a sign from You." But he answered
> and said to them, "An evil and adulterous generation seek
> after a sign, and no sign will be given to it except the sign of

the prophet Jonah. For as Jonah was three days and three nights in the belly of the great fish, so will the Son of Man be *three days and three nights* in the heart of the earth."

Friday to Sunday is not three days and three nights. Tradition will have to take a back seat. But where has traditional Christianity got this wrong for all these years?

Well, the Scriptures tell us that Jesus' body had to be buried before the Sabbath. Because the Jews celebrate the usual weekly Sabbath on a Saturday the assumption was made that Jesus died on the day before the weekly Sabbath, the Friday morning.

However, in that particular week, the Jews were celebrating the annual feast of Passover (Lev. 23:6-7), or Unleavened Bread, and there was also a Sabbath, a high or holy day, on the Thursday of that week in the month of Abib, Abib is also the month of Nissan (March – April). The Bible called the day before this the day of Preparation. The day that Jesus spoke about prior to his death with His disciples. In John 19:38 Joseph of Arimathea asks for the body of Jesus to prepare the body for burial, according to Jewish custom (John 19:38-42). Along with Nicodemus, Joseph went to prepare the body and the tomb. Verse 42 repeats: "..because of the Jews' preparation day."

Luke 23:54 says:

"That day was the Preparation and the Sabbath drew near."

John 19:31 says: "The Jews therefore, because it was the preparation, that the bodies should not remain upon the cross on the sabbath day, (for that day was a high day,) besought Pilate that their legs might be broken, and that they might be taken away." It was a feast lasting all week, which Jesus had anticipated. If this was the day that Jesus' body was placed in the tomb, then His death would have been the day prior to that, mid-week, on a Wednesday, the day of Preparation, making it three full days and nights to early on resurrection Sunday. Jesus was brought out by Pilate to The Pavement, or Gabbatha, on the Preparation day of the Passover, and about the sixth hour, John 19:13-14, just before He was crucified.

The disciples went to the tomb early, the first day of the week. Not a Monday, as is our first day in this century, but on the Lord's day, which was known as the first day of the week, a Sunday morning, to find that the Lord Jesus had already risen from the dead, sometime from the night before (at sundown Saturday) to the early part of Sunday morning when they went to the tomb to anoint his body. Mark's gospel says in 16:2:

"Very early in the morning, on the first day of the week,
they came to the tomb when the sun had risen." and adds in verse 9:
"Now when he rose early on the first day of the week,
he appeared first to Mary Magdalene..."

Luke 24:1 confirms it was "very early in the morning on the first day of the week." John 20:1 says "While it was still dark." So, Jesus was most likely crucified mid-week allowing three full days and nights before His resurrection.

Jesus already told us that no other sign would be given "this evil and adulterous generation" than that of the prophet Jonah. For just "as Jonah was three days and nights in the belly of the great fish", so would Jesus Himself be in the heart of the earth. See Matt.12:40. And yet the whole of Christendom still doesn't even question the truths of this message, whilst most believe unthinkingly that Jesus died and was buried three days before He rose again, they go on the theories of theologians and other teachers, and meanwhile still accept worldly tradition – just because they do not study to show themselves approved, or because they would not want to challenge centuries of widely accepted Church tradition. Hence the "Good Friday" myth, because Jesus Christ said Himself: "After three days I will rise again." Surely this is worth more than a second glance; shouldn't we look for the promise within the sign that He gave to the whole world? The Bible does not say Jesus died on a Friday.

The Resurrection is the pivotal point of the Christian faith and doctrinal teachings. To think that Jesus had not kept His word would be incomprehensible. He always does, this is no different. It is probably not heretical to say that Good Friday is the day of the death if Jesus, but it is simply untrue. It is an error to teach that He died on a Friday, which many do, and to practice the Good Friday observance.

Acts 12:3 mentions the days of unleavened bread, followed by a mention of the word Passover, or Pesach, which has erroneously been translated in many Bibles as "Easter." It should read Passover which was celebrated by Jesus and his followers. Luke 22:11,15; Mark 14:14; Matt.26:2, 18,19 and John 18:28,39; 19:14. The New King James uses the word Passover, but most other versions use the word Easter which relates to the pagan goddess Ishtar or Astarte, a false pagan deity which was celebrated at that time. Hence, "Easter eggs", a tribute to the fertility goddess, Eostre, along with the wee bunny rabbits and the fluffy chicks.

God tells us that people perish for a lack of knowledge, it is ignorance and apathy to not examine this aspect of Christian doctrine. Whilst Spirit-baptized believers aren't yet seeking proof per se, we already believe, yet there may be many seekers who would possibly be converted with correct biblical preaching on this subject. Maybe if believers had the correct theological teachings on this matter in our day, then we would be ready to give an answer to those seeking and asking serious questions about the Christian faith who may just believe if they heard some sound teaching about Resurrection day rather than some tradition-based message about the feasts of the Christian faith.

Christians who have not considered that it was not a Good Friday can become quite defensive and reactionary if their traditional viewpoint is threatened. However, at the risk of sounding pedantic, I submit my Scriptural study and hope to blow a hole in Good Friday tradition, even if by doing so someone might believe and this may make the difference between eternal life with our Lord Jesus, or an eternal damnation and separation from God; it probably won't. But then, "Ash Monday" and "Maundy Tuesday" would really mess up the religious calendars and church programs, wouldn't it?

In Romans Paul is addressing disputable matters regarding dietary issues, and mentions the observation of days in verse 5-6 of chapter 14. In verse 17 he states that the kingdom of God is not in eating and drinking but in righteousness, peace and joy in the Holy Spirit. This is likely a matter of conscience. Those of us who serve Christ are not Jews, so we are not bound by the law to observe the feasts of Israel. However, Jesus made provision for celebrating Passover, and we now celebrate the Lord's day. In Acts 20:7 and 1 Corinthians 16:2 the disciples came together to break bread as in Acts 2:46. They were told to lay something aside for collections of finances. So, we see that the first day of the week may have been celebrated by the early church as the Lord's day, which is usually celebrated in the churches and in the fellowship gatherings of believers, although the fellowship gatherings of the believers at that time may have been every day of the week, as elsewhere stated in the Scriptures.

The Gospel is a message of blessing to those who will receive it. God promises that His people will prosper and be blessed. 1 John says: "Brethren, I pray that you may prosper and be in health even as your soul prospers." This isn't to imply that we make a separate doctrine or "another gospel" out of this teaching. It is actually a greeting. God's divine power has given us everything that pertains to life and godliness, says the Bible, through the knowledge of Him who has called us by glory and virtue, says 2 Peter. And we have been given God's promises so that by these we may be partakers of the Divine nature, having escaped the corruption that is in the world through lust. Through diligence we are called to add to our faith virtue, knowledge, self-control, perseverance, godliness, brotherly-kindness and love. God says we will not fall as we do this, nor be unfruitful in the knowledge of our Lord and Saviour, Jesus Christ (verse 8). Jesus tells us that we will bear fruit through abiding in Him in John 15. This brings glory to God. Verse 6b assures us that if we're bearing fruit we will ask what we desire from the Father and He will give it. This is providing we are walking in love.

Jesus prayed for His disciples according to the will of the Father, in John 17, that He may be glorified. That they would keep his Word and believe on Him, be kept through His name and be one, and not be lost, that they would have His joy fulfilled in them, that they would be kept from the evil one, and be sanctified by the truth of God's Word, for the world to believe and to receive God's glory, to be one with the Godhead, and perfect, to know the Father's love, to be with Jesus and behold His glory, and for the Father's love to be in His people.

GOD IS FORGIVING AND THE FORGIVER OF INIQUITY

It has been said that "Forgiveness is the fragrance that the flower leaves on the heel of the one that crushed it." Psalm 103:3 tells us that God forgives all our iniquities and heals all our diseases; that he has not dealt with us according to our sins or rewarded us according to our iniquities. The shed blood of Jesus Christ has been given as an offering for sin to appease the justice of a holy God. When we come to God and confess our sins God is faithful and just to forgive us our sins and to cleanse us from all unrighteousness says 1 John 1:9. In Romans 6:1 Paul says: "Shall we continue in sin that grace may abound?" Clearly not. The very reason we are crucified with Christ is that the body of sin might be destroyed and so we may no longer serve sin (Rom.6:6). He goes on to say that one who is dead is freed from sin and we are to reckon ourselves as dead to sin, but alive to God (verse 11). Therefore, we are to subdue the flesh nature and not allow sin to reign in our mortal bodies, to not submit to its lusts, but to yield ourselves to God as instruments of righteousness not allowing sin to have dominion over us. If we are serving sin, or the sinful nature, we cannot be serving God. Sin is enslavement. Righteousness and holiness are our aim, and we can live such a life as far as we are surrendered to Christ by the power of the Holy Spirit.

Romans 8:1 says that we are free from the law of sin and death as long as we are walking in the Spirit and living by the Spirit. It is a mindset; either the carnal or flesh nature is obeyed and in control in its lusts and desires, or we yield to the Holy Spirit. Paul promises that in Christ we are "more than conquerors through Him that loved us" (8:37) and that God's love will not permit us to be separated from Him because of Christ Jesus. In Matthew 6:12 Jesus says in this prayer that we are to forgive our debtors (verses 14-15), and that if we do so, our heavenly Father will also forgive us our trespasses. It is conditional. Ephesians 4:32 says that we are to be kind and tenderhearted, forgiving one another, even as God, for Christ's sake, has forgiven us. Therefore, to walk in an attitude and lifestyle of love. God likens marital love to that of Christ and the Church in Ephesians 5:22-33. This is a mystery; The wife showing reverence to her husband and the husband loving the wife and cherishing her as his own body. Psalm 32:1 says "Blessed is the man whose transgression is forgiven, whose sin is covered." Luke 6:37 says: "Forgive, and ye shall be forgiven." and in 17:3: "If your brother repents, forgive him." Colossians 3:13 says that as Christ forgives, we are to do so also. We cannot move forward in the Christian life if we are in an attitude of unforgiveness; It gives the devil a foothold for other areas of our lives to be entangled as well as being displeasing to God. The Lord wants us to cancel the record of offences toward us; Not to keep an account of wrongs, for love keeps no record of wrongs, it says in 1 Corinthians 13. We must hit the "delete" button. If the" angry dog" rises up when someone's name is mentioned, or when a certain person comes to mind, or we face particular situations where there are forgiveness issues, then the matter ought to be resolved. We usually want our "pound of flesh" when someone has done us wrong, we want to exact justice and have revenge, even if that means chipping in our "two cents worth" and putting the other person in the right as we see it. But God says; "Vengeance is mine, I will repay." Which is why we ought to pray for our enemies or those who have miss-used us in some way, for "it is a fearful thing to fall into the hands of the living God." God disciplines those He loves, says the writer of Hebrews, yet it is far better to yield to His chastening hand than to dig our heels in and rebel.

In my experience God has been gracious and merciful. I can testify to His goodness and kindness even when I have been wrong and sinned or off track. Gently, as a Shepherd, He leads us back to Himself and to the way of righteousness. In His way is genuine pleasure, and true joy of a far-lasting kind. Here, there is no room for bitterness of soul. God loves a meek and quiet spirit; It is in the sight of God "of great price." Also, a gentle answer turns away wrath and being peaceable is of great value to God. Psalm 130 verse 4 tells us that there is forgiveness with the Lord, so that He may be feared. The God who forgives is known in Hebrew as El Nasa. (Psalm 99:8). If we even knew the matchless holiness of the God we serve we would be embarrassed by saying we have no need of further repentance, that all sins are automatically erased. Repentance is a daily need. God is always willing to receive our confessions. His ears are open to the meek and humble.

He is indeed a faithful God who is able to forgive those who come to Him.

GOD IS FAITHFUL AND TRUE

God is faithful. He is just and true in all His ways and He will not forget His promises; He is true to His Word. He has proven His faithfulness in the lives of the heroes of faith, for us to witness. Abraham, Moses, Joseph, King David and the Apostle Paul, to name a few. The Word of God says: "His faithfulness reaches to the clouds" (Psalm 36:5). In Psalm 89:1 it says that He makes His faithfulness known to all generations. Palm 92:2 says He shows His faithfulness every night and in Lamentations that His faithfulness is great and His mercies new every morning. "Great is thy faithfulness" says the Bible. 2 Thessalonians 3:3 says that the Lord is faithful and in 1 John 1:9 that He is faithful and just to forgive sins. Revelation 21:5 says His Words are faithful and true, and in Psalm 31:23 that He preserves the faithful. Faithfulness is a quality that God looks for in His people. He will not overlook even the smallest act or attitude of the faithful servant; He is sure to reward in His time. The very fact that the sun comes up each morning and that the moon and stars shine each night, is testimony to the faithful nature of the Almighty God of creation, as is the witness of the rainbow.

God is faithful. "His faithfulness reaches to the heavens," says the Psalmist. God will not let us down or disappoint. He is true to His Word. Often, we may feel short-changed in life, or that life has not been kind, or is unfair, but God can be trusted. He may not give a "yes" answer to our every request - usually it is because He has something far better in mind. But He does answer our heartfelt prayers and meet our deepest longings, sometimes in the most remarkable ways.

In Nehemiah's prayer he extols God's virtues, saying that God is ready to pardon, gracious and merciful, slow to anger, abundant in kindness and that He did not forsake His people even though they disobeyed Him greatly during their time in the wilderness. Nehemiah 9:19 goes on to say that God still did not forsake them in His manifold mercies. He gave them a cloud by day to lead them and a pillar of fire by night for light. He gave His Spirit to instruct them, gave them manna, water, sustained them, so that they lacked nothing and even their clothes did not wear out neither did their feet swell, and He brought them into a fruitful land, already prepared, and yet they rebelled against His goodness. God's attribute of faithfulness means that He will not fail us. Whatever He says, He will do. He keeps His promises. The words of a well-known hymn, *Faithful One*, ring true:

Faithful One, so unchanging; Ageless One, You're my Rock of peace
Lord of all, I depend on You, I call out to You again and again,
I call out to You, again and again.
You are my Rock in times of trouble;
You lift me up, when I feel down
All through the storm Your love is the anchor,
My hope is in You alone.

2 Thessalonians 3:3 says: "The Lord is faithful, who shall establish you, and keep you from evil." And in 1 Thessalonians 5:24 the Word says: "Faithful is He who calls you." His faithfulness is mentioned in 1 Corinthians 1:9. He is loyal, remaining true. Psalm 92:2 speak of the elements; the sun coming up each morning to reveal God's faithfulness, and in Lamentations 3:23 that His mercies and compassions never fail. In Revelation 1:5 Jesus is called "The faithful witness," and in Revelation 21:5; also, that His words are faithful and true in Revelation 22:6. In 2 Timothy 2:13 the Bible says that even if we are faithless, God remains faithful – He cannot deny Himself. It is His very nature. He is "abounding in faithfulness" says the Psalmist (Psalm 86:15) and "all His work is done in faithfulness" (Psalm 33:4). Hebrews 10:23 reminds us that "He who promised is faithful" and in Hebrews 11:11 Sarah, it says, "considered God faithful." Psalm 36:5 says that His faithfulness reaches to the clouds, and in Psalm 111:7-9 that the "works of His hands are faithful and just." Psalm 89:1-2 says "In the heavens your faithfulness will be established" and in Exodus 34:6 that the Lord is abounding in steadfast love and faithfulness."

God reveals His faithfulness through His promise to never, never leave us nor forsake us, in Hebrews 13:5. We can be sure God is true to His Word, which will never pass away (Matt.24:35). When we are tempted, God is faithful, who not allow us to be tempted beyond our ability, and will provide a way of escape, says Paul, in 1 Corinthians 10:13. Also the Lord says that He has good plans for us, and to give us a hope and a future, in Jeremiah 29:11-13, and that He has continued His faithfulness to us with an everlasting love (Jer. 31:3).

In Deuteronomy 7:9 the Word tells us that "the faithful God keeps covenant and steadfast love with those who love Him and keep His commandments, to a thousand generations." In the Holy Scriptures we can see that God is faithful and His Word is true. He promises to keep every covenant He has made. There are numerous testimonies throughout Scripture where the faithfulness of God is proven true. Though the Jewish people have been scattered throughout the world, God promised they would return to their land, and He is fulfilling that promise to the Jewish people as they return to their homeland, Israel. Gods faithfulness is shown concerning the promised Messiah which was fulfilled in the New Testament when He sent the Saviour to atone for our sins and through whom we have everlasting life. Psalm 89:8 says that God's faithfulness surrounds Him. Psalm 119:89 says: "Forever, O Lord, Thy word is settled in heaven. Thy faithfulness unto all generations: thou hast established the earth and it abides." In Psalm 91:4 we read how God protects us, saying that He covers us with His feathers, and that we can trust under His wings as His truth shall be our shield and buckler. In the Gospels Jesus said: "He that is faithful in that which is least, is faithful also in much" (Luke 16:10). He requires that we be faithful even with "the unrighteous mammon" (the least), and this will ensure that we will be entrusted with "true riches" – the currency of God's kingdom; such as wisdom, understanding, knowledge, prudence and discretion as well as the fruits of the Holy Spirit; love, joy, peace, patience, kindness, goodness, gentleness, faithfulness, and self-control. These qualities cannot be bought. These are the lasting riches, along with a meek and quiet spirit, which is in the sight of God, of great price.

THE PROVIDENCE AND SUFFICIENCY OF GOD

In a place of need we find a greater joy of blessing through answered prayer which increases faith in the providential care of God. In a pluralistic, post-modern society it is so gratifying to find that there are still some absolutes, that there is still a true standard, a plumb-line, a compass, an anchor, something to count on that does not change with fashion, something that has constant values, ethics, morals and standards that are not affected by the winds of change. I am not here speaking of churches, doctrines or even church people. No, man is fickle. It is only God and his Word that remain true. YHWH, the Lord of creation, and his living Word – Jesus Christ, without whom we are men most pitiable. Through Jesus, God has provided a way to come to Himself, to be at peace with him and be reconciled. In Paul Billheimer's book: "*The Mystery of His Providence*" the author says that God is much more interested in what we become than in what we achieve. "If failure works better than success to make us unselfish, considerate, sympathetic and helpful to others, if it matures in us agape love, then God may permit failure because our eternal promotion is involved. He goes on to say that this may include seeming failure even in God's work because God is interested primarily in our entire consecration to Him, and not even our ministry must come before Him. Whether God is permitting hardship in order to teach us some heavenly values or to discipline us for wrong doing, it is always in love and to draw us closer to Himself. Often, He comes in the clouds, when the skies seem darkest and the lesson may be for the purpose of building trust or forging some other character-building trait into our nature. God will test us to see if we will remain faithful to Him even in trying times. Sometimes it is only when hardship comes to us, in whatever form, that God can finally get our attention."

The cross was unbearably heavy. How can we ever think to partake of that cup of suffering without sharing in the burden of pain? If we suffer with Him, we shall indeed reign with Him. Yet we do not want to suffer. We want the gloss, not the cross. We want the blessings, the healings, the wholeness, the miracles and the prosperity of earthly kinds and we want it all now. We demand instant healing without understanding the reality of the pain, instant cures and an easy, comfortable life, without having to face the consequences of our own sin. We want godly character without trials. Patience without testing. Good physical health without a righteous life-style. We want to walk in victory without being fully surrendered. We want to have all the answers to prove to others that we have it all together, that we are being blessed by the Almighty, and have His favour resting upon us. We want pain-free glorified bodies now, without the cost of personal sacrifice. We don't want to appear weak before our fellow man, rather, strong and together. We are afraid to strip off the plastic veneer, to become transparent and authentic. We don't want to say; "I need you" to another, especially not to someone else who appears less spiritual in our eyes. We want to force our views upon others, refusing to hear their concerns and opinions as valid and relevant. Their deeper needs become glossed over by simplistic answers. Genuine questionings are regarded with contempt and trampled upon. The problem of human pain and suffering is met with trite solutions. The person is not cherished or held dear. Feelings are ignored. Wounds are opened and the precious pearl is trampled. Good God, forgive us. Yet suffering forges character into the core of one's soul. Fibre is built into one's being through trials and testings. Lessons are learned in the school of pain which are afforded in no other area of life. There – one is caused to trust in One greater than himself and thereby learn the art of utter dependency.

There is joy in the presence of God, that even in the place of great personal difficulty or hardship, can sustain a person's soul. Mental anguish and psychological pain are often the hardest to endure and may accompany physical pain, which in and of itself can be traumatic. Yet, God, in His mercies, is able to uphold the weak and supply our needs. He truly is the one who provides under every circumstance, as we lean upon Him. In Him we find an enduring happiness, regardless of circumstances. Even in our losses He will meet us. "For to live is Christ, and to die is gain," says the Apostle Paul. As we die to self and the carnal nature He fills us with more of Himself.

Material need is most often the thing that calls us to prayer. Yet Paul says to "present our requests to God, and His peace will guard our hearts and minds" (Phil.4:6-7). In the Psalms David prayed and reminds us that there is no want to them that fear Him (Psalm 34:9) and in Psalm 37:4 that as we delight in the Lord He will give us the desires of our heart. The previous verse shows us that as we do good we shall dwell in the land and be fed (verse 3). Also, that the meek shall inherit the earth and delight themselves in the abundance of peace (verse 11).

Jesus tells us not to worry, but to seek first God's kingdom and righteousness in Matthew chapter 6. Worry may be one of the sins most dishonouring to God since He is worthy of all our trust, and we have no need to be concerned with God as our heavenly Father. His grace is sufficient. In the third epistle of John, the writer says in the form of a greeting: "Beloved, I wish above all things that you may prosper and be in health, even as thy soul prospereth." verse 2. It is my belief that John is referring to the essence of the people he was addressing here. That YOU may prosper. YOU spiritually. The *spiritual you*. Elsewhere the Scriptures tell us: "For ye are dead, and your life is hid with Christ in God." Paul says in Colossians 3:3. Before this he says: "If ye then be risen with Christ, seek those things which are above, where Christ sitteth on the right hand if God. Set your affection on things above, not on things on the earth." verses 1-2. Why is it then, when speaking with the carnally-minded person the verses about prospering is so often quoted with relevance to the material? "That you may prosper..." does not imply a new house, car, boat or aero plane, but rather those spiritual qualities and virtues relevant to the maturity of the believer, such as grace, love, mercy, wisdom, understanding and the like. Such things that are eternal in nature. "...and be in health" refers to the physical state, an added blessing of healthy bodily function. This verse, a foundational Scripture reference for the "Prosperity Gospel" preachers is mis-applied and mis-used by those who rely upon it as validation of their material success. "That you may prosper..." means the spiritual inner man, for the Word elsewhere tells us: "What is a man profited, if he shall gain the whole world, and lose his own soul?" Matthew 16:26. Here, Jesus says to deny ourselves, take up our cross, and follow Him. God is not interested in our material gain, but in our Christ-likeness. In the "Sermon on the Mount" Jesus said to not lay up for ourselves treasures on earth, but in heaven (Matthew 6:19-21).

The accumulation of possessions and worldly wealth only tends to pride and self-sufficiency, an alienation from God and a lack of dependency upon our Creator. In the Old Testament God blessed those who were obedient with wealth, undoubtedly, but this was before the cross, which secured for believers the riches of Christ. Even King David suffered ill health at times as the Psalms attest, and in the New Testament, all were not healed, as we read in 2 Timothy 4:20 where Trophimus was left at Miletum sick. Also, Epahroditus was described as "sick nigh unto death" (Phil. 2:27), but we are told that God had mercy on him. Paul himself had "a thorn in the flesh" which may have been a physical illness, and he may have had a problem with his eyesight. God simply told Paul that His grace was sufficient.

The God we love and serve is sufficient. He is able to meet all our need. We need not be convinced to pursue money in mega amounts in order to be considered successful. Even the concept of having to achieve success is not what God is looking for, but our demonstration of faith. Jeremiah the prophet says: "Let not the rich man glory in his riches" (9:23b). In 1 Timothy the Bible speaks of those who do not adhere to sound doctrine, in chapter 6, and verse 5 says: "...perverse disputings of men of corrupt minds, and destitute of the truth, supposing that gain is godliness: from such withdraw thyself." We are warned here to withdraw from such people, not to follow them, but to pursue godliness and contentment.

GOD IS PATIENT

Love suffers long…says 1 Corinthians 13. To be longsuffering is to be patient. We have a God who is longsuffering. In Exodus 34 it speaks of God's nature as merciful, gracious and longsuffering. He bears with us. Numbers 14:18 echoes this, saying that He is longsuffering and of great mercy. In Nehemiah the Word says that for many years God was patient with His people and that He delivered them many times. He is a God of compassion, gracious and longsuffering says the Psalmist (Psalm 86:15). In the New Testament Paul expounds on God's attributes of goodness, forbearance and longsuffering in Romans 2:4. In 2 Peter 3:9,15, 20 it describes the same quality in that God is not willing that any should perish, but that all should come to repentance and that the longsuffering of our Lord is salvation. It is through faith and patience that we inherit His promises says the writer of Hebrews and in James 1:3-4 that the trying of our faith works patience, bringing completion or perfection. Jesus Himself commends the Church for her patience in Revelation 2:2,3,19 and refers to the patience of the saints. This is a key attribute for the godly since Jesus, our Lord, learned obedience through the things which He suffered. James 5:10-11 says: "Take, my brethren, the prophets, who have spoken in the name of the Lord, for an example of suffering affliction, and of patience. Behold, we count them happy which endure. Ye have heard of the patience of Job and have seen the end of the Lord; that the Lord is very pitiful, and of tender mercy." We have all heard of the patience of Job, yet Jesus endured far greater suffering.

How did Jesus learn patience? I believe if we look at His life experiences on this earth we can glean a better picture. Before His death on the cross Jesus endured suffering. He was considered without honour among His brethren and family. He experienced deep loneliness when even His own disciples could not watch and pray with Him for one hour prior to His death. The religious leaders of His day, those who were the most respected of society, virtually all disregarded His authority. He made Himself of no reputation, the Bible says. The ultimate was then His suffering of being flogged and tortured on that cruel cross. Not only that, Jesus had been in the presence of the Father before coming into this world. He would have been awaiting the reunion of being in the Father's presence once again. This must be one of the most necessary of virtues. The Bible speaks of the patience of the saints in Revelation 14:12; and of the patience of Jesus, in Revelation 1:9.

Patience is needed when awaiting the birth of a baby. It is needed when waiting for a bus, or for a visitor to arrive; when waiting for an appointment or for flowers to bloom once the seeds have been sown. Patience is required whilst awaiting test results from an exam, or from the medical doctor; It is needed when standing in an elevator, or in a line at the grocery store. In all areas of life, patience is needed. Patience is needed whilst waiting for seasons to change, or even for the next day to arrive. Patience is needed especially with other people when they are being impatient. Patience is needed for personal growth; for development of character. Government elections require patience. Most of all, trials take patience. Love suffers long. There is no such thing as short-term patience. It is a virtue to be desired and cultivated. With patience there is no sense of hurry or rushing into things. No sense of immediacy or imminence. Where patience is absent, frustration shows up; anger rears its ugly head; ill temper arises. In the presence of patience there is a calm; a stillness; a quietness and a peace. Most often suffering in some sense is necessary for patience to be developed. Patience is one of the fruits of the Holy Spirit mentioned in Galatians 5:22. God is committed to accomplishing the good work He has begun in His people. He wants us to grow to become more like Jesus our Saviour; growing more into maturity, towards perfection, or completion. This takes time. Patience is a much-needed virtue.

In describing the character of love, the Word of God first says in 1 Corinthians that love suffereth long. It is patient. God's long-suffering is shown numerous times throughout the text of Scripture. His patience was shown long ago to those rebellious people while Noah was building the ark through to the words in Revelation concerning Jezebel, to whom God gave time to repent of her evil deeds and continues today. God's patience is shown in and through His creation, and it shows in our lives. He patiently waits for us to return to Him, as He did with Hosea's wife who had turned to prostitution. This story of the magnitude of God's love reveals what a patient nature He has. Often, we might think that our sins and misdemeanors would separate us, but for His grace, and yet He still bestows upon us His people the mercies we do not merit. He allows the sun to rise and the rain to fall on the just as well as the unjust. His unparalleled affection for all He has made is revealed through His Word, the Holy Scriptures. His patience ought not to be confused with His permissiveness toward us. He is not a God to withhold good even when we err, for His love is constant. But the Word of God also says: "Behold therefore the goodness and severity of God" Romans 11:22a, and we are to continue in His goodness. Patience is one of the fruits of the Holy Spirit mentioned in Galatians, it's counterpart may be considered as impatience or lacking tolerance. The Scriptures also tell us to bring forth fruit with patience, that tribulation worketh patience, that the trying or testing of our faith works patience and that we are to run the race set before us with patience, says the book of Hebrews.

GOD IS SLOW TO ANGER

In the modern worship song entitled, 10,000 reasons, the chorus says - "You're rich in love, and You're slow to anger; I'll worship Your Holy Name." Were it not for God's restraint and this attribute of being slow to anger, we would have been duly dealt with many a time. His anger is but for a moment, says Psalm 30:5. Psalm 103:8-9 says that He is slow to anger and will not keep His anger for ever. Also, in Psalm 145:8 and in Nehemiah 9:17; Joel 2:13; Nahum 1:3; Micah 7:18 and Jonah 4:2. Psalm 2:12 says to "Kiss the Son, lest He be angry." Psalm 78:38 says that many a time God turned His anger away. Also Psalm 90:11 David says: "Who knows the power of Your anger?" and in Jeremiah 4:8; 12:13; 25:37 and 36:7 the Bible says that God's anger is fierce.

The sins of the people and serving other gods was something that provoked God to anger, as revealed in the Scriptures, His anger was kindled, it says in Exodus 4:14; 1 Kings 16:2; Jeremiah 32:29. Psalm 78:58 tells us that Israel's building of idolatrous high places provoked God to anger, and worship of graven images, Jeremiah 8:19. In Psalm 106:32 "they angered God at the waters of Meribah." In Ezekiel 43:8 God says: "I have consumed them in my anger." In Hosea 8:5, His anger is kindled, and in Micah 5:15 that He will execute vengeance. Zephaniah 2:2 speaks of the day of the Lord's anger. Yet in Isaiah 48:9 we read that God's anger was deferred.

The Bible has much to say about man's anger. In the Proverbs it says: "It is better to be slow to anger" (Prov.16:32) and that "a gift given in secret pacifies anger" (Prov.21:14) and in Proverbs 22:24 not to make friendship with an angry man. In Ecclesiastes 7:9 it says not to be hasty in your spirit to be angry and Psalm 37:8 says to cease from anger and forsake wrath, that it does no good. Also, Ephesians 4:26 tells us not to sin in our anger, and verse 31 continues; "Let all bitterness, wrath, anger, be put away from you." Colossians 3:8 says to put off anger and wrath and in 3:21 to not provoke your children to anger. Titus 1:7 says to be not self-willed, not soon angry. The fruit of the spirit of self-control is a guard against angry outbursts.

The elder brother of the Prodigal son was angry and wouldn't go in and enjoy the home-coming celebrations of his long-lost brother. Says Henry Drummond in his book, a treatise on love, "*The Greatest Thing in the World*": "Look at the elder brother, moral, upright, hard-working, patient, dutiful – let him get all credit for his virtues – look at this man, this baby, sulking outside his own father's door. "He was angry," we read, "and would not go in." Look at the effect upon the father, upon the servant, upon the happiness of the guests. Judge of the effect upon the Prodigal – and how many prodigals are kept out of the Kingdom of God by the unlovely characters of those who profess to be inside? Analyze, as a study in Temper, that thunder-cloud as it gathers upon the Elder brother's brow. What is it made of? Jealousy, anger, pride, uncharity, cruelty, self-righteousness, touchiness, doggedness, sullenness – these are the ingredients of this dark and loveless soul. In varying proportions, also, these are the ingredients of all ill-temper. Judge if sins of the disposition are not worse to live in, and for others to live with, than sins of the body. Did Christ indeed not answer the question Himself when He said: "I say unto you, that the publicans and the harlots go into the Kingdom of heaven before you." There is really no place in heaven for a disposition like this. A man with such a mood could only make heaven miserable for all the people in it. Except, therefore a man be born again, he cannot, he simply cannot, enter the Kingdom of heaven. For it is perfectly certain – and you will not misunderstand me -that to enter heaven a man must take it with him." (page 55).

Frequently people are prone to complain about their lot in life. The Israelites did so in the wilderness provoking Moses to anger, and he struck the rock and water gushed out. (Num.20:11; Psalm 106:32-33). Most of us have food and water every day, we have our faculties, our limbs probably, clothes on our back and a roof over our head as well as people who care about us, yet we are still prone to discontentment. It seems to be very much a part of human nature. Indeed, there are many in poverty, but if we who have even the basics do not acknowledge with gratitude all that we have from our Maker's bounty, what use is it to even consider giving to others from a mean and stingy heart? God commands us to be thankful in everything (1 Thess.5:18; Col.3:16), to give – even if we have little; to do good and share – even if our resources are limited. What we have, small though it may be, could be another person's treasure. Giving with joy is God's way. A little given with love has a way of multiplying. Stewardship is not just about managing money. It's about managing effectively our time, talents, energy, resources, career, personal development and all that God blesses us with (2 Thess. 1:11-12). We are to give with a right spirit also. 1 Corinthians 13 tells us that even if we should give our bodies to be burned and have not love, it profits nothing. There is one occasion in the New Testament when we see Jesus become angry. This was in the temple. There were people selling wares in His Father's house and making merchandise out of people. This action on the Lord's behalf was not what we know to be a loss of temper. Jesus made a whip of cords. This would have taken time. We do not see Jesus here flaring up. What He did was in honour of the Father. He made a vehement expression of anger, which in this case was a godly action, what we call righteous indignation. There is a time for anger since it can be a motivator to act in righteous causes where there is injustice.

GOD IS A JEALOUS GOD

The Scriptures refer to God as a jealous God. This means that we are not to think of Him in any other way than is revealed of Him through His Word. The Israelites made a golden calf, an idol, and worshipped this image. God called it idolatry. Pictures, statues or other artifacts seeming to represent God, Jesus or the Holy Spirit are no less dishonouring. They diminish God's glory and simply fail to do Him justice. Even words could never be sufficient to portray the magnitude of God, for He is truly great. Words are limiting. Pictures lend towards a creation of imagery that is binding, yet God is limitless. The Holy Spirit descended upon Jesus in the form of a dove, yet the Holy Spirit is not a dove, as we know it. God took on the very nature of man when Christ came to earth, yet He is not now a man, He is God who came in human form, now risen and exalted. When the Scriptures speak of God being jealous, it is in the sense of Him being protective over us. He wants our affections and is desirous of our love, and that we give Him first place in our lives. His love is expressed throughout the Word of God.

Some time ago a church-goer passed on to me a picture supposedly representing "Jesus"- painted by a young girl. He looked middle-aged, rugged and very handsome with dark curly hair, as if he'd just walked out of an expensive hair salon. I had long since de-throned some posters I had acquired from the screen shots of the film: "The Passion of the Christ"; pictures showing what was supposed to be Jesus on the cross. I had them filed away. In my recent house-cleaning, whilst God was purging me, I came across them also. I was reading John 15 and Psalm 53, speaking of purging and the pruning that takes place. The Word of God was washing me clean and sanctifying me. I began afresh tearing down the idols in my life. It first had to be addressed in the heart, before the outward riddance would come. Little did I realize -this was one of them. I was reminded sharply: "Thou shalt have no other gods before me. Thou shalt not make unto thee any graven image, or any likeness of any thing that is in heaven above, or that is in the earth beneath, or that is in the water under the earth: Thou shalt not bow down thyself to them, nor serve them: for I the

Lord thy God am a jealous God…" Exodus 20:3-5a. Could his possibly be a violation of the first commandment in the Bible? I wasn't literally worshipping the pictures. But why did I have them in my possession even? I may not have been giving oblations to them. But why did I have them at all? As a reminder? A reminder of what? They aren't even true representations! How often, when we show someone a photograph we will say "That's Mary" or "That's John." Really? It's a picture of Mary or John, but that's definitely not them. They used to look something like that, if it is a good enough shot - but it isn't truly "them." No, it's an image. And quite possibly a false one. Any image or picture representing Christ is merely some artist's representation of Him. As an artist, I have studied art for years, my training both in Book Illustration and more importantly, in the Bible, for over three and a half decades has stood me in good stead. I learned about the gift of art. I studied iconography, from both perspectives. I was convicted early on in my Christian walk to never paint a picture to represent Christ. But surely having a picture of "our blessed Saviour wasn't idolatry! No? The Israelites set up the golden calf. And how severely they were dealt with by God. And yet again and again the nation fell into sin. Are we so far from God that we need a picture – yes – an "image" -to remind us of Him? Surely, if our lives are entrenched in the Word of God and prayer and worship, He will be as sweet to our soul as honey, His Word will be our truth, our light and our life! Any image of God, no matter how pleasing to the eye – is in no uncertain terms – idolatrous. God says to de-throne them! Yes, smash them to the ground, burn them! Read the Bible and meditate on the Word of God. Seek after truth and get to know the true and living God. He will meet your every need. Nothing else can be a match for His presence.

To be a Christian who worries may be like being an artist who is colour blind, or a veterinary surgeon who is afraid of animals. The two would be utterly inconsistent and incongruous. Worry and fear are conditions that are diametrically opposed to the call of a committed believer. Trust, and faith in God, are elementary principles of the life of a victorious believer, and they are earmarks that characterize the life of the believer in such a way that leaves no room for the worrisome or fearful disposition. We need look no further than the parables of Jesus and His message of the lilies of the field or the sparrow. Worries about money, food, clothing, possessions and health are to be laid aside, as we offer our implicit trust into the hands of our Creator and loving heavenly father. To fail to do so is sin and reveals a lack of confidence in the God who is more than able to care for us and to lovingly meet our every need. All we need do is ask -and it shall be given, as we ask in faith, and in accordance with the will of God. Doubt and unbelief are also sinful, and as with worry and fear, these are toxic to the spirit, and the antithesis of faith. The antidote to fear, worry, anxiety, unbelief, and depression is prayer. Prayer is a lifestyle and is a constant communication or dialogue with the Holy Spirit. This internal dialogue is necessary in order to renew the mind. Intentional prayer dispels fear and worry. As you pray you enhance your own brain health. The Bible tells us to pray at all times, and in everything by prayer and supplication, with thanksgiving to let our requests be made known to God. Most mental health problems are born out of worry and misplaced fear. Toxic thinking is common to all mental health problems. These are not medical illnesses and are diagnosed medical conditions that are not scientific. God says to worship Him with the whole mind in the Gospels and in Paul's letter to the Romans that we are to be transformed by the renewing of our minds. In Ephesians, Paul further states that we are not to walk in the vanity of our minds as the Gentiles do (Eph.4:17), but to be renewed in the spirit of our minds, verse 17. In chapter 5 he goes on to say that it is how we walk and talk. Transformation involves the very form, shape and structure of our minds. We are to take every thought captive to the obedience of Christ, as Paul says in 2 Corinthians. The brain has the capacity to restore itself. The brain is subservient to the mind. We have free will, and with our minds we can choose to serve Christ and choose life as it says in Joshua chapter one. In James 1:21 it says that the implanted Word of God is able to save our souls. God has a redemptive nature in that He draws all things back to Himself with restorative power and He makes all things beautiful in His time, as Ecclesiastes says. Isaiah speaks of the Restorer of streets to dwell in. He is in the business of restoration. We are to consider our resources of space, time, energy, talents and money, and allow God to be Lord of all these areas of our lives.

What is on my heart is to share how very much God loves us. Yes. You have heard it before, but He really does. The Word of God says that your worth is far above rubies, and they are costly, yet God is saying that we have even more value than these precious gems. A second Scripture passage is in Romans 8. Read verses 28 to 39 and you'll get the picture; that nothing can separate you from the love of God once you're His child. Nothing. It says you're justified in God's sight -that is- made righteous with God, at peace with Him, because of what Jesus did on the cross. So, no one can condemn you, if you are a believer. It says tribulation, distress, persecution, famine, nakedness, peril or sword…. No- in all these things we are more than conquerors. Not only that, not death, life, angels. principalities, powers, the present or future, height or depth, nor any other created thing shall be able to separate us from the love of God which is in Christ Jesus our Lord. A third passage is from Ephesians 4 and 5 where Paul is saying to "walk the talk" in love. And as you have received Christ so walk in Him. So, first, be assured of God's love for you, even ask Him for personal revelation through His Word. Then recognize that He will never leave you because his love is steadfast, and thirdly go and walk it out and share His love with others. What you give away comes back to you. Sow the seeds of the fruits of the Holy Spirit into the lives of others and watch the harvest return to you for the glory of God. You don't need confirmation from "10 angels" on Facebook. God declared His love already and demonstrated it through sending His Son. Receive His love, get filled up by the Holy Spirit, then go out into all the world and share His love, into a world that is hungry for both truth and love. Know the truth - what God already says about you, and get your foundation solid through His Word, then you'll be an effective evangelist for Jesus Christ. God's Word never fails. His promises are true. Be the effective person He made you to be and live a life of love and truth knowing that you are accepted by God.

Getting the above right on a vertical level enables us to do the do-able and get the horizontal in order – our relationships with others. If we try to live out the Christian life whilst unconvinced of the basics – namely – Gods love for us – we'll be ineffective in reaching a lost and dying world. Jesus said to love others as we love ourselves. Once we have the vertical relationship in order, the horizontal pans out. We are supernaturally equipped to share the good news of the Gospel. If we are uncertain of our relationship with God and unconvinced of our right standing with Him, this inconsistency will be apparent in our dealings with our fellow man and will affect all of our relationships.

Forgiveness is a life style – a way of life. First, to be in right relationship with God we need His forgiveness. It is not hard. Repentance for our sins from a sincere heart will bring this into order. From that point on we are to walk in forgiveness towards others. No matter what the offence, we must cancel the debt, clear the record, press the "delete" button, learn from it and forget about it. If we don't a root of bitterness develops, as mentioned in Hebrews, and by it many become defiled. Then further offence climbs on to the back of an initial offence and a spirit of unforgiveness develops to the extent that we are unable to shake it. It has taken hold. Jesus says, when we come to prayer – the very first thing is to forgive, as we have been forgiven. It is in the Lord's prayer, and He spoke about it in the parables too. Paul mentions it in Ephesians, to be "tenderhearted. Forgiving one another, just as God for Christ's sake has forgiven you." Face it! If you feel a queasy feeling in your guts when a certain someone's name is mentioned, or you find yourself avoiding eye contact when in someone's company – something needs to be addressed. "Oh… but they wronged me." Regardless, whether the offence was caused by another person or not, if we are at odds with another, and we are a Christian, it's always our call to go and put it right. Jesus said to leave your gift there at the altar and go and make amends with your brother or sister, and then we are free to come and worship God in Spirit and in truth.

When there are no outstanding issues with our fellow man in our lives, we can literally walk in freedom. We are, as far as possible, to live in peace with all people. The majority of strife and divisive issues are fixable if we have the humility to deal with them as Jesus commanded. Only then will we be able to "Enter His gates with thanksgiving, and His courts with praise," as David said in Psalm 100:4, and be able to worship and reverence God as we ought and see answers to our prayers. Where there is division and very often, complaining and criticism, there is no blessing. If we have a complaint against someone, we are to deal with it responsibly and with maturity. God hates complaining. Look at what happened to Miriam. She and Aaron complained about Moses and she became leprous! The Israelites complained in the wilderness, and they wandered for 40 years. When the whining stops we position ourselves for God's favour. Not that He doesn't bless us anyway, He still does, for He is kind even to the unthankful, but we experience a deeper measure of the goodness of God when we are walking in forgiveness and when we are at peace with others. God speaks of unity as the "precious oil that runs down Aaron's beard." He looks with favour on those brothers and sisters who seek peace. He tells us to "seek peace and pursue it." God loves unity.

Even if we happen to be happier without certain "toxic people" in our lives, it's important to resolve issues amicably wherever possible and at least to come to agreement. This doesn't imply that we need to maintain an ongoing relationship with them thereafter, but simply to be living in harmony. God wants us to be at peace with Him, with ourselves and with others and be willing to seek resolution as far as possible with others.

Having made amends wherever possible, we are freed in our conscience, and this is the state God wants; not to owe any man anything – but to love one another, as Romans 12 says. If we are retaining people's sins and harbouring grudges we will live miserable lives. As far as possible we are to make peace. A life of true worship is a natural flow from there on in. Making peace won't just happen. In fact, the longer an offence continues, the harder the human heart grows. As believers, we are to pray for those who have offended us. Jesus goes as far as to say: "Bless them…" and "Do good to them…" We can and ought to pray for them. Pray for God's grace to permeate their lives. Pray for a softened heart. Pray for repentance and for receptivity. Once we begin to bring another soul to the foot of the cross, there is no end to the manner of godly prayers that may flow from us and rise to the throne of grace. As we do this, we find that it is we, ourselves, who change. God supernaturally changes our hearts. We become malleable and pliable. God humbles us.

The Word of God says that when a man's ways please the Lord, He makes even his enemies to be at peace with him. Not only this, but in Proverbs it says that it is a man's honour to overlook an offence. And in the Psalms, David said: "Great peace have they that love thy law: and nothing shall offend them." Psalm 119:165. This may be understood as a literal offence, or a deeper meaning may be that of "causing to stumble" Jesus was a "stone of stumbling" and a "Rock of offence" for those who did not believe. And see how many are offended in Him and at the Gospel message! If we are walking right with the Lord, we will overlook minor matters. Life is too short for petty grievances. There are, however, certain matters, concerning truth and equity and justice that must be fought for.

But often we hold on to something on a matter of principle when we would be just as well to ditch our so-called principles and put the matter right. Walking in the way of peace is God's design. His Kingdom is a Kingdom of peace. Paul speaks of "righteousness, peace and joy in the Holy Ghost" as foundational in God's Kingdom. Peace is found in the quiet heart. We are meant to be mediators on Christ's behalf. Yes, there is only One mediator between God and man – the Man, Christ Jesus, however, God wants His people to "stand in the gap" and be intercessors, which we cannot possibly do from the vantage point of un-rest or dis-ease, which is where unforgiveness resides.

GOD IS HOPE

"Love hopeth all things" says 1 Corinthians 13:7. This part of the Father's intrinsic nature. We, too are to exhibit the virtue of hope. We are looking forward to the day of Christ's glorious appearing. Man cannot live without hope. It is vital to human life. One may be able to live a loveless life, or even a life without faith, but not without hope. Some years ago my Dad penned an article about hope which is as follows: -

This little world is often plagued by misfortune. Were it not for the indefatigable spirit of human nature which transcends all its experience in the pursuit of hope, there would be little to be pleased about.

Daily, for those who are alive to it, and aware of it, the spirit of hope and goodness calls out with its many gestures. In the midst of madness, it can be heard – if you will listen or look.

Even in the hurly-burly world of commerce there are the jewels not seen by blind eyes; the pleasure of dealing with a gentle man or gentle woman who comes with clean heart, innocent of the traps of commerce, but trusting.

The satisfaction of this utter confidence and returning it in abundance. The sheer delight of seeing the pleasure it gives. Joy!

The innocent unsullied query of the little child who naively questions, the humour evoked sometimes voices words that reach to the core of life or truth.

Amidst life's chores – the unexpected gift or gesture; The trust exhibited by a dog devoted to its master. The early dawn's sunrise, the first twitter of the morning bird. The shrieking of sea gulls. The still of starry night. So much, so little lived. So short a time to understand. But there for all of us – God's heaven on earth amid the hell – to give us answers if we listen should somber thoughts or unhappiness abide – the truth of hope and all its expectations.

Ernest D'Ambrosie 24th May 1976

Hope is replete with expectation. It is a joyful anticipation, a looking forward. The Bible says that those of us "who are of the day, be sober, putting on the breastplate of faith and love; and for an helmet, the hope of salvation."

1 Thessalonians 5:8. Salvation is also something we look forward to, something that God has appointed us to through our Lord Jesus Christ. This passage is speaking of a future time when we will live together in glory. It is also saying that for now, we are to live as children of light in these dark days. Previously words of comfort are spoken regarding the Lord's return. This refers to the Second Coming of Christ, the Parousia. There is a sense of great anticipation in these words in chapter 4:13-18. That we have something of great significance to look towards. A day when we will once again be together with now deceased loved ones who have died in the Lord. Also, it is a day when Christ Himself, the King of all glory, will return. "He will descend from heaven with a shout, with the voice of the archangel, and with the trump of God." (4:16). What a glorious event this will be!

There is also warning to not be living in darkness, neither to be found sleeping or drunk, but to be watchful and sober. The people who do not yet know Jesus as their personal Lord and Saviour are still living without hope. They are not living with the expectation of His soon return as described in this passage. Paul says they are in darkness. It is for us to light the way. Ann Spangler, Author of 'The Names of God,' says: "Hope isn't false. It doesn't pretend away our sorrow but rises up inside it. It's a brightness that can't be quenched, a gift for this life that's meant to carry us into the next." Isaiah 40:31 says: "Those who hope in the Lord will renew their strength."

I don't know about you, but on those sultry autumn afternoons when thunder and lightning strike I think of what is known as the Parousia. As the lightning cracks through the heavens my thoughts are transported to the Second Coming – the Parousia, when Jesus will break open the skies, coming with clouds, and every eye will see Him. The Second Coming of Christ is little addressed in current literature, or even in modern sermons. There were several books on the shelves of Christian bookstores in years gone by although much of it based on errant theology. Yet this is our hope. The blessed hope. We are assured in Scripture that Jesus Christ will return. The Bible tells us that since the beginning His attributes are clearly seen (Rom. 1:20).

SEPARATION AND TEMPERANCE IN GOD

Temperance may be applied to appearance. The matter of sexual purity is highly relevant for the believer. Paul, the Apostle mentions in the Bible the matter of remaining sexually pure. The topic of homosexuality is also mentioned in Revelation. Either way, we, as believers in the Lord Jesus, are to live a pure life, and the Bible says that homosexuality is an immoral way of life. Sodomy is not natural and is illegal in many countries still. This subject is difficult to address, yet I believe it warrants attention. Because the Scriptures tell us not to judge, many think this refers to behavior, when the Word is clearly speaking about heart motives. Jesus did not directly address the issue of homosexuality, but He did talk about marriage between a man and a woman. Being a practicing Jew He held to the law of Moses, which clearly addresses this matter. The Church appears to have become increasingly more tolerant towards anyone living an alternative lifestyle. Paul spoke about keeping a pure life. Separation is necessary. When a man marries, he has chosen his wife above all other women and committed himself to be faithful to her alone. So, he willingly chooses a life of separation, that of being set apart for the love of his life, and she, likewise. With homosexuality in general, there tends to be the view of promiscuity, that one is practicing sodomy with a variety of individuals on a regular basis, as a loose man or woman may do if they are heterosexual when involved in several illicit relationships. Both would be the sin of fornication. Either way it is wrong in God's eyes. In the book of Acts, chapter 15, it is written; "But that we write unto them, that they abstain from pollution of idols, and from fornication, and from things strangled, and from blood." In the Bible, if something is repeated it is usually of great importance. This verse is repeated again in verse 29 of the same chapter, and again in chapter 21 verse 25. Later, in Galatians Paul is again writing and addresses the subject in Ephesians 5:19-21: "Now the works of the flesh are manifest, which are these; Adultery, fornication, uncleanness, lasciviousness, idolatry, witchcraft, hatred, variance, emulations, wrath, strife, seditions, heresies, envyings, murders, drunkenness, revellings, and such like: of the which

I tell you before, as I have told you in time past, that they which do such things shall not inherit the kingdom of God." He goes on to say what is the fruit of the Spirit, which is quite the contrasting picture, and say that if we live in the Spirit, let us walk in the Spirit, in other words, to not practice such things as were mentioned above, but rather to live godly lives. Romans 1:21-32 describes also those who are given over to a reprobate mind, as Paul describes it. This passage addresses fornication, and the unnatural use of the body. In 1 Corinthians 6:9-11 it is written: "Know ye not that the unrighteous shall not inherit the kingdom of God? Be not deceived: neither fornicators , nor idolaters, nor adulterers, not effeminate, not abusers of themselves with mankind, not thieves, nor covetous, nor drunkards, nor revilers, nor extortioners, shall inherit the kingdom of God. And such were some of you: but ye are washed, but ye are sanctified, but ye are justified in the name of the Lord Jesus, and by the Spirit of our God." Hebrews 13:4, James 4:4, and Revelation 21:8 also make reference to this matter with severe warnings. In the Old Testament references can be found in Leviticus chapter 20, where the punishment was death by stoning. Thank God for Jesus! God calls His people to be holy, sanctified, set apart. He wants a holy people for Himself. He longs for us to live pure lives consecrated to Him. "For this is the will of God, your sanctification, that ye should abstain from fornication" (1 Thess. 4:3), and "That each of you should know how to possess his own vessel in sanctification and honour." Paul further adds in Romans 12: "I beseech you therefore, brethren, by the mercies of God, that ye present your bodies a living sacrifice, holy, acceptable unto God, which is your reasonable service." So in effect, God is giving instructions about how we should conduct ourselves amidst a perverse generation, and this applies to our habits, appearance, behavior and lifestyle. This is not written with condemnation towards homosexuals. Anyone practicing a sexually promiscuous lifestyle needs to repent. This is the way forward.

The Bible says in Ephesians 5:18-21 to be filled with the Spirit. However, this Scripture goes on to say how to be filled… "*by* speaking to yourselves in psalms and hymns and spiritual songs, singing and making melody in your hearts to the Lord, giving thanks always for all things unto God and the Father in the name of our Lord Jesus Christ; submitting to one another in the fear of God." This actually means in a sense, from the original language, "*be* being filled" or as we would say, "keep on being filled." This matter of being filled with the Spirit is not at all describing a once and for all experience, but rather a process, a walk, or a way of life.

The Bible speaks of being temperate. Many believers choose not to drink alcohol. This may be to be a more effective witness for Christ. It is also another matter that can be the cause of division, as is the eating of certain foods. The Apostle Paul instructed Timothy, however, to drink a little wine for his stomach's sake. Whilst the Scriptures condemn drunkenness, Jesus Himself turned water into wine at the wedding of Cana, His first recorded miracle in the New Testament. Paul did not instruct Timothy to drink goat's milk, therefore wine must have had some medicinal value. However, later Jesus said that He would not drink of the fruit of the vine until He drinks it anew with us in the Father's kingdom.

The book of Proverbs makes reference to drinking wine or strong drink and says to not look at the wine whilst it is full red in the cup. In Europe and Latin countries wine is very much a part of the cultural lifestyle. I lived in several European countries for a few years in the late 1970's and in Italy and Spain found that the tap water was not potable. In people's homes drinking wine was the norm, with dinner. The Bible does warn, however, about drunkenness and says frequently to be sober. In a similar manner people often rely on other recreational substances to get a high, drugs of various kinds, including prescription pills as well as street drugs, and now that marijuana is legalized in many countries it has become a form of regular use for intoxication. It is exactly that. In limited doses, drugs may be used to alleviate pain, but they are addictive and therein lies the problem.

Eating real food is good for the body. Preferably organic, non-GMO, (not genetically modified) natural whole foods. A good diet is vital with a lot of water to keep hydrated. We are intended to honour God with our bodies, and to love God with our whole heart, mind, soul and strength. For many people, the Pineal gland located in the brain has already been calcified by the use of junk foods and other toxins but can be treated and improved function is possible with a healthy diet and some food supplements. The Pineal gland may be referred to as "the seat of the soul." It is important to glorify God in our bodies as well as in the Spirit and with the mind, emotions and will. It is the Hindus who are most concerned with the pineal gland which is also known as the Third Eye. This is relating to chakras and other things, such as the

Kundalini awakening of the serpent spirit at the base of the spine, that do not concern the Christian. This is Hinduism. Yoga also comes from the Hindu religion. Treating our bodies well is one way of glorifying God but God does not communicate with us through the Third Eye.

Temperance is not only in what we eat and drink but includes our habits. The big monster in the living room of most homes is a cause of deep concern. Here are some statistics: - In the United States, according to a Nation Master survey in 2002, the average American watches 35 hours of T.V. per week, in the U.K about 28 hours. The average American youth has watched 1,200 hours of T.V. per year, having witnessed 150,000 violent acts by the age of 18. In addition, in the U.S. 55 minutes of T.V. programming is seen on P.C.'s or mobile devices per day. In the U.S. 99% of households have a T.V, and 65% have three sets or more. My Dad would call it: "The one-eyed monster." There is the story about a Christian man who had purchased a new T.V. set and was awaiting delivery one day; It arrived with a banner across the box which said: "Brings the world right into your home." He sent it back. The content on T.V. leaves little to be desired. Someone said that "Television is a mass hypnotist to the global mind." Most of that which comes out of Hollywood is tainted with secular values; the message is usually regarding sex, violence or money. The news is mostly influenced by agendas from those with many biases, particularly anti-Semitic, in most countries. And the remaining viewing is frequently from an atheistic viewpoint, such as the nature documentaries. The advertising is a huge influence which persuades the viewer to want more. The comedy is usually laced with foul language. These are hardly the values that our God would want for us to be influenced by. Without a television, it is possible to receive information through the internet, and to watch carefully selected videos or other programming. We need to be discerning. The programming conditions people to a particular world view. This is manipulation and control since all of the facts are not presented. Someone said: "Television is the most powerful weapon of psychological warfare in history." For many people it is the primary member of the family. It represents an altar, a religious altar of information that one is worshipping before. It controls people without their conscious awareness. It invokes a hypnotic state of the mind due to the flickering of the images which are not consciously seen, causing a vulnerability to manipulation. It also creates a unified mindset among the majority of the population.

In the United States, CNN is even broadcasting blasphemous advertising promoting a false antichrist, Maitreya. The Church has forgotten who it is. It has become spellbound by the witchcraft of the enemy. God calls us to live separate lives from that of the world. As Christians our lives should be consecrated to the Lord. We cannot sit in front of the television for hours each day and be influenced by a Satanic agenda, then enter into God's presence.

We are not to let anyone into our house who brings not the doctrine of the true Gospel and yet many sit daily under heathen indoctrination without too much of a thought being mesmerized by daily television viewing. Both temperance in lifestyle and separation are essential if we want to live a holy life. The Bible says that we are a peculiar people. This is not so much meaning odd, as it is distinctive, as the Mirriam-Webster dictionary asserts. We are unique, not weird.

PAIN AND SUFFERING

Of the most heinous crimes known to man there are several matters which I believe most affect the very heart of God. One of the most painful would be that of murder, namely abortion. According to records the abortion rates have been declining, possibly owing to the use of contraception. As it turns out, the number of abortions per year have declined every year since 1990, when 1,429,577 were performed in the U.S. In fact, abortion is currently at historic lows: **540,537 abortions were performed in 2014,** which is the smallest number since 1972. To put it in perspective, that's only one-third as many abortions as were performed in 1982, the peak year for abortion in America (1,573,920 foetuses were aborted). The Bible does not mention the word abortion, but it does mention the murder of persons; the unlawful taking of someone else's life. In the Bible the unborn are called children. Exodus refers to a woman with child being harmed, so that her fruit depart from her…then thou shalt give life for life. (Ex.21:22-23.) The punishment was the same for the unborn as it was for adults. The Scriptures often speak of prophets being called "from the womb" as in Isaiah 49:1 saying: "The Lord hath called me from the womb; from the bowels of my mother hath he made mention of my name." See also verse 5. King David speaks in Psalm 51:5 a: "Behold, I was shapen in iniquity; and in sin did my mother conceive me." In Jeremiah 1:5 the Word of the Lord says: "Before I formed thee in the belly I knew thee; and before thou camest forth out of the womb I sanctified thee, and I ordained thee a prophet unto the nations." The Bible also speaks about the birth of Jesus in Matthew 1:20b-21 "…Fear not to take unto thee Mary thy wife; for that which is conceived in her is of the Holy Ghost. And she shall bring forth a son, and thou shalt call his name JESUS: for he shall save his people from their sins," A child in the womb is capable of sensing emotions; Luke 1:41 and 44 say that the babe in Elizabeth's womb leaped for joy. We read that the unborn are known personally and intimately by God. The unborn are persons therefore abortion is morally wrong. It is the deliberate termination of a pregnancy. According to records 30% of American women will have an abortion by the age of 45. Genesis 9:6 is a stark warning; Whoso sheddeth man's blood, by man shall his blood be shed: for in the image of God made he man." Since the moment of formation in the womb God has been involved. Family planning is a part of responsible parenthood, but this is through contraception, not abortion. The Bible says to both fill the earth and subdue it, in Genesis 1:28, which means to "moderate," suppress," or "restrain." This is a form of bringing under control.

Very often in life we tend to think of our own pain and suffering, and focus on the injustices we have incurred through this passage of life; but I wonder what God feels when His beautiful creation is marred with such disdain and carelessness? We see the very heart of God's compassion as Jesus wept over Jerusalem (Luke 13:34.) The Father heart of God is grieved over the pain, and sorrows over it also. On the other hand, the Bible tells us the Jesus learned obedience through the things which He suffered. He was tempted in all points as we are, says the Bible, yet He was without sin. We are tested to make us more mature as believers. Someone has said: "What doesn't kill you will make you stronger." In truth, most of us would admit, at the time of testing, that we should not wish to be so strong at all. Rather than bemoaning our losses, it would serve us well to bear in mind the sensibilities of this awesome God we so love and serve. He has compassion. He weeps along with us in our time of sorrow; at the tomb of Lazarus we read: "Jesus wept" – the shortest verse in the Bible.

Not only abortion, but paedophilia is a crime that must grieve God deeply. I know it is heavy on my own heart the number of missing children that go astray each year across the globe. Some are trafficked and used as sex-slaves by their abusers, others are involved in Satanic ritual abuse. The numbers are increasing. Hundreds of thousands of children go missing annually across the earth. Many are never found. One source says: "Child sexual abuse is a devastating crime whose victims are those least able to protect themselves or speak out and whose perpetrators are most likely to be repeat offenders. Many paedophiles follow career paths that provide steady contact with children and earn them the trust of other adults. Priests, coaches and those who work with troubled youth are among the professions that child molesters have gravitated toward.

Unfortunately, child sexual abuse is also a significantly under-reported crime that is difficult to prove and prosecute. Most perpetrators of child molestation, incest and child rape are never identified and caught." This is a matter requiring much prayer, where offenders are often likely to be close family members or even trusted leaders. In cults there is a high rate of paedophilia, as seen throughout my research into this area, where child victims are afraid to report to anyone of the crimes against them. In an article entitled: *The Hard Facts about Satanic Ritual Abuse,"* the writers mention the following: "True believers among therapists, alleged adult survivors, law enforcement officials, journalists, and Christian leaders unanimously call for the public to believe the stories, to change the justice system so recovered "memories" alone can bring convictions in criminal court, and to rise up against this astonishingly powerful satanic conspiracy. If the alleged victims' allegations are true, then such reactions are to be expected. If they are false, then countless families and reputations are being destroyed for nothing, truth is being ignored, biblical standards of evidence and testimony are being discarded, "survivors" are being trapped in long-term, destructive therapeutic situations, and Satan is getting more credit than he is due" (Bob and Gretchen Passantino, article ID DO040). Some say that between 40,000 and 60,000 persons per year are ritually murdered (statistic attributed to Dr. Al Carlisle of the Utah State Prison System by Jerry Johnston (*The Edge of Evil* (Dallas: Word Books, 1989)) and others).

This calls for true believers across the globe to be constant in prayer and to be pro-active in bringing perpetrators to justice. We must be vigilant. 1 Peter 5:8 says: "Be sober, be vigilant; because your adversary the devil, as a roaring lion, walketh about, seeking whom he may devour."

Human trafficking is yet another area of great concern. In Britain, the A21 campaign functions to help protect against this slavery. Kevin Hyland, anti-slavery commissioner says: "The A21 Campaign has developed a powerful presentation depicting an appalling truth—that modern slavery exists today within our communities, on our streets, and before our eyes. Millions around the world, and thousands in the UK, are deprived of life and liberty at the hands of evil slave masters. Whether farm or factory, brothel or building site, car wash or cannabis farm, we are seeing growing numbers of adults and children abused and exploited in criminal conditions. We cannot simply watch and wait while this persists. I hope that through this A21 initiative people will open their eyes to the vulnerable and that together we will see victims rescued, criminals pursued, and perpetrators punished." The A21 site says that slavery is a hidden crime, yet it is happening in plain sight. It is happening on a daily basis in places across the UK that people interact with on a daily basis such as nail bars, restaurants and car washes. In response to recent statistics *"Can you see me?"* highlights these two particular types of slavery to educate members of the public on common scenarios where victims may be found. "Our aim is to not only help people understand the issue but also to do something about it. By partnering with law enforcements, governments businesses and NGO's (non-governmental organisations) our goal is to turn awareness into action. We hope that through collective action, human trafficking identification and rescue will increase, thereby making it more difficult for human traffickers to operate." Human trafficking is currently the most common and prevalent type of exploitation in the UK.

One other area of deep pain and suffering which is for the most part unnecessary is that of animal abuse prior to slaughter. There are many organisations who are pro-active in defending the rights of those who cannot speak for themselves. After witnessing many videos online, it is to me undeniable the amount of suffering that is caused the world over for the sake of a meal! Truthfully many people do not even consider their food sources, and yet millions of animals are cruelly treated daily across the globe in slaughterhouses. We shut our ears, defending our "God-given right" to a peaceful life and bury our not-so-holy heads in the sand while animals endure unbearable torture on a daily basis, all because of the demand for the food we want. I will spare the reader the details for the sake of those who are especially sensitive and empathic. I often find myself crying out to God, the Lord our Righteousness, to have mercy and defend these impoverished creatures and bring about justice. The Scriptures tell us: "For we know that the whole creation groaneth and travaileth in pain together until now." This speaks of awaiting redemption of our bodies. I believe this is saying that the animals are included. Joel 1:18 also says: "How do the beasts groan…" Jesus was speaking to the Pharisees about Sabbath-keeping when He addressed the matter of a sheep falling into a pit. It was obvious He was saying they should pull it out; that this would not constitute a violation of the Sabbath (Matt. 12:11), rather that they should do well on the Sabbath days, including treating animals well. In Proverbs 12:10 the Bible says: "A righteous man regardeth the life of his beast: but the tender mercies of the wicked are cruel." And indeed, how cruel they are!

UNITY AND THE HEART IN GOD

Much can be learned from the animal kingdom. Wolves are one of the most feared predators and have a legendary status around the world. I feel that we have a lot to learn from them. Wolves have exceptional survival instincts and are highly adapted to their environment. Watch them work together as a pack and you will see just how complex their social relationships are and what they can achieve together.

Some early humans modelled themselves on the behaviour of wolf packs because they noticed how successful wolves are as a species. Today, there are still many things we can learn from these creatures. Wolves are fiercely loyal to their pack, they are the ultimate team players. Many families, businesses and sports teams could learn a thing or two from the teamwork that wolves demonstrate. Understand your place, follow the rules and be loyal to your "pack."

Wolves will do anything to protect their family, even if it means sacrificing themselves. They work together to achieve a common goal that benefits the whole pack. Wolves thrive in some of the most extreme environments and make the most of the resources they have available and accept the situation they are in. Wolves have been found living in more places in the world than any other mammal, apart from humans. The strict hierarchy in a wolf pack means that youngsters have a great respect for their elders. Humans tend to take far more than they need, which means we are gradually ruining our planet. If we were as resourceful as wolves the world would be a much better place. Wolves get cast out of a pack just like some people do in society, disregarded and considered worthless. Lone wolves aren't worthless, they become perfectly well adapted to looking after themselves. A lone wolf learns how to look after itself. They may suffer a life of loneliness or they could eventually be accepted back into the pack. Wolves are expert communicators, able to direct an entire pack with a howl, snarl, growl, look or using their body language. They also use scent and touch to communicate to members of the pack and rival packs. The communication between wolf pack members seems effortless. When you watch them hunt they just seem to know what to do, where to be and how to help each other. It's what makes them such successful predators. Wolves show affection to each other by licking, grooming, nuzzling and even nibbling one another. They are not afraid to show affection when they feel it, or a pack member needs it. Life gets so intense and we are often moving so fast that we forget to show affection. Wolves will take the opportunity to have a bit of fun or play when there is nothing pressing to do. We humans often miss the chance to indulge in a little fun. Wolves will save their energy whenever they can, so that when they need to hunt they have as much strength as possible. Us humans on the other hand, don't seem to truly understand the concept of rest these days. Rest is extremely important. (Adapted from Kiri Nowak's article on wolves).

In looking at wolves we learn that they are among the most loyal creatures in the world. They hunt in packs and bring down prey much larger than themselves. This brings to mind the Scripture verse which tells us: "How should one chase a thousand, and two put ten thousand to flight, except their Rock had sold them, and the Lord had shut them up?" (Deut. 32:30). We can accomplish more in unison. Territorial skirmishes between neighbouring wolf packs can be ferocious. As well as the life lessons we can glean from the way wolves behave, we are also to be mindful that the Lord uses wolves in a negative sense in the Scriptures to describe the type of person to avoid. He calls false teachers "Ravening wolves" in Matthew 7:15. They are dangerous predators. In this case, they wear sheep's clothing. In other words, they are dressed to appear to be sheep. They look the part, they talk the talk. But this passage goes on to say that they are known by their fruit. Here Jesus says that they will be able to have prophesied in the name of Jesus, cast out devils in His name, and in His name will have done many wonderful works, so they say. But Jesus will say "Depart" to these deceitful workers of iniquity. He does not tell us to begin to do the work of deciding who they are now but says to let the wheat and these tares grow together until the end of time when the angels will do the work of separation. But the Bible does say to test all things, to be discerning and to look for good fruit in another's life so that we know a true believer from a false one. The Bible does say, however to mark them which cause divisions contrary to the doctrine which we have learned and to avoid them. This means warning other people. We can learn about unity by studying God's creation.

"*Life Together*" is a very insightful book written by Dietrich Bonhoeffer. In this book, the renowned Christian minister, professor, and author of "*The Cost of Discipleship*" recounts his unique fellowship in an underground seminary during the Nazi years in Germany. Giving practical advice on how life together in Christ can be sustained in families and groups, Life Together is bread for all who are hungry for the real life of Christian fellowship.

"The physical presence of other Christians is a source of incomprehensible joy and strength to the believer", says Bonhoeffer. "It is easily forgotten that the fellowship of Christian brethren is a gift of grace. A gift of the kingdom of God," he says. It is something we so often take for granted, until it is taken from us. We are not guaranteed Christian fellowship. For the lonely, it is not a daily provision, nor for the believer in prison. The Holy Bible says to not give up meeting together, not to forsake the assembling together of ourselves, and to do so even more in the light of Christ's soon coming. The early believers met together daily it says in the book of Acts. They came together having all things in common. They sold their possessions and shared according to the need. And they continued daily with one accord in the temple and breaking bread from house to house eating their food with gladness and singleness of heart, praising God says Acts 2:44-46. As a result, they had favour with all. And the Lord added daily to the Church. They were not without occasions of disagreement, as Paul and Barnabbas did at one time. Both were right in what they were concerned about, from their own perspectives, and the disagreement was resolved amicably after time. Very often we have a parting of ways over some minor issue when it is not even necessary. We are to pursue peace with all. Unity takes work. It is a work of God, but it requires our willingness to achieve it. James speaks of God's wisdom as being peaceable and easy to be entreated. These are qualities which are required if unity is to be maintained. Also, agreement in the truth. Unity can be achieved through correct teaching, or doctrine as well as the right spirit. "The Christian lives wholly by the truth of God's Word in Jesus Christ," adds Bonhoeffer. Without true fellowship we are apt to be picked off by the enemy, Satan, who prowls around as a roaring lion, looking for someone to devour.

In the book by Elizabeth Elliot *"Through Gates of Splendour"*, there is an opening hymn expressing the unity and care we are to have for each other: "Give of thy sons to bear the message glorious, give of thy wealth to speed the on their way, pour out thy soul for them in prayer victorious, and all thou spendest Jesus will repay." This is the story of five men who went to take the Gospel to the Auca Indians in Ecuador. Nate Saint, Jim Elliot, Pete Flemming, Ed McCully and Roger Youderian were men who were not ashamed of the Gospel of Christ. They fearlessly faced the Auca tribe, the Quichuas, in South America as a team working for our Lord and Saviour, Jesus Christ. Even though they all died as a result of their work there, yet "thousands of people in all parts of the world pray every day "that the light of the knowledge of the glory of God" may be carried to the Aucas, a people almost totally unheard of before." (*Through Gates of Splendour*, page 190). The work goes on today.

End of the Spear is a 2005 drama film that recounts the story of Operation Auca, in which the five American Christian missionaries attempted to evangelize the Huaorani (Waodani) people of the tropical rain forest of Eastern Ecuador. Based on actual events from 1956 in which five male missionaries were speared by a group of the Waodani tribe, the movie tells the story from the perspective of Steve Saint (the son of Nate Saint, one of the missionaries killed in the encounter), and Mincayani, one of the tribesmen who took part in the attack. The two eventually form a bond that continues to this day. Without true Christian unity and a common purpose this would not have been accomplished. In the film *"The End of the Spear"* which portrays the life of Jim Elliot and the other missionaries who went to the Waodani tribe in South America, there is a quote worth recalling: "Some people say that in a world of irreconcilable differences we still haven't found a way to change the human heart."

The Bible speaks beautifully of unity in Psalm 133, where it says: "Behold, how good and how pleasant it is for brethren to dwell together in unity! It is like the precious ointment upon the head, that ran down upon the beard, even Aaron's beard: that went down to the skirts of his garments; as the dew of Hermon, and as the dew that descended upon the mountains of Zion: for there the Lord commanded the blessing, even life for evermore." It is also referred to in the letter of Ephesians which speaks of endeavouring to keep the unity of the Spirit in the bond of peace, verse 3, and till we all come in the unity of the faith, verse 13. Unity involves believing and speaking the truth in love. It is a one-ness of mind, a singular mindset. We are to have a common purpose, and the Lord has given ample instruction in His Word as to what that is. There are some grey areas of doctrine to which we all may not agree, but to maintain unity we must all agree on the central doctrines of the Christian faith.

There are two types of unity in the Bible. In Ephesians 4:3, Paul says that we are to be diligent to preserve the unity of the Spirit in the bond of peace, as mentioned. The unity of the Spirit is already a fact for believers, but we must be diligent to preserve it. Then in Ephesians 4:13, after talking about the ministry of pastors and teachers who equip the saints for the work of ministry, Paul adds, "… until we all attain to the unity of the faith, and of the knowledge of the Son of God, to a mature man, to the measure of the stature which belongs to the fullness of Christ." This unity of the faith is not yet a reality but is attained to as we grow to maturity in Christ. We might call this "positional unity," which is a fact; and "practical unity," which is a work in progress.

We see the same thing in our text: In verses 21 & 22, of John 17, Jesus prays that those who believe in Him would be one, even as He and the Father are one. That prayer was answered when the Holy Spirit baptized all believers into the one body of Christ (1 Cor. 12:13). Yet Jesus also prays that believers may be "perfected in unity" (John 17:23), which implies a process of growth. It Is much like sanctification: We are positionally sanctified in Christ (1 Cor. 1:30; 6:11); yet, we must grow in sanctification (2 Cor. 7:1; 1 Thess. 4:3). (From Pastor Steven J. Cole's teaching). Christian unity is based upon our common salvation in Jesus Christ. Jesus' prayer was answered on the Day of Pentecost, when the Holy Spirit came on all believers, uniting them in the one body of Christ. Since then, all who believe the apostolic witness to Christ share new life in Him (1 Cor. 12:13): "For by one Spirit we were all baptized into one body, whether Jews or Greeks, whether slaves or free, and we were all made to drink of one Spirit." This is the unity of the Spirit that Paul talks about (Eph. 4:3). It is a fact, and yet we must be diligent to preserve it. In part, the glory that Christ has given us is the glory of our salvation, received and sustained by abundant grace. By our visible unity with all true believers, we proclaim to the world the truth that God sent His Son to pay for sins and give eternal life to all that believe, adds Cole. Also, by our love for one another is how the onlooking unbelieving world takes notice.

The Gospel of John speaks often of the unity between the Father and the Son, Jesus Christ. Jesus says in John 10:30: "I and my Father are one." And in 14:11a: "Believe me that I am in the Father, and the Father in me." John 3: 34-35 says: "For he whom God hath sent speaketh the words of God: for God giveth not the Spirit by measure unto him. The Father loveth the Son, and hath given all things into his hand." Jesus says in John 8:28-29 that He does nothing of Himself, but as the Father has taught Him, He speaks these things, and He always does what pleases the Father. With the Godhead there is unparalleled unity. In John 16:28 Jesus tells us that He came forth from the Father, and in 17:21-23 He prays to the Father: "That they all may be one; as thou, Father, art in me. And I in thee, that they also may be one in us: that the world may believe that thou hast sent me. And the glory which thou gavest me I have given them; that they may be one, even as we are one.: I in them, and thou in me, that they may be made perfect in one; and that the world may know that thou hast sent me, and hast loved them, as thou hast loved me." These verses portray the unity between the Godhead, Father, Son and Holy Spirit.

In Watchman Nee's book: "*The Life that Wins,*" he says about the life ordained for Christians, in his opening words, page 1: "From the Holy Scriptures we may see that the life as ordained for Christians is one full of joy and rest, one that is uninterrupted communion with God, and is in perfect harmony with His will. It is a life that does not thirst and hunger after this world, that walks outside of sins, and that transcends all things. Indeed, it is a holy, powerful and victorious life, and one that constitutes knowing God's will and having continuous fellowship with Him. The life which God has ordained for Christians is a life that is hid with Christ in God."

Not only wolves, as mentioned previously, but geese work together, as do many of the animal kingdom. We learn to get along together and to live in harmony by being united in the truth. We are called "the body of

Christ" in the Bible. We are knit together. Jesus says we are His friends if we lay down our lives for one another. We are deeply connected to Christ, the true vine. The True Vine in Hebrew is HaGefen Emet (John 15:1,4-5). The symbolism in the Scriptures is rich. God has given us examples of unity in nature. The following is a series of lessons extracted from nature from notes on Canada geese by Milton Olson, original author.

1. Sharing a common goal: As each goose flaps its wings it creates "uplift", an aerodynamics orientation that reduces air friction, for the birds that follow. By flying in a V-formation, the whole flock achieves a 70% greater flying range than if each bird flew alone. The lesson we can learn here is that people who share a common direction and goal can get where they are going more quickly and with less effort because they benefit from the momentum of the group moving around them. Make sure your team is aligned towards a common goal.

2. Increasing visibility: Flying in a V-formation increases the visibility as every goose can see what's happening in front of them. The lesson here is to make our organizations visible in both org-chart directions. Having top-down visibility enables leaders to stay connected with the edges of the organization to make better informed decisions. Bottom-up visibility enables employees to see the bigger picture, engages them, and empowers them to better align themselves with the organizational objectives.

3. Having humility to seek help: When a goose falls out of formation, it suddenly feels the friction of flying alone. It then quickly adjusts its mistake and moves back into formation to take advantage of the lifting power of the bird immediately in front of it. The lesson we can learn here is to be humble to admit the challenges we face and to seek help as soon as we get stuck. This humility will enable you, your team, and your group to move faster and achieve more.

4. Empowering others to lead: When the lead goose in the front gets tired, it rotates back into the formation and allows another goose to take the leadership position. The lesson here is to empower others to also lead. Micro-managing and keeping tight control will burn you out. It will also disengage and demotivate others around you. People have unique skills, capabilities, and gifts to offer. Give them autonomy, trust and a chance to shine, and you will be surprised with the outcomes.

5. Always recognizing great work: The geese honk to recognize each other and encourage those up front to keep up their speed. The lesson here to make sure we praise people and give them the recognition they deserve. Lack of recognition is one of the main reasons employees are unsatisfied at work and quit. It's very common for people's efforts to go unnoticed by their peers in a busy and fast-moving work environment. However, remembering to constantly provide recognition and encouragement is vital and keeps teams motivated to achieve their goals.

6. Offering support in challenging times: When a goose gets sick or wounded, two geese drop out of formation and follow it down to help and protect it. They stay with it until it dies or is able to fly again. Then, they launch out with another formation or catch up with the flock. The lesson here is to stand by each other in difficult times. It's easy to always be part of winning teams, but when things get difficult and people are facing challenges, that's when your teammates need you the most.

7. Staying committed to core values and purpose: The geese migration routes never vary. They use the same route year after year. Even when the flock members change, the young learn the route from their parents. In the spring they will go back to the spot where they were born. The lesson to learn here is to stay true to our core values and purpose. Strategies, tactics, and products may change in order for an organization to remain agile, but great companies always stick to their core purpose and values and preserve them with vigour.

Whilst these lessons have been made to fulfil business objectives, they nevertheless remain a good example for the Church as a whole to maintain unity and peak performance. It is very important in the Church to share a common direction; to not fly alone, but to travel on the strength of one another; to take advantage of the lifting power of the one in front; take turns in doing the hard tasks; honk from behind and be supportive; stand by each other and help each other, and to remember that we have got to learn to fly! In our walk of faith we must align ourselves with God's plans and purposes. God has a master plan and a personal plan. Every single thing in our lives is being used by God. God is after our heart.

It has been said: "What is in the well of you heart is bound to come up in the bucket of your speech." What we truly embrace and believe will be evident in our actions and lifestyle. Jesus said that the heart is where the root of the problems lies when He said: "But those things which proceed out of the mouth come forth from the heart; and they defile the man. For out of the heart proceed evil thoughts, murders, adulteries, fornications, thefts, false witness, blasphemies; these are the things which defile a man" Matthew 15:18-20a. An old Cherokee Indian once told his grandson: "There is a battle inside us all. One evil; It is anger, jealousy, resentment, envy, sorrow, regret, greed, arrogance, self-pity, guilt, resentment, inferiority, lies, false pride, superiority and ego." "The other is good: It is joy, peace, love, hope, serenity, humility, kindness, benevolence, empathy, generosity, truth, compassion and faith." The boy thought about it and asked his grandfather: "Which wolf wins?" The old man replied: "The one you feed." This is an interesting tale with a positive moral to it. We have a choice to either follow that which is good or not. If we do good, the result will be good fruit.

We are intended to pursue good. In order to do good, we are to take every thought captive to the obedience of Christ. The connection between the mind and the body is real. Allegedly 87% of current illnesses today begin in the head; the result of the thought life. The brain takes eighteen years to grow, but a lifetime to mature. The Bible also says to think on whatsoever things are just, pure, lovely, of good report, things of virtue and those things that are praiseworthy. The brain cannot defragment until there is right thinking.

In Romans 12:1-2 the Bible talks about being transformed by the renewing of the mind to God's will and the Word also tells us that it is the entrance of God's Word that gives light. The heart requires transformation. This comes about by grace and through our yieldedness to God. In nature we can learn from the example of the oyster. "The oyster creates a pearl out of a grain of sand. The grain of sand becomes an irritant to the oyster. In response to the discomfort, the oyster creates a smooth, protective coating that encases the grain of sand and this provides relief. The result is a beautiful pearl for an oyster. An irritant becomes the seed for something new. If we respond to life's discomfort appropriately, the smooth, protective coating that encases the irritant will result in a beautiful pearl. We can look for ways to rid ourselves of the irritant, or, with acceptance, condition ourselves towards a beautiful response, thus relieving ourselves of the discomfort, and bringing forth beauty." (From *"Mind over Mood"* by Greenberger and Padesky).

HUMOUR IN GOD

The topic of seeing ourselves in others is for me one of the healthiest forms of humour. We laugh at our mistakes and learn to take ourselves less seriously. We see the frailty of our humanity in the sight of our decisions and we are humbled at the awareness of our foolish pride made evident in those embarrassing moments. We begin to see ourselves more clearly. Among the most popular topics of comedy belongs the matter of the mundane daily routines of life as well as that of romantic relationships and of seeing ourselves in others, especially their faults and embarrassing behavior. Themes may be related to social or cultural issues, the economy, class distinction, national, historical or political matters, as well as religious beliefs. The Bible has little to say about the subject, except to mention to not be given to course jesting which is not fitting. But this does not mean that we are to see life so seriously. Good humour is vital. It can help us get through the most difficult of circumstances. It is good when it is not at someone else's expense. Comedy in romantic love relationships brings relief to a serious subject. Most people can identify. If not for the hilarity of some situations we encounter, we would otherwise be crying.

As a result of Western society's changing values, religion has become much the focus of comedy especially with television talk shows. There is an increasing disdain towards the evangelically-minded Christians in society and towards the truth we represent. This is targeted through comedy, but not necessarily with good humour. In difficult circumstances humour is a way of helping us to stay sane and sound of mind. It helps us to survive.

An elder who once counselled me said to me that if it were possible to add to the Beatitudes, he would quote: "Blessed are the balanced, for they shall live sanely." But we shall not add to the Word. There is a mention in the book of Proverbs where King Solomon writes: "A merry heart doeth good like a medicine: but a broken spirit drieth the bones" (Proverbs 17:22). Modern medicine has revealed that the chemical dopamine is released in the brain with joyful laughter, and likewise that with tears of deep sorrow toxins are released from the body that are not otherwise expelled except by this means. A Webster dictionary definition says that humour is: "Playful and indulgent treatment of the absurd; incongruous or ludicrous; sportive fancy or imagination; capacity or habit of mind which apprehends and appreciates the ludicrous sympathetically." Often with good humour we see the pathetic reality of our weak temperaments, and we laugh because we have been there, and we don't like to admit it!

In Nehemiah the writer says: "The joy of the Lord is your strength." Joy is one of the fruits of the Holy Spirit. The Word tells us in Psalm 126: 2 "Then was our tongue mouth filled with laughter, and our tongue with singing." Psalm 2 is especially insightful where the wicked are raging against the people of God and this shows us the response of the Lord: "He that sitteth in the heavens shall laugh: the Lord shall have them in derision." James 4:9 talks about letting our laughter be turned to mourning, and our joy to heaviness at the presence of sin and pride.

GOD IS SALVATION; GOD'S GRACE

The Scriptures tell us that God loves the whole world in John 3:16. That He makes the sun shine on the just as well as the unjust alike. However, to please God or to be approved by Him requires something else. That is faith. It is not by doing good, however righteous this may be, or having high moral standards, or any other ideal, but that man can come to the Creator by faith alone, through the grace of God, which He bestows upon those who seek Him. To believe that He exists at all is to have faith. Belief implies more than mere intellectual assent to a fact; it means something like being in agreement with or having allegiance to. The King James Bible says: "Believe that He is." Other versions say; "that He exists." I believe there is a deeper meaning here. The words of the Almighty spoken to Moses were: "I AM that I AM." This verse could be interpreted as: "God who is", or to "believe that He is the One."

Further, God rewards those who diligently seek Him. Such find favour with God. Jesus said; "Seek and you will find." In Jeremiah it says: "You will seek Me and I will be found by you, when you search for Me with all your heart." Not only is there the reward of finding God through seeking Him, but the added joys and benefits of gaining His approval by virtue of doing His desired will by longing to know Him. This is not to say God has gone anywhere, when I say, we find Him. He is not far from any one of us, says Acts.

It is God who bestows upon people the gift of salvation, which comes by grace through faith. It is all of His goodness, not man's doing. Faith in Christ as Saviour and Lord is what is needed. Nothing can earn salvation. It is the precious gift of God. Because it is such, God gets all of the glory and credit due to Him. Ephesians 2:8-9 says: "For it is by grace that you are saved, through faith, and this not of yourselves, it is the gift of God, not of works, so that no-one can boast." Hebrews 11:6 says: "Without faith it is impossible to please God, for he that comes to God must believe that He exists, and that He rewards those who diligently seek Him." This verse addresses the distinction between God's love and His approval.

Through these passages timeless truths may be extracted to support the facts that God declares to be true about Himself, and to confirm the principles of His Word in order to help us grow in our understanding of who He is, as well as to help bring us into maturity causing us both to be fruitful in good deeds and to be more Christ-like in moral character and in every other way. To know of God's grace, we need only to turn our eyes upon Jesus. Look to the cross where our blessed Saviour died and there we will see the limitless grace of God.

INTIMACY AND CONTENTMENT IN GOD

"To be content is to be satisfied with God", says Joseph M. Stowell in his booklet "*Experiencing Intimacy with God.*" "Finding satisfaction, sustenance, and security in our relationship with God is a process. Too many of us have become discouraged in the pursuit of God by expecting that the product will be ours quickly and that the experience will be in line with our expectations of what it ought to be. The first task in the pursuit of intimacy with God is to deal with the disconnectedness that keeps us far from Him. This is our responsibility. God looks for repentant, radically reliant hearts in which to set up His residence. The next step is starting on a pilgrimage toward God by being routinely faithful to the realities that trigger an experience with His fulfilling presence. Each of us will experience Him differently. The consistency and constancy of His reality in our lives will be a lifelong growth experience. Intimacy with God must not be defined in terms of experiential elements. Experiences are too subjective, varied and individualized to nail down as universal scenarios of intimacy. God doesn't meet all of us in the same way – emotionally, intellectually, or spiritually. Each of us perceives things in a unique way. If we define intimacy by what it looks and feels like, we will inevitably be defining it as one individual sees it, thus setting up other people for disappointment. "Draw near to God and He will draw near to you" (James 4:8). That is a process statement. The pursuit of intimacy is an intentional commitment to take steps toward God and, in the process of that Godward motion, to grow more deeply conscious of connected to, and confident in Him alone as the only source to satisfy, sustain, and secure. The pursuit of intimacy with God embraces a way of life that increasingly fills the soul with the satisfaction, sustenance, and security of His presence. The pursuit of intimacy is about growing more deeply connected to Christ as the ultimate source for all that is needed."

With intimacy there is a contentment. His presence satisfies. We are no longer seeking the gifts, but the giver, looking to His face and not His hand. In 2 Corinthians there is a beautiful passage which refers to the comfort of God: "Blessed be God, even the Father of our Lord Jesus

Christ, the Father of mercies, and the God of all comfort; who comforteth us in all our tribulation, that we may be able to comfort them which are in any trouble, by the comfort wherewith we ourselves are comforted of God. For as the sufferings of Christ abound in us, so our consolation also aboundeth by Christ." God can comfort us is many ways. Often it is through the Holy Scriptures, which it says, that through the comfort of the Scriptures we might find hope. It can be by other means. It is entirely possible that this comfort can come through the tearful hug from a close friend or loved one; or even through the warm embrace of a family pet – even if it is a cat! Who is to say how such comfort may come. It doesn't always have be by such super-spiritual means. It may come quietly, in the deep, inner recesses of the human heart. God's love is so very practical and relevant. It has been said that "Some people are so heavenly-minded, they are no earthly good." We must guard against all forms of bigotry. We ought to express tolerance towards the views of others. It is not always necessary to have our say when others are voicing their opinions. Silence does not always mean complicity. It can foster understanding, when we are willing to forego our opinions so that others can feel heard and understood. In a sense, this is showing to them that comfort which God has shown us. Simply listening to others is a dying art these days, it seems. When hearing of street people in an interview, one of them, lying in a gutter, refused both food and money asking only for someone to talk to. Often when a friend or loved one is going through difficulty we may feel it is our place to give advice, and whilst it is often helpful to do so, it is also vital to hear the person out before we offer solutions, which is often not the need. Very often, people have within themselves the very answer to their problems; It takes a man of wisdom to draw this out, says the Bible. In this way, we are communicating the comfort of God. This lends towards a deeper level of intimacy in human relationship, and towards our Maker.

Stowell continues: "Our primary purpose in life is to embrace the transcendent God by faith and to worship Him in purity and service. This life focus is a directional thing. Intimacy is not about God doing things for us. It is not about Him making us feel good. He wants for us to embrace Him and to pledge to worship and serve Him no matter what happens. Intimacy begins by giving self away. It gives self to God as the ultimate gift of our love. It should be sufficient to see and hear about God at work in the lives of others and to learn to rest and rejoice in the fact that God does marvelous things in others' lives. We need to be forever grateful for His daily presence; His quiet work behind the scenes; His grace that is sufficient; His mercy that stays His judgment; and heaven. God has already done more for us than we deserve, by redeeming us, cancelling hell and guaranteeing heaven That ought to be enough to launch us into praise and worship for the rest of our lives. God has already dramatically intervened in a major way in our lives when He opened up the story of the cross to us and bid us come by the power of His Spirit. When we embraced that rugged cross and felt the weight of our sin leave us and were washed by that cleansing blood, it was enough -more than enough to keep our hearts lovingly grateful. God is probably doing a lot of things for us that we don't even know about. These may not be big dramatic things, but God's Word teaches us that He stands like a sovereign sentinel at the gates of our lives, keeping out anything that is more than we can bear (1 Cor. 10:13). He lets only those things that by His power and with our cooperation, will turn to His glory and gain to our good (Romans 8:28).

When God thinks of intimacy He thinks of a heart relationship with us. Of course, our loved ones like to bless us with gifts, but what they really want is a love relationship with us. Intimacy is about a love relationship, not a gift exchange. When we live expectantly, serve Him purely, slow down and spend seasons on our knees with His Word in prayer and meditation, He fills our souls with Himself. It's not what He does for us that we should be loving; it's God Himself, not the other things we are attracted to, not all the provisions we expect from Him."

A closer look at Psalm 23 will show us the attainable outcomes of a deepening personal relationship with the Lord; He will satisfy our souls, sustain our lives, and secure us in the face of great danger. In many of the Psalms there is this same confidence expressed in the providential care of our Maker. Psalm 91 brings a similar message of protection from evil. In drawing near to God, we become more confident of His protection, that He is true to His promises. Intimacy with God is the very reward of a life well lived before God. Things cannot satisfy. They all perish. Jesus spoke of the illusiveness of material gain and said to not pursue it. Many seek after the blessings from God in terms of materialism, and whilst He does meet our need, yet He desires rather an intimacy in relationship with Himself. In the Proverbs King Solomon prayed: Remove far from me vanity and lies: give me neither poverty nor riches; feed me with food convenient for me." (Prov.30:8). There is such a thing as "enough."

Closeness with God and the fruit of good Christian character are far to be desired over material gain. The Proverbs speaks much about desiring the imperishable riches of intimacy with God over material wealth. Intimacy, says Stowell, requires "a steady pouring out of our hearts in praise to God and prayer, and the steady absorbing of His Word into our hearts." Psalm 1 describes the godly person who is absorbing the Word of God and calls them blessed. The influence is the Word of God, not the trappings of the world system. This drawing close to God leads to an abundant life, a life of meaning and purpose, one that is well organized and clean, that is driven by what ultimately satisfies. Both Bible reading and praying aloud are very helpful. This method keeps the mind from wandering, as does journaling, which helps to make one's thoughts more concrete. Faithfulness is key, and a deeper relationship with the Lord is the reward. Most often, earthly pleasures intended to bless us, can dull our appetite for God. The Bible says: "Seek first the kingdom of God and His righteousness..." in the Gospels. Another poem I have written is called Abiding:

> *Trust and obey, always abiding*
> *No other way, here is the blessing*
> *Peace found in Jesus, constant and still*
> *No other desire, only His will*

Often in the Old Testament, God blessed the obedient with material prosperity as a means of satisfying them and rewarding them. We have His Son today, living in our hearts. The blessings of the kingdom are not the material benefits we so desire. God will grant them accordingly, but these are not intended to be our pursuit. Wealth is not the earmark of the godly life. God's presence is. There is, however, the contentment of aspiration which differs from the contentment of acquisition; To be constantly in the pursuit of developing truly Christ-like character involves discontentment of aspiration; with our character, relationships and values. To become more wise, deeper, and more loving. Here, there is a sense of dissatisfaction, if you will, that motivates a person to strive for higher ideals, to reach the mark, that high and holy calling spoken of by the Apostle Paul in the Bible. Money has no lasting value, and God reminds us to be content with having our daily needs met. We have much more than this in the Western world, where necessities include so much more. Money and possessions can give a false sense of security, but they give no assurance of heavenly wealth. The Bible reminds us "to be rich toward God" Luke 12:21. Seeking first God's kingdom and His righteousness is what truly counts. Gary Inrig says in "*Cultivating a Heart of Contentment*": The seduction of prosperity theology attempts to sanctify what God has called us to flee; a consumerist, materialistic, philosophy of life. We are not merely to flee, however. The call of the Christ-follower is to do just that, to follow the Lord. "Follow after righteousness, godliness, faith, love, patience, and meekness." 1 Tim. 6:11b." He adds: "There is a richness to life when we use the abilities and resources that God has made available to us to make a difference in the lives of other people. And there is a huge difference between living with a thirst for pleasure and living with a sense of purpose. The richest times in life come when we use our money to further God's kingdom. That is real living, and its value extends far beyond the present world into eternity." Even a cup of cold water given in the name of Jesus will not be overlooked by God. Hebrews 13:5 says: "Let your conversation be without covetousness; and be content with such things as ye have: for he hath said, I will never leave thee, nor forsake thee," King Solomon wrote: "Labour not to be rich: cease from thine own wisdom. Wilt thou set thine eyes upon that which is not? For riches certainly make themselves wings; they fly away as an eagle toward heaven." And in Ecclesiastes, he wrote: "Behold that which I have seen: it is good and comely for one to eat and to drink, and to enjoy the good of all his labour that he taketh under the sun all the days of his life, which God giveth him: for it is his portion. Every man also to whom God hath given riches and wealth, and hath given him power to eat thereof, and to take his portion, and to rejoice in his labour; this is the gift of God." It has been said: "He is no fool, who gives what he cannot keep, to gain what he cannot lose."

A SOUND MIND IN GOD

No doubt many of us will agree that we are indeed "fools for Christ", as the Apostle Paul said. But this does not mean that we don't have soundness of mind. "For God has not given us the spirit of fear, but of power, and of love, and of a sound mind." 2 Tim. 1:7. In Romans 12:2 the Bible also says: "And be not conformed to this world: but be ye transformed by the renewing of your mind, that ye may prove what is that good, and acceptable, and perfect, will of God." Also, in 2 Corinthians Paul is addressing the mind when he says: "For the weapons of our warfare are not carnal, but mighty through God to the pulling down of strong holds; Casting down imaginations, and every high thing that exalteth itself against the knowledge of God, and bringing into captivity every thought to the obedience of Christ."

Peter, likewise, in addressing the assaults of the devil, speaks about the perfection, establishing, strengthening, and settling of the believer following affliction, in 1 Peter 5:10. There is much to be said for having soundness of mind. There is no merit in becoming "loopy" or "flaky" for a believer. We are meant to be solid (as a rock).

In this world there is the rise in statistics of mental illness, which includes various forms of depression. This covers a whole range of disorders. Many are diagnosed by the medical profession as having a disorder, which may be treatable with certain medications. I would add that for a life in Christ, a level of stability can also be attained through prayer, meditation and practice of the Word of God, a lifestyle of worship and right living. Medications do have a role to serve in many cases, as it is with diabetes, or heart disease, for example. As Christians we don't seem to have difficulty with a fellow brother or sister using medical assistance and hospitals in order to have a hip replacement, and yet in some circles, there is often a subtle message conveyed regarding the other matters mentioned, as if the sufferer is lacking faith to be taking medications or being treated by a medical doctor. Here, this is not referring to strange shamans, but to qualified practitioners. The adverse effects of misunderstanding in this area can lead to devastation.

We are living in a world which is described as Satan's domain in the Bible. God made it all and declared it good, but the prince of the power of the air, the devil, rules this world. He has been defeated on the cross, yet he still has rule in the heavenlies until Christ returns. We are meant to overcome him, not in our own strength, but in God's power, and that requires vigilance. I believe at the cross, Satan was defeated, and cast down, as it says in Revelation 12:9: "And the great dragon was cast out, that old serpent called the devil, and Satan, which deceiveth the whole world: he was cast out into the earth, and his angels were cast out with him." Some say that the devil, being the accuser of the brethren has the capacity to go before God, as he did in the days of Job, and accuse us. He did do that in those days, having access to the heavenly throne room, it seems, or at least, into the presence of God. See Job 1:6-7. Here the devil was in the very presence of God and even had access to roam earth also. In Revelation, the verse mentioned says he has been cast out of that heavenly realm, not the immediate realm above earth, but the highest heaven, where he once used to go and worship God as the chief worship angel. It is my belief that since the Cross, the devil has been cast out, he has been defeated. He no longer has that authority to go and bring accusations about God's people. He will have us believe he does, and many Christians still believe what it says in Job, as if the same scenario is occurring today; but since then Jesus won the victory on the Cross over death and hell. Jesus is victor! Jesus has conquered our heavenly foe and he no longer is able to do what he did in the days of Job. He has lost his power. Death has lost its sting. This revelation ought to release many from fear.

Revelation 12:10 goes on to say: "And I heard a loud voice saying in heaven, Now is come salvation, and strength, and the kingdom of our God, and the power of His Christ: for **the accuser of our brethren is cast down**, which accused them before our God day and night." This has come about by the victory Christ has won on the Cross. This is all to say that we, as believers need no longer live in fear of what the devil may do or say before God, as so many still do. In fact, we have more to be concerned about, in fact, with what we say before God about one another, never mind the devil!

This leads to a more balanced view and stable mindset, knowing that our foe is already defeated. As Romans 8:31-39 tells us: "We are more than conquerors through Him who loved us." Most likely, the major cause of mental illnesses and disorders of the mind, is rooted in fear. It is said the fear is: False Evidence Appearing Real. It is deceptive. Fear can immobilize a person. God wants to be the object of our utmost respect and awe. When we place fear in something else we are giving that object the reverence due only to God Almighty. Fear does that. It has the ability to cause us to serve something or someone else other than God. Yet the Holy Scriptures are replete with passages speaking of fear and reverence towards God. The devil is like a bee without a sting. Jesus has taken the sting at Calvary. He deserves all our reverence and awesome fear in the truest sense of the word.

People are beset with all kinds of fears; fear of danger, the fear of potential loss or harm, the fear of seemingly losing control or whatever it may be, but these are mostly illusions. The Bible has something to say about them all, and how to deal with them, which we will find, if we search the Scriptures. "Perfect love casts our fear" 1 John 4:18 is one verse that comes to mind. "I will not fear what flesh can do to me" Psalm 56:4; "Be not afraid of sudden fear." Prov.3:25; Conversely, Jesus says in Luke 12:4-5: "And I say unto you my friends, Be not afraid of them that kill the body, and after that have no more that they can do. But I will forewarn you whom ye shall fear: Fear him, which after he hath killed hath power to cast into hell; yea, I say unto you, Fear him." This is a sobering message.

When it comes to the matter of mental illness, it is treated quite differently in the Church than a physical problem, where one might readily recommend a physician. In such cases it is often seen as a spiritual cause. if we immediately dismiss the possibility of mental illness, or a chemical imbalance, and automatically assume spiritual deficiency, our actions amount to spiritual abuse. I know those are powerful and pointed words. Very often, in the cases of Schizophrenia-like disorders, and bipolar illness, there is an underlying physiological cause, which, with the correct treatment wholistically (not holistically), it can be remedied, thus avoiding serious consequences. Soundness of mind is attainable for even the bipolar sufferer. These are labels given by modern medicine, but in the days when Jesus walked this earth other illnesses were addressed, such as the palsy. The labels keep changing to avoid stigmatization, but they still exist. In Jesus' day there were times when He did cast out devils from possessed people. Very often though people with bipolar, for example, are suffering from something other than "devils." A head or brain injury can be a root cause, emotional dysfunction, poor nutrition, inadequate sleep, poor discipline, and often disobedience to God can cause an onset of all types of depressive illness, but not in all cases. We have a tendency to blame ourselves in such cases, which compounds the problem. If our belief system is wacky, there is an unstable foundation. It is just like building our house on sand, as Jesus said. We operate from fear, guilt and shame instead of freedom. Jesus said: "If ye continue in my word, then are ye my disciples indeed; And ye shall know the truth, and the truth shall make you free. If the Son therefore shall make you free, ye shall be free indeed." John 8:31-32,36.

A sound mind brings freedom. In the Bible this is also termed "liberty." In Luke 4:18 –19a Jesus was quoting the prophet Isaiah when He said: "The Spirit of the Lord is upon me, because he hath anointed me to preach the gospel to the poor; he hath sent me to heal the brokenhearted, to preach deliverance to the captives, and recovering of sight to the blind, to set at liberty them that are bruised, to preach the acceptable year of the Lord." The mentally unwell are surely such as these. There needs to be understanding and compassion towards those among us who are sufferers, not condemnation. They do not need to be shunned. Jesus would want us to extend our hands and hearts towards these people and aid in their recovery and healing. It is possible. "With God all things are possible."

KNOWING GOD THROUGH PRAYER

The most reliable way of knowing God is through His Word. In His Word He has revealed sufficient about Himself for us to have a relationship with Him. Through prayer we become intimately acquainted with God. The disciples asked Jesus: "Lord, teach us to pray", and Jesus shared with them the Lord's prayer. In this prayer, Jesus made requests as He did when praying to the Father in John 17. Elsewhere the Scriptures speak of making requests with thanksgiving to God and presenting to Him our supplications. Today there is much talk of what is called "contemplative prayer." It has become one of the most seductive teachings among Christians today. This comes from the Eastern mystics. With biblical meditation we are logically employing Scripture verses and meditating on God's precepts, as David did, not by emptying the mind. People are often invoking demon spirits by uttering mantras during yoga or contemplative prayer. Pastor Joe Schimmel of Blessed Hope Chapel, California, warns against the dangers of contemplative prayer saying that "it is very important that Christians realize there is mass deception going on and the Emerging church leaders are opening up their followers to these demonic hosts -whether knowingly, or unknowingly." Contemplative prayer is an esoteric tradition. "It is one of the most dangerous deadly things that is moving into the Church right now," says Pastor Michael Hoggard. Prayer includes making requests to God and communing with the Father, not getting in contact with some "higher self within", or some interior void, which is New Age mystical practice.

It is said: "Nothing leaves heaven until something leaves earth." Whether this is true or not, God is responsive to the expressed need of the human heart. The great men of faith in the Holy Scriptures were people of prayer. Communion with God includes praise, worship and prayer. Worship is invariably preceded by praise. Prayer can take various forms, including adoration, confession, supplication and intercession, which is making requests to God. Much of our communication with our heavenly Father flows from a heart that knows Him through a relationship with Him, oftentimes through a knowledge of Him by His Word, the Holy

Scriptures. The Word testifies to the very nature of God and reveals who He is. We can pray God's Word back to Him by affirming declarations of who He is, and by declaring His promises.

J.C. Ryle says that "Prayer is to faith what breath is to life." He adds: "Words said without heart are as utterly useless to our souls as the drumbeating of the poor heathen before their idols." There is no prayer without heart. Ryle continues: "The great majority of men either ask nothing of God or do not mean what they are saying when they do ask, which is just the same thing." People are sadly wanting in their desire to pray to God. We enjoy all the benefits He has granted us, yet we do not acknowledge Him for all His goodness. J.C. Ryle also says: "Diligence in prayer is the secret of eminent holiness." Prayer is simply speaking to God. We do not sufficiently realize the blessings and privileges of prayer.

THE WORD OF GOD

The Bible is a unique book that has a thread through it and is written over a period of 1,600 years from 1400 BC to AD 100 by more than 40 authors writing under the inspiration of the Holy Spirit. It is called the Word of God, to which I have also referred as the Holy Bible or the Holy Scriptures throughout this book. Jesus is also called the Word of God in the book of Revelation. The canon of New Testament Scripture was made up of documents and writings from the 1st Century. In 331 AD the Roman Emperor Constantine sent a letter to Eusebius asking him to complete a Bible. The Codex Vaticanus and the Codex Sinaiticus were written. It was forty years later when a final list of the 27 letters of the New Testament were canonised by the Church of the time. The Gospels are written with eye-witness testimony. The gnostic Gospels were written later between the 2nd and 4th centuries.

The Bible was written in three languages; Hebrew, Aramaic and Greek. The first translation of the Bible was the Septuagint, a Greek translation from the Hebrew Old Testament in the 3rd century BC. The Bible consists of 66 books; 39 in the Old Testament and 27 in the New Testament. The first English translation began in 1382 and was completed in 1384 by John Wycliffe. The first Bible printed in movable type was the Gutenberg Bible in 1455. It was a version of the Latin Vulgate. Martin Luther first translated the New Testament from Greek into German in 1534. William Tyndale printed the first English translation of the New Testament in 1535. The first legal translation was published in 1535 by Coverdale. The Geneva Bible was published in 1560, the first one to be brought to America; It was known as the Pilgrim's Bible. The Bible is the bestselling book in the history of the world. The writers of the Bible understood that they were speaking on behalf of God, often reiterating: "Thus saith the Lord" throughout the writings. The Bible is infallible; It is all about Jesus from beginning to end. The Septuagint added the Apocryphal books. These were written between the Old and New Testaments but were not included as canonical texts. The Septuagint is the Greek translation of the Old Testament. The Hebrew Scriptures were already written at the time when Jesus Christ walked the earth. The Masoretic text is dated 1006. The Dead Sea scrolls were found in caves in Qumran in 1947. These texts pre-dated the Christian era by just a few years. They contained 19,000 scroll fragments from about 200 BC, the entire Old Testament except the book of Esther, and it is it virtually identical to what we read today.

The accuracy and integrity of all copies found is phenomenal. The final book of the Old Testament is Malachi. The Apocryphal books written afterwards were only included in the Catholic Bible and some Protestant ones. Matthew, Mark and Luke were probably written before the fall of Jerusalem. The Latin Vulgate was the only version of the Bible available before Wycliffe who opposed the tyranny of the Roman Catholic church. The church threatened to kill anyone who read the Bible in any language other than Latin. Erasmus translated the Bible from the corrupt Latin Vulgate and published the Greek/Latin parallel New Testament in 1516. The Latin part was his own translation from the original Greek. Martin Luther became the first person to translate the Bible into the language of the common people with the Luther Bible. Then, the Catholic church burned people at the stake for the crime of reading the Bible. In 1526 the first printing of an English translation was made by William Tyndale, who was arrested and deemed a heretic. He was burned at the stake after being strangled to death. Eventually in 1541 Henry the Eighth allowed the printing of the Bible in English. God was accomplishing His will to bring His Word to the people. In 1604 James the 1st authorized the printing of the Bible into English.

"Next to prayer there is nothing so important in the Christian life as reading the Bible." Says J. C. Ryle. There is no other book in existence written in such a manner as the Bible. These are the very words of the eternal God. The men who wrote it spoke from God as they were carried along by the Holy Spirit. The books of the Old and New Testament are all inspired truth; every chapter, word and verse is from God. 2 Timothy 3:16-17 says: "All scripture is given by inspiration of God, and is profitable for doctrine, for reproof, for correction, for instruction in righteousness: that the man of God may be perfect, thoroughly furnished unto all good works" and 2 Peter 1:20-21 says: "Knowing this first, that no prophecy of the scripture is of any private interpretation. For the prophecy came not in old time by the will of man: but holy men of God spake as they were moved by the Holy Ghost." In addition, Paul says in Galatians 1:11-12: "But I certify you, brethren, that the gospel which was preached of me is not after man. For I neither received it of man, neither was I taught it, but by the revelation of Jesus Christ."

Without Bible knowledge man has no lasting attainment. Bible truth provides enough for a man's soul to be saved. The Bible gives us God's plan of salvation; His plan to receive, pardon, and save to the uttermost. The Bible gives us knowledge of the character of Jesus Christ. It gives us history of men and women of God, as well as those who despised reproof and ruined their souls. The Bible contains precious promises. It also speaks of heaven and hell. It speaks of the future prospects of every true Christian. It is the true judge of the thoughts and attitudes of the heart. The Word of God as a title in Hebrew is D'war Adonai.

This book turned the whole world upside down in the days of the apostles; In a few generations they changed the face of society. The abominations of Roman Catholicism became distinctly visible as society became affected by God's Word. Reading the Bible ought to be done with humility and heartfelt prayer. The indwelling Holy Spirit will illuminate the reader's mind. Love of the Word is characteristic of the true child of God.

The men of the Bible loved the Word; King David said: "Oh how I love thy law." It is the armoury from which great men have drawn their weapons. Love of the Bible is one of the great points of agreement among all converted men and women. The Bible is the only book which can truly comfort a person in the last moments of their life. It is enduring. "There is no conversion in the coffin," says Ryle. We have opportunity now to read and hear the Word of God. It is able to convert the soul. "There is but one fountain of comfort for man drawing near to his end, that is the Bible" adds Ryle. "All comfort from any other source is a house built upon the sand." The King James version of the Bible is, and always has been the greatest threat to Roman Catholicism because it is the only Bible in use today that can be traced back to the true Christians in Antioch. The King James version has produced more spiritual fruit than all other Bibles combined and the King James version's Textus Receptus is backed up by over 95% of all ancient Greek manuscripts.

THE WRATH OF GOD

Many focus on the love of God alone, some even deny that there is a hell, saying it is not mentioned in the Bible, even though Jesus addressed hell on more occasions than He talked about heaven. God, in order to be just must have anger. His anger is not a loss of temper, as human anger is very often. The wrath of God is fearsome. The Bible talks of both the goodness and the severity of God. The Old Testament gives examples where God meted out vengeance on mankind, such as the great flood of Noah's day. God will forgive sin if it is confessed, which is why it is important to address the Hyper-grace movement here once again, which teaches that we no longer need to confess sin once we come to Christ, saying all future sin is automatically forgiven. 1 John says: "If we say that we have fellowship with him, and walk in darkness, we lie, and do not the truth: But if we walk in the light, as he is in the light, we have fellowship with one another, and the blood of Jesus Christ his Son cleanseth us from all sin. If we say that we have no sin, we deceive ourselves, and the truth is not in us. If we confess our sins, he is faithful and just to forgive us our sins, and to cleanse us from all unrighteousness" (1:6-9). We see here that a provision is made in the case of sin. But it needs to be appropriated.

In Hebrew the Lord, God of Vengeance is El G'mulah YHWH, Jer. 51:56 and the God who avenges for me is El nathan n'qamah, Psalm 18:47.

Committing any sin is forgivable when it is confessed and forsaken, regardless of what it is. Peter denied the Lord, and resisted the Holy Spirit, yet was forgiven. The unpardonable sin is not committed in words alone. Peter cursed at Christ and said he did not know Him. The heart must be engaged, not only words. Very often people may despair and turn from God out of sorrow or fear. God is always waiting for them to return. The Word of God says to not neglect so great a salvation, and to not be given over to pleasures. There is an everlasting hell. A place of torment, where "the worm never dies." This is the conscience. We are to make our calling and election sure, the Bible says. In 1 Corinthians there is an account of a man who was living a licentious lifestyle. Paul says: "Deliver such a one to Satan for the destruction of the flesh, that the spirit may be saved in the day of the Lord Jesus" in 1 Cor. 5:5. Paul adds: in verse 13b: "Therefore put away from among yourselves that wicked person." Paul later addresses the matter in 2 Corinthians 2:6-11. The man had been punished and disciplined by being excluded from the fellowship of believers and had repented. Paul says to comfort him and forgive him, lest perhaps such a one should be swallowed up with too much sorrow and Satan get the advantage. I find it interesting, however, that initially Paul had said to deliver the man to Satan, so that his spirit would be saved in the day of the Lord Jesus. Here, is some hopeful truth. The Bible elsewhere speaks of falling away to the point that this puts Christ to shame, and is considered trampling underfoot the Son of God, Hebrew 6:6; 10:29; 12:15-17. And yet in the passage about the man who had fallen into temptation and sin, Paul still says that his spirit would be saved. There is, however great loss of rewards for a life not lived to the glory of God, as Corinthians speaks of in 1 Corinthians 3:10-15. In hell there is an ever-increasing knowledge of being lost, of being cast away from God for all eternity. There will be given to lost souls an eternal body that cannot be consumed and there will be weeping and wailing and gnashing of teeth. It is a place where man's lusts will burn forever and not be satiated. Men will seek death and not be able to find it. Five times Scripture calls hell the lake of fire. The Bible even says that the majority of mankind will be going there, as the way to eternal life is narrow, and few there be that find it. 1 Peter 4:17-18 says: "For the time is come that judgment must begin at the house of God: and if it first begin at us, what shall the end be of them that obey not the gospel of God? And if the righteous scarcely be saved, where shall the ungodly and the sinner appear?" Other than the unpardonable sin, it is still a necessary requirement to repent of known sin and to confess sins to God as necessary and receive forgiveness.

There is no light in hell. It is described as a place of outer darkness. It will be a world of transgressors and the ungodly. Nothing of the present joy of the presence of the Holy Spirit as it is even on earth today. It will be torment. Those in hell will suffer the vengeance of God. Those in hell are not in the hands of the devil; they are in the hands of an angry God. This is the wrath of God unleashed. We can be assured of our salvation by turning to Jesus Christ. Today is the day of salvation.

GOD IS OUR FUTURE

In our study of eschatology, which is referring to death, judgment, and of the final destiny of the soul and of humankind, we learn of God's sovereignty. The Bible, versus other religious books, tells us what the future holds. It foretells the future. There have been hundreds of prophecies in the Bible which have already been fulfilled. There are no prophecies in the Hindu Vedas, the Qur'an, the book of Mormon, the Tripitaka, the Bhagavad Gita or the Upanishads. The Bible can substantiate its claims to be divinely authoritative. Jesus speaks of the signs of the times in His discourse on Mount Olivet; He warned of great deception four times more than anything else. Satan does not want us to be aware of the signs of Christ's return. In the Old Testament Zechariah prophecies of the Second Coming of the Lord in chapters 12-14; he writes apocalyptically, commenting on what is happening in the heavenlies with what is taking place on the earth. The book of Zechariah is one that connects; he speaks of Jesus coming on a donkey, but also of His return.

The first major event in the prophetic timeline is an imminent event – the coming of Christ for His Church (1 Thess. 4:16). When a true Christian dies the spirit goes to be with God in heaven. The body goes into the grave, asleep, awaiting resurrection. In 1 Thessalonians 4:17 the Bible says that we who are alive and remain shall be caught up together with them in the clouds to meet the Lord in the air. This is speaking of the actual removal of people from the earth. Jesus will be there before us! The Bible adds that we shall not all die but that we shall be changed, in the twinkling of an eye. We will be given heavenly bodies and will be taken to heaven. Jesus is going to usher His followers into His presence in heaven where we will be re-united with loved ones who have died in the faith. After Jesus comes for His Church there will be what the Bible calls "the Bema seat" judgment (2 Cor. 5:10). This is not a judgment of salvation, but one to determine the authenticity of our works so that rewards, or else loss, will be recompensed. All believers will be there face to face with Christ. This is an evaluation of what the believer has done for the Lord in regard to service. 1 Corinthians 3 speaks of the testing of these works, and whether or not they will survive the fire. It is a testing of our motives; God will assess what we have done with the life He has given us; our time, talents, gifts, resources, service and finances. We must redeem the time, as the Scriptures tell us, for time is short. Let us be living for the King of kings, working wholeheartedly for the Lord.

A tribulation period is mentioned in the Scriptures where God will pour out His wrath upon the earth. The antichrist will rise to power and God will be pouring out a series of judgments on the world, mentioned in Matthew 24. Some of these things are also mentioned in Revelation. During this time there will be great trouble on the earth. It is known as "the time of Jacob's trouble." This will extend for a period of seven years. Some of these judgments include; an outbreak of wars (Rev. 6:4), deadly famines (6:8), huge fires (8:7), an asteroid crashing into the sea and killing a third of the living creatures, and destroying a third of the ships (8:8-9), demons being unleashed and able to torment unbelievers who have taken the mark of the beast (9:1-5), a prolonged drought (11:6), incurable sores (16:2), everything in the ocean will be killed (16:3), heat will scorch the earth and its inhabitants (16:8-9), darkness across the planet (16:10), a world-wide earthquake (16:19), island disappearing and mountains crumbling (16:20), huge hailstones of about 100 pounds each that come down out of heaven upon men (16:21). About half of the world's population will die. It is a time of the great wrath of God. This is God's judgment upon sin. Yet even during this time God is going to make the Good News of salvation available to mankind. Many will wake up, but many will also lose their lives for converting. It is far better to be reconciled to God today.

In Ezekiel chapters 38-39 God speaks of the Jewish people being gathered again to their homeland. Israel was declared a nation in 1948, and the Bible says that various nations would invade Israel. The nations against Israel have a demonic hatred for the Jewish people. The invasion that Ezekiel prophesied could happen in our generation. Ezekiel says that God Himself is going to rise up in Israel's defense and He will make Himself known. "They will know that I am the Lord." It may be at this time that the Jewish people will rebuild the temple. The antichrist will stand in a rebuilt temple declaring himself to be God. The battle of Armageddon will occur during the end time of tribulation. This will be a worldwide revolution starting in Megiddo. While this is going on,

Matthew 24 tells us that the sun will be darkened, the moon will not give its light and the stars will fall from the heavens, then the Son of Man will come in power. He will descend on a white horse with the clouds and every eye will see Him. The resurrected saints will come with Him, following on white horses to descend in Israel. All of the angels of heaven will accompany Him and the believers. Zechariah 14:4 says that His feet will stand on the Mount of Olives. Jesus will put an end to the deceptive rule of the antichrist, says the Bible. The tribulation period and the battle of Armageddon will now be at an end. Following will be the judgment of the nations; that of the sheep and the goats, in Matthew 25. This is not the final judgment. Then comes the thousand-year reign of Christ, also known as the Millennium. The wicked will have been cast out. Satan will be locked up for a thousand years and Jesus will be King of the world, ruling and reigning from Jerusalem. There will be a world-wide knowledge of God (Is.11:9.) Idolatry and false idol worship will be cut off. The apostles will rule over the twelve tribes of Israel. All weapons of war will be destroyed, there will be no more sickness, there will be fruitful and joyful labour to do and we will build homes and plant vineyards There will be a restoration of one language for us to speak, says Zephaniah 3:9. The animal kingdom will enjoy perfect peace, says Isaiah 11:6 where the wolf (not the lion), will lie down with the lamb, and the lion will eat straw like the ox… a child with play with an asp. There will be no harm there. There will be wonderful changes to the environment; the desert will blossom and waters will break forth in the wilderness. At the end of this thousand years Satan will be unleashed for a short time to face his demise in the bottomless pit. Then follows the great white throne judgment. After this thousand years there are people who will be resurrected to stand before God; these are the unrepentant sinners spoken of in Luke 16. Great books will be opened with details of every sin This will be a terrifying thing. Those unforgiven sinners will be cast into the lake of fire where they will be eternally separated from God. Today is indeed the day of salvation!

Romans 10:9-10 says: "That if thou shalt confess with thy mouth the Lord Jesus, and shalt believe in thine heart that God hath raised Him from the dead, thou shalt be saved." After these things, God tells us in Revelation 21 that He is going to create a new heavens and a new earth. 2 Peter 3 says that this present heavens and the earth will pass away. It has been contaminated by man's sin. God is going to place the New Jerusalem on this new earth. It is a glorious gigantic city, with walls made of jasper, and the city will be of pure gold with foundations garnished with precious stones. Believers are going to live in that city and will be able to go in and out on the earth. It will be a wonderful place where there will be no more death, nor sorrow, crying or pain. There will be fulness of joy. Most of all, we will be with Jesus, the One whom we have loved and served, and He who has made us and shown us so much love. Not only will we be with our Lord, Saviour and Friend, but we will have all the spiritual blessings in Christ as joint heirs, we will sit on His throne and reign with Him for ever and ever. Hallelujah!

Parousia is another of my poems: -

> *The trumpet soon sounding*
> *The day is at hand*
> *The angels awaiting*
> *To do His command*
> *Each eye shall behold Him*
> *In clouds He will come*
> *With power and glory*
> *To gather us home*

INDEX

73	Ex. 34:6	Gracious
50	Ex.34:14	El Kanno/ Qanna
85	Ex. 48:35	Jehovah-shammah
111	Lev. 11:44a	Pure and Undefiled
118	Lev. 19:2	Sacred
25	Lev.19:3	Adonai Eloheikhem
30	Lev.21:12b	Anointing Oil
37	Lev. 23:2 b	One Who Celebrates
33	Num.6:24	One Who Blesses us
42	Num. 6:24-26	God's Countenance
68	Num. 10:10	Found in His Appointed Feasts
95	Num.14: 18a	Longsuffering
82	Num.24:17	Israel's Living Star
24	Deut.3:24	Adonai-Adonai
41	Deut. 4:24	Consuming Fire, Esh Oklah
68	Deut. 4:29	Found by Those who Seek Him
52	Deut.4:31	El Rachum
56	Deut.4:39	Elohim Bashamayin
25	Deut. 6:4	Adonai Eloheinu
64	Deut.7:9	Faithful, El Aman, El Emunah
50	Deut.7:9	El Hanne'eman
80	Deut. 8:2	One Who Humbles and Tests us
41	Deut. 8:5	Corrects and Disciplines His Children
48	Deut. 10:17	El Gadol Gibohr Yare
75	Deut.28:58	Hashem
82	Deut. 29:29	Intimate
46	Deut. 32:4	El Aoreok
47	Deut. 32:18	El Chuwl
55	Deut. 33:26	El Yeshurun
105	Deut.33:27	Olam Zerowa
51	Deut. 33:27a	El Kedem
130	Deut. 33:29a	Sword of thy Excellency, Jehovah Chereb
47	Joshua 3:10a	El Chay, El Ghah'y
83	Joshua 18:3	Jehovah Elohim Ab
71	Joshua 22:22a	God of gods
56	Joshua 24:19a	Elohim Kedoshim
28	Judges 6:12	Angel of the LORD

82	Job 33:23	Intercessor
107	Job 37:16	Perfect in Knowledge
29	Psalm 2:2	Anointed One
91	Psalm 2:4	Laughs
92	Psalm 3:3	Lifter of my Head
57	Psalm 4:1	Elohim Tsedeq
118	Psalm 4:8	Safety
54	Psalm 7:11	Elohim Shofet Tsadik
25	Psalm 7:17	Adonai Elyon
54	Psalm 7:9b	El Tsaddik
23	Psalm 8:1	Adoneinu
101	Psalm 10:16a	Melekh
96	Psalm 12:5	Lord Adon
24	Psalm 13:3	Adonai Elohay
113	Psalm 14:6	Refuge of the Poor
108	Psalm 16:5	Portion of my Inheritance
53	Psalm 17:6	El Shama
52	Psalm 18:2	El Palet, Jehovah Mephalti
59	Psalm 18:46	Elohei Yishi
52	Psalm 18:47	El Nathan N'Qamah
99	Psalm 19:7	Makes Wise the Simple
115	Psalm 19:9	Righteous
27	Psalm 19:14	Adonai Tsuri v'goali
59	Psalm 20:1	Elohay Yakob
84	Psalm 20:9	Jehovah-hoshiah
81	Psalm 22:3	Inhabits the Praises of His People
108	Psalm 22:16b	The Pierced Messiah
63	Psalm 22:19	Eyaluth
85	Psalm 23:1	Jehovah-roh'i
114	Psalm 23:3	Restores the Soul
40	Psalm 23:4	Comforter
42	Psalm 23:5	Cup
102	Psalm 24:8	Mighty in Battle, Gibbor Milchamah
89	Psalm 24:9	King of Glory
26	Psalm 24:10	Adonai-Tzva'ot
85	Psalm 27:1	Jehovah-ori
32	Psalm 27:4	Beautiful

56	Psalm 62:8	Elohim Machase Lanu
98	Psalm 63:3	Lovingkindness
117	Psalm 66:7	Ruler
82	Psalm 68:4	JAH
31	Psalm 68:5	Avi, Father
54	Psalm 68:19	El Yehuatenu
51	Psalm 68:20	El Mohshahgoth
55	Psalm 68:24	Eli Maelekhi
119	Psalm 72:13	Saves the Needy
104	Psalm 72:17	Name Endures Forever
43	Psalm 82:3	Defender of Widows and Fatherless
129	Psalm 84:11	Sun and Shield
97	Psalm 84:12	LORD God of Hosts
40	Psalm 86:15	Compassionate
84	Psalm 89:18	Jehovah-maginnenu
99	Psalm 90:1	Ma'on
81	Psalm 90:2	Immutable
53	Psalm 91: 1	El Shaddai
98	Psalm 91:2	Machseh, Fortress
23	Psalm 93:4	Addiyr Mahrom Jehovah
122	Psalm 94:1-2a	Shophet
133	Psalm 95:1	Tsur Yeshuato
26	Psalm 95:6	Adonai Osenu
23	Psalm 97:5	Adon, LORD
98	Psalm 98:2	Makes Known His Salvation
84	Psalm 98:6	Jehovah-ha-Melech
44	Psalm 98:7-9	Divine Judge of all things
51	Psalm 99:8	El Nahsah
61	Psalm 102:12	Eternal
42	Psalm 102:25	Creator of All Things
67	Psalm 103:2-3	Forgiver of Iniquities
101	Psalm 103:8	Merciful and Gracious
124	Psalm 103:19	Sovereign
95	Psalm 106:1	The LORD
54	Psalm 109:1	El Tehilati
23	Psalm 110:1	Adoni
79	Psalm 111:3	Honourable

68	Prov. 14:27	Fountain of Life
63	Prov. 15:3	Eyes are on All
76	Prov. 15:29	Hears Prayer
136	Prov.16:2	Weighs the Spirits
129	Prov.18:10	Strong Tower, Migdal Oz
69	Prov. 18:24	Friend that Sticks Closer than a Brother
131	Prov.21:2	Tests the Hearts
37	Prov. 21:30	Cannot Be Thwarted
122	Prov. 30:5	Shield
98	Eccl. 3:11	Makes Everything Beautiful
88	Eccl. 12:13-14	Judges All
92	Song of Sol. 2:1	Lily of the Valleys, Rose of Sharon,
32	Song of Sol. 2:4	Banner
139	Song of Sol. 2:7-8	Yesua Habibi
112	Isaiah 1:18	One who Reasons with man
26	Isaiah 1:24	Adonai Jehovah Tsaba Israel
24	Isaiah 3:1	Adon Jehovah Tsaba
49	Isaiah 5:16	El Hakkadosh
85	Isaiah 6:3b	Jehovah Sabaoth
110	Isaiah 9:6	Prince of Peace
92	Isaiah 10:17a	Light of Israel
49	Isaiah 10:21	El Gibor
127	Isaiah 11:1	Stem of Jesse
126	Isaiah 11:2	Spirit of Knowledge and Understanding
115	Isaiah 11:4a	Righteous Judge
116	Isaiah 11:10	Root of Jesse
54	Isaiah 12:2	El Yehuati
25	Isaiah 17:7	Adonai Elohei Y'Israel
41	Isaiah 25:1	Counsels us
100	Isaiah 25:4	Maowz Dal
25	Isaiah 25:8a	Adonai Elohim
83	Isaiah 26:4	JEHOVAH
138	Isaiah 26:7	Yashar
68	Isaiah 28:16	Foundation
51	Isaiah 30:18b	El Mishpat
54	Isaiah 30:29	El Tzur
23	Isaiah 33:21a	Addiyr Jehovah

86	Isaiah 33:22	Jehovah-shaphat
25	Isaiah 38:5	Adonai Elohe David
88	Isaiah 40:25	Kadosh
83	Isaiah 40:28	Jehovah-bore, Creator of all things
79	Isaiah 41:14b	Holy One of Israel
121	Isaiah 42:1	Servant
106	Isaiah 42:6	'Or Goyim
103	Isaiah 42:13	Mighty Warrior
139	Isaiah 43:3a	Yeshua
32	Isaiah 43:15	Bara Y'Israel , Creator of Israel
34	Isaiah 43:25	One who Blots out Transgressions
139	Isaiah 44:6	YHWH of Hosts, Sabaoth
77	Isaiah 45:15	Hides Himself
112	Isaiah 48:10	Refiner
83	Isaiah 49:7	Jehovah-aman
42	Isaiah 49:8	Covenant to the People
84	Isaiah 49:26	Jehovah-Moshiekh
99	Isaiah 53:3	Man of Sorrows
129	Isaiah 53: 4-5	Suffering Servant
73	Isaiah 54:5	God of the Whole Earth
40	Isaiah 55:4	Commander
138	Isaiah 55:10-11	God is One Whose Word Never Fails
81	Isaiah 57:15	Inhabits Eternity
48	Isaiah 57:18	El Erekh Apayim avi ha tanchumim
71	Isaiah 60:1	Glory of Israel
22	Isaiah 60:16	Abir Jacob, Jehovah Goelekh
102	Isaiah 60:16b	Mighty One of Israel
76	Isaiah 61:1	Healer of the Broken-hearted
35	Isaiah 62:5b	Bridegroom
29	Isaiah 63:9	Angel of His Presence
63	Isaiah 60:19	Everlasting Light
35	Isaiah 62:5b	Bridegroom
72	Isaiah 63:16b	God of thy Father
108	Isaiah 64:8	Potter
59	Isaiah 65:16a	Elohay Amen
67	Isaiah 66:1	God's Footstool
73	Jer. 3:12b	Grants Favour

32	Jer.8:22a	Balm of Gilead
90	Jer. 10:7	King of Nations
47	Jer.10:10a	El Chaiyim
96	Jer. 16:21	LORD Jehovah
103	Jer. 17:13	Miqweh Y'Israel
86	Jer. 23:6	Jehovah-tzidkenu
80	Jer. 23:23-24	Immanent
52	Jer. 31:3b	El Olam
102	Jer. 32:18	Mighty God
57	Jer.32:27	Elohim of all Flesh
92	Jer. 33:6	Life's Guarantor of Joy and Health
133	Jer. 33:15	Tsemach Tsedahah
84	Jer. 51:6	Jehovah-gmolah
49	Jer. 51:56	El G'moolah Jehovah, El Gemuwal
101	Lam. 3:22-23	Mercies are Great
122	Ezek.7:9	The Lord that Smiteth
32	Ezek. 20:29	Bamah
85	Ezek. 48:35	Jehovah-shammah
82	Hosea 2:16	Ishi – my Husband
87	Hosea 2:22	Jezreel
95	Hosea 2:23	Lo Ammi
72	Amos 4:13	God of hosts
43	Obad. 15	Day of the Lord
47	Jonah 4:2b	El Channun
70	Joel 3:16b	Gives us Hope
122	Nahum 1:2-3	Slow to Anger
70	Hab. 3:18-19	Gives Joy and Strength
114	Zeph.3:17	Rejoices
46	Dan. 2:23	Elah-avahati
69	Dan. 2:28a	Gelah Raz
46	Dan.2:47b	Elah Elahin
58	Dan. 3:17	Elohim Yakol
62	Dan. 4:3	Everlasting Kingdom
28	Dan. 7:13	Ancient of days
67	Dan. 9:9	Forgiving
60	Mic.6:6a	Elohay Marom
44	Haggai 2:7	Desire of Nations

24	Zech.6:5	Adon Kol-ha'arets
35	Zech.6:12	BRANCH
100	Zech. 9:9	Mashiach
34	Zech. 10:4	Bow of Battle
125	Zech. 12:10	Spirit of Grace and Supplication
95	Zech. 14:9	Lord of the Earth
48	Mal.2:10a	El Echad
102	Mal.3:1	Messenger
129	Mal.4:2	Sun of Righteousness
133	Mal.3:6a	Unchanging
122	Matt.1:1	Son of Abraham
38	Matt.1:16	Christ
123	Matt. 1:18	Son of Mary
86	Matt. 1:21	Jesus
61	Matt. 1:23	Emmanuel
73	Matt. 2:6	Governor
38	Matt.2:11a	Christ Child
104	Matt. 2:23	Nazarene
33	Matt.3:17	Beloved Son
107	Matt.5:48	Perfect
66	Matt. 6:9	Holy Father
69	Matt.7:13	Gate for the Sheep
76	Matt. 8:16	Healer
68	Matt. 11:19	Friend of Sinners
101	Matt.11:29	Meek and Lowly in Heart
121	Matt.12:18a	Servant of the LORD
37	Matt.13:55	Carpenter's Son
123	Matt.15:22b	Son of David
116	Matt. 16:18	Rock
33	Matt. 17:5	Beni Yedidi
123	Matt.18:11	Son of Man
81	Matt. 18:20	In our Midst
80	Matt.21:9	Hupistos
97	Matt.22:32	Lord of the Living
100	Matt.23:8	Master
60	Matt. 27:46	Eli
115	Matt.28:6	Risen Son of Man

87	Mark 1:9	Jesus of Galilee
108	Mark 2:17	Physician
37	Mark 6:3	Carpenter
34	Mark 11:9-10	Blessed
22	Mark 14:36a	Abba
66	Mark 14:62	At the Father's Right Hand
59	Mark 15:34	Eloi
123	Luke 1:32	Son of the Most High
72	Luke 1:68	God of Israel
80	Luke 1:69	Horn of Salvation
43	Luke 1:78	Dayspring
124	Luke 2:11	Soter
31	Luke 2:12	Babe
41	Luke 2:25	Consolation of Israel
97	Luke 2:26	The Lord's Christ
92	Luke 2:32	Light of the Gentiles
126	Luke 4:18-19	Spirit of the Lord
78	Luke 4:33-34	Holy One of God
97	Luke 6:5	Lord of the Sabbath
89	Luke 6:35	Kind
101	Luke 6:36	Merciful
33	Luke 9:35	Beloved Son of God
40	Luke 9:20	Christ of God
100	Luke 9:20	Mashiach Ha Elohim
75	Luke 11:2	Hallowed
106	Luke 11:13	Paraclete
89	Luke 19:38	King
127	Luke 20:17-18	Stone
43	Luke 22:20	The Cup of the Blood
110	Luke 24:44	Prophecy Fulfilled
71	John 1:1,2	God
137	John 1:1	Word, Logos
91	John 1:4	Life
92	John 1:9	Light of the World
27	John 1:14	All-Glorious
56	John 1:18	Elohim Ben Yachad
102	John 1:41b	Messiah

91	John 1:29b	Lamb of God
87	John 1:45	Jesus of Nazareth
111	John 1:49b	Rabbi
130	John 3:2	Teacher Come from God
106	John 3:16	Only Begotten
125	John 4:24	Spirit
119	John 4:42b	Saviour
94	John 4:14	Living Water of Life
79	John 5:22-23	Honoured
35	John 6:33	Bread of God
35	John 6:32	Bread of Heaven
35	John 6:51	Living Bread
123	John 6:69	Son of the Living God
92	John 8:12	Light
69	John 8:23	From Above
44	John 10:7	Door of the Sheep
69	John 10:10b	Giver of Abundant Life
72	John 10:11	Good Shepherd
115	John 11:25	Resurrection
136	John 11:35	Weeps
89	John 12:13b	King of Israel
63	John 13:15	Exemplar
70	John 13:31	Glorified
109	John 14:2-3	Preparing a Home
136	John 14:6	The Way, Truth and Life
40	John 14:16	Comforter
127	John 14:16-17a	Spirit of Truth
116	John 14:26	Ruach Ha Kodesh
134	John 15:1	Vine, Husbandman
132	John17:3	True God
89	John 19:19	King of the Jews
112	John 20:16	Rabboni
97	John 20:28	My Lord and my God
73	Acts 2:19	God of Wonders
110	Acts 3:15	Prince of Life
110	Acts 3:22	Prophet
87	Acts 4:10-12	Jesus Christ

71	Acts 4:27	God's Holy Child Jesus
62	Acts 4:29-30	Eved ha Kadosh
116	Acts 5:9a	Ruach Adonai
109	Acts 5:31	Prince
88	Acts 7:52a	Just One
81	Acts 10:34-35	Impartial
95	Acts 10:36	Lord of all
71	Acts 10:38a	God's Anointed
87	Acts 10:42	Judge of the Living and the Dead
117	Acts 16:7	Ruach Yeshua
120	Rom.1:16	Saviour of Jew and Gentile
62	Rom. 1:20	Eternal Power and God Head
134	Rom. 5:1	One who Vindicates
34	Rom. 5:11	Blood Atonement
96	Rom.6:23	Our Lord
126	Rom. 8:2	Spirit of Life
125	Rom.8:9	Spirit of Christ
117	Rom. 8:9	Ruach haMashiach
125	Rom. 8:15	Spirit of Adoption
70	Rom. 8:32	Gives Freely
22	Rom. 8:15	Abba Avinu
120	Rom. 9:33	Scandalon
61	Rom. 10:4	End of the Law
90	Rom.10:9	Kurios
107	Rom. 10:13	Personal
134	Rom.11:33	Unsearchable
43	Rom.11:26	Deliverer
132	Rom.12:2	Transforms us
95	Rom.14:9	Lord of the Dead
107	Rom. 15:5	Patient
79	Rom. 15:13	Hope of the World
96	1 Cor. 1:6-8	Lord of Glory
137	1 Cor. 1:24-25	Wisdom of God
107	1 Cor. 5:7	Passover Lamb
118	I Cor.5:7b	Sacrifice
31	1 Cor. 8:6	Avi'ad
127	1 Cor.10:4	Spiritual Rock

34	1 Cor. 11:24	Body
66	1 Cor.15:23	Firstfruits
29	1 Cor. 15:25-26	Annihilates Satan's Plans
91	1 Cor. 15:45	Last Adam
120	I Cor. 15:47	Second Adam
41	1 Cor.15:55,57	Conqueror
34	2 Cor.1:3	Blessed of God
31	2 Cor. 1:3	Avi HaRachamim
126	2 Cor.3:3	Spirit of the Living God
126	2 Cor.3:17	Spirit of Liberty
106	2 Cor. 618	Pantokrator, Almighty
28	2 Cor. 9:8	All-Sufficient
69	2 Cor. 9:15	Gift of God
74	2 Cor. 11:31a	Ha'Av L'Yeshua HaMashiach
120	Gal.3:16	Seed of Abraham
126	Gal.5:22-23	Spirit of Peace
105	Gal. 6:7	Not Mocked
33	Eph1:6	Beloved
127	Eph.1:12-13	Spirit of Promise
45	Eph. 1:13b,14	Earnest of our Inheritance
117	Eph. 1:17	Ruach Hechazon
103	Eph. 1:21	Name Above Every Name
75	Eph. 1:22-23	He that fills all in all
107	Eph.2:14	Peace
38	Eph.2:20b	Chief Cornerstone
118	Eph. 3:8b-9	Ruler of His Creation
102	Eph. 3:20-21	Mighty in Power
106	Eph. 4:5-6	One
30	Eph. 4:8	Ascended
75	Eph. 4:15	Head of All Things
79	Eph.4:30	Holy Spirit
67	Eph. 4:32	Forgiver
78	Phil.2:9-10a	Highly Exalted
36	Phil. 3:10	One Who Can Be Known
138	Phil. 4:6	Worthy of Thanksgiving
128	Phil. 4:13	Strengthener
101	Phil. 4:19	Meets Every Need

97	Col. 1:2b	Lord Jesus
66	Col.1:15	Firstborn of Every Creature
42	Col. 1:16	Creator
27	Col. 1:17	All in All
75	Col.1:18	Head of the Church
109	Col.1:19-20	Preeminent and Supreme
103	Col. 2:2	Mystery of God
131	Col. 2:9	Theotes
132	Col.2:15	Triumphant
136	1 Thess. 4:3	Will of God
79	1 Thess. 4:6	Holy and True Avenger
124	1 Thess.4:16-17	Soon Coming King
136	1 Thess. 5:3	Will of God
131	2 Thess. 1:2	Theos
89	1 Tim. 1:17	King Eternal, Immortal Invisible
100	1 Tim. 2:5	Mediator
112	1 Tim.2:6	Ransom
99	1 Tim. 3:16	Manifest in the flesh
119	1 Tim. 4:10	Saviour of all Men
108	1 Tim.6:15	Potentate
120	2 Tim.2:8	Seed of David
129	2 Tim.2:19a	Sure Foundation
82	2 Tim. 3:16-17	God's Inspired Word
62	2 Tim. 4:1	Eternal Judge of Quick and Dead
70	Titus 2:13	Glorious
111	Titus 2:14	Purifier
76	Heb. 1:1-2	Heir of all Things
30	Heb. 1:2	Architect
80	Heb. 1:3	Image of the Invisible God
66	Heb. 1:6	First begotten of the dead
37	Heb 2:10	Captain of Man's Salvation
30	Heb.3:1	Apostle
36	Heb. 3:4	Builder of All Things
115	Heb.4:10	One who Rests
88	Heb. 4:12	One who Judges the Motives
74	Heb. 4:14	High Priest
30	Heb.5:9	Author of Eternal Salvation

36	Heb.6:17-18	Cannot lie
67	Heb. 6:20	Forerunner
90	Heb. 7:2	King of Peace
61	Heb.7:15-16	Endless
109	Heb 7:17	Priest
133	Heb.7:24	The Unchangeable one
133	Heb. 7:26	Undefiled
98	Heb.8:1b	The Majesty
117	Heb. 9:14	Ruach Olam
131	Heb.9:16	Testator
67	Heb.10:17	One who Forgets our Sins
74	Heb. 10: 19-22	Great High Priest
94	Heb.10:31	Living
22	Heb. 11:6	God is
36	Heb. 11:10	Builder
82	Heb. 11:27	Invisible
111	Heb.11:40	Provider
66	Heb. 12:2a	Finisher of our Faith
38	Heb.12:6	One who Chastens
31	Heb. 12:9	Avi Ha Ruchot
117	Heb. 12:28b-29	Ruach haKodesh u Vaesh
104	Heb. 13:5b	Never Leaves us
76	Heb. 13:6	Helper
118	Heb. 13:8	The Same
74	Heb.13:20-21a	Great Shepherd
70	James 1:5	Gives Liberally
130	James 1:13	Tempts no one
65	James 1:17	Father of Lights
69	James 1:17	Giver of Good Gifts
105	James 1:27	God is not Religious
68	James 2:23	Friend
45	James 3:17	One who does not show Partiality
40	James 5:8	Christ's Second Coming is Near
62	James 5:9	Eternal Judge
135	James 5:11	Very Pitiful and of Tender Mercy
119	1 Pet. 1:2	Sanctifier
31	1 Pet. 1:3	Avi Yeshua Hamaschiach Adoneinu

78	1 Pet.1:16	Holy
38	1 Pet.2:9	Chosen of God
94	1 Peter 2:4	Living Stone
41	1 Peter 2:7	Cornerstone
60	1 Peter 2:6	Elect and Precious
34	1 Pet.2:25	Bishop of Souls
29	1 Pet. 3:22	Angels are Subject to God
125	1 Pet.4:14a	Spirit of Glory
38	1 Pet.5:4	Chief Shepherd
37	1 Peter 5:7	One who Cares
61	1 Peter 5:10	Eternal Glory
44	2 Pet. 1:3a	Divine
44	2 Pet.1 :4a	Divine Son
63	2 Peter 1:17	Excellent Glory
43	2 Peter 1:19b	Daystar
137	1 John 1:1	Word of Life
112	1 John 1:5	Radiant One
107	1 John 1:9	Pardons
27	1 John 2:1b	Advocate
111	1 John 2:2	Propitiation of the Sins of the World
37	1 John 3:5	Cannot Sin
138	1 John 4:2	Word made Flesh
97	1 John 4:8	Love
120	1 John 4:14	Saviour of the World
131	1 John 5:7	Three in One, Equal and Eternal
123	1 John 5:12	Son of God
123	2 John 1:3	Son of the Father
67	3 John 11	God's Followers are good
22	Jude 24-25	Able
110	Rev.1:5-6	Prince of the Kings of the Earth
33	Rev. 1:8	Beginning and Ending
66	Rev.1:11 a	First and Last
64	Rev. 1:13-15	Eyes Like a Flame of Fire
24	Rev.1:18	Adonai
27	Rev.1:18a	Alive For Evermore
132	Rev.2:7b	Tree of Life
99	Rev. 2:17	The Manna

78	Rev. 3:7	Holds Key of David
104	Rev. 3:12	New Name
28	Rev.3:14b	Amen
64	Rev. 3:14b	Faithful and True Witness
131	Rev. 3:21	God is on His Throne
121	Rev. 4:5	The Seven Spirits
28	Rev. 4:8b	Almighty
94	Rev.4:10-11	Lives for Ever
138	Rev.4:11	Worthy
93	Rev. 5:5	Lion of the Tribe of Judah
113	Rev. 5: 9-10	Redeemer
91	Rev. 5:12	Lamb who was Slain
91	Rev. 5:13	Lamb Upon the Throne
44	Rev. 6:10	Despotes
115	Rev. 11:15	Returning King
40	Rev. 12:10	Christ' s Anointed
40	Rev. 14:4b	Christ the Lamb
90	Rev. 15:3b	King of saints
88	Rev. 15:4	Judgments are made Manifest
108	Rev. 15:8a	Power of God
106	Rev. 16:5	The One Who Is, Was, and Is to Be
90	Rev. 17:14a	King of kings
118	Rev. 19:1	Salvation
88	Rev. 19:2a	Justice
105	Rev. 19:6b	Omnipotent
109	Rev.19:7	Preparing His Bride
64	Rev. 19:11	Faithful and True
42	Rev. 19:12	Crowned with Many Crowns
137	Rev.19:13	Word of God
74	Rev.19:16	Ha Kadosh Barukh Hu
101	Rev. 19:16	Melech Ha Melachim
20	Rev 21:6	Alpha and the Omega
90	Rev. 22:1	Lamb
130	Rev. 21:22	The Temple
115	Rev.22:12	Rewarder
116	Rev.22:16b	Root and the Offspring of David
36	Rev. 22:16	Bright and Morning Star

MY PERSONAL TESTIMONY

In pursuit of truth, inner peace, and a purpose in life, I arrived at the little village of Bluche, Switzerland, at the age of twenty-two. My first time on skis, I conquered Plaine Morte at 12,000 feet high. It was not bravery, just blissful ignorance. Then the following year I attempted to walk from John O'Groats, Scotland to Land's End on my own. My knees buckled after about two hundred miles and eleven days into my journey I found myself weeping in a tiny village chapel near Kincraig. I tried many other pursuits on my travels, with many risqué adventures and other wild activities in a bid to find what I was looking for. I had the usual series of failed relationships, substance abuse, and other pacifiers which did not work, so I turned to some unconventional religious endeavours such as biorhythms, yoga, marginal occult practices and the modern-day theologians of the me generation, self-psychology. When I was in Switzerland I was asked if I was a Christian. I reckoned I was good enough, having been schooled in a convent, and replied: "Well, I suppose so, I haven't killed anybody." That question caused me to ponder my eternal destiny.

As a child, I was raised in a loving environment with good parents. They encouraged me to paint and helped me to become a better person in life. My dad was a compassionate gentleman and an honest man. My mother cared for the needy and they raised eight children. I was the oldest girl. I left home at the age of seventeen for London, England and travelled throughout Europe, back-packing and working as I travelled for eight years before leaving for Canada. I had been to several countries, but my dreams were unfulfilled. Then my older brother died at the age of twenty-nine from Hodgkins' disease, which caused me to query further the reason for living. I left home again and worked in a Zoo in France, having already lived in Italy for some time. My spoken Italian and French helped me to get around and assisted in the working environment. Eventually I went to Canada and after some time was married. I still hadn't found the answer to the "why" of my existence, not did I have the inner peace that had long eluded me despite the awesome majesty of those beautiful Swiss mountains, and the breathtaking splendor of the bonny hills of Scotland.

On one of my aero plane trips between Canada and England a young woman spoke to me and we exchanged beliefs. I had been raised Roman Catholic, so I had a basic belief in the God of creation and accepted this from my youth. She shared with me her views on life, and when I asked what her belief was, she said: "To love God above all things and your neighbor as yourself." A seed was sown. Then shortly after that on my visit in England I met up with a school teacher who simply said on parting, "Seek and you will find." On this visit I went to see a friend who had multiple sclerosis. On other occasions Joss would raise an angry fist heavenward and curse his Maker. He had suffered a great deal for several years and had lost his motor functions. He was then dependent upon his loving mother. He even dubbed himself: "The cheerless cynic." This time Joss was different. His face was radiant, and he was no longer angry. We talked at length, and upon parting he said through stammering lips and a shaking head: "The kingdom of God is within us all – if only people knew." Joss was almost totally incapacitated, but I had seen and heard words of life and a powerful testimony. He died shortly afterwards, but I'd witnessed something that I would never forget and it would change my life.

Further circumstances led me to read the Bible. I had also been in a twelve-step program which often referenced the Bible in its material and was founded on the Ten Commandments and the Sermon on the Mount. This had helped me draw nearer to the peace I was seeking at the time. Once back in Canada I was led to go to a local Christian bookstore. At the time, my marriage was unstable due to my spouse's former drinking habits and lifestyle, and eventually he left. Even the group I attended did not give the level of peace in my life that I sought. I read some of the material that I brought home with me from the bookstore, and one pamphlet spoke directly to my heart where Jesus said: "I am the way, the truth, and the life: No man cometh to the Father except through me." The pamphlet mentioned admitting one's own sinfulness and asking for God's forgiveness. At first I found it difficult to admit to my sinfulness because I thought I was quite a good person until the Holy Spirit began to convict me and show me that I was no different than all the people I was reading about in the Bible; Mary Magdalene, who had lived a sinful life of self-abuse, Zacchaeus, who selfishly took from others for personal gain, the woman at the well, who had seduced men and claimed several husbands, or even the religious zealots of that day who claimed to be good and righteous but were inwardly deceived. I was compelled to agree with that inner Voice that indeed: "All have sinned and fall short of the glory of God." And that "all" included me.

Many times, prior to this I had found myself weeping on my knees, usually because of my destitute circumstances and personal dissatisfaction with life, but this time I wept for my personal need for God, for my spiritual poverty. In March 1982, I repented of my sins and received Jesus Christ as my personal Saviour and Lord. Tears of joy followed shortly afterwards, although I wasn't fully aware at the time of what had actually taken place. I soon began going to a church and was baptized by immersion. I had a renewed appreciation for life. A purpose for living, and the peace I longed for was in my own heart. Jesus Himself is the truth and he had filled me with the knowledge of Himself as my very own Saviour, and I had a love for God, my heavenly Father, to whom I owe my all.

During the following years I graduated from Sheridan College in Canada with a major in Interpretive Book Illustration, and later in England I completed the B. Ed. Degree in Education and training at Sunderland University. During these years my faith was tested through a chemical imbalance but the Lord has proved Himself faithful to keep me. Difficulties can be a means of God forging character into the human soul, often it is a means of humbling us. In the earlier years of my Christian walk I was involved in the hyper-Charismatic movement. The first church I attended was reasonably sound in biblical doctrine but was quite cultic sociologically. This influence was not helpful during that time, when I was a new believer. This continued for several years until the Lord brought me to a place of mental soundness and stability many years later. "For God has not given us the spirit of fear, but of power, and of love, and of a sound mind." After many years of continuing to seek God I came to a place of joy and peace. It is that of being on a solid foundation, but only after searching and crying out for truth. The exposés in this book have come about after years of research and study, whilst praying for wisdom and insight into the truth and the errors of false teaching, which had influenced me as it has the rest of the body of Christ. My involvement in the Hyper-Charismatic movement contributed towards the instability I suffered for many years. I can only thank God for bringing me out of it all, by His grace.

As an artist, much of my work has been painted during times of deepest struggle and internal conflict; and was born out of my own search for meaning and understanding. I see art as an integral part of God's creation and draw inspiration daily from the beauteous perfection of all his work. Therefore, I strive for excellence in my work, seeking to excel and to honour God with my labours. I also see my work as a painter to accompany the written Word of God, not as a medium on its own, but to amplify Scripture.

Not everyone can paint a picture or write or sing a song. Visible talents are not a mark of maturity though. Many have unseen talents that are used to bring glory to our Creator and these may speak volumes about the reality of Jesus in this world than the ore obviously talented. It is not ability that counts, but availability and willingness.

My artist's mission statement is as follows: To communicate to the individual our unique and inestimable worth and the love of our Creator, through the combined media of the Holy Scriptures and the visual arts; And to thereby elevate the mind by offering a message of hope, purpose, direction, encouragement and pleasure." My success is found in reaching towards the goal set before me in Christ. My quest for truth, peace, and purpose has all been found in Christ. The process has begun; and the Bible says that He will complete the good work He has begun in me. Even though it seems hard to believe, in heaven "It is finished."

Owing to my experiences, however difficult, the Lord has given me the capacity to understand others who suffer from similar disorders, just as Jesus came and can identify with us in order to fully understand our humanity. God uses this for His glory in our lives and in the lives of others. God's power is made perfect in weakness, not through personal strength, but through vessels that are wholly surrendered to Him. I believe that what happens to us is for our spiritual refinement, to prepare us for an eternity in the presence of our Lord and King. C.S. Lewis once said "God whispers in our pleasure, speaks in our conscience, but shouts in our pain. It is His megaphone to rouse a deaf world."

There came a pivotal point in my life some years ago when I began to walk in forgiveness and gratitude. This came about after years of having issues in relationships, and the Lord Jesus touched my life in a very powerful way so that I simply forgave from the heart all those with whom I had disagreements. I no longer had a list of offenders. At that time, I began to walk in gratitude and contentment. Until this point I had not been truly content, but this was a work of God in my heart. I refer to this as my personal epiphany.

I find this contentment is a gift. I live very simply and know that the Lord will meet all my need. More importantly, it is what happens in us, and through us that matters most. Jesus tells us to seek first His kingdom and His righteousness. I live now looking for His coming, anticipating that glorious day when Jesus shall come for His bride. It is truly wonderful to be a part of what He is doing on earth in these last days. Praise God!

In conclusion I would like to add the words from a well-known hymn, entitled "In Christ Alone." In the final verse there is a powerful line: "From life's first cry to final breath, Jesus commands my destiny." Amen.

APPENDIX - GOD - I AM

CPSIA information can be obtained
at www.ICGtesting.com
Printed in the USA
LVHW072023051021
699576LV00013B/816